Not Alone in NICU

of related interest

Anything for My Child
Making Impossible Decisions for Medically Complex Children
Stephanie Nimmo
ISBN 978 1 80501 027 2
eISBN 978 1 80501 028 9

Letters from the Grief Club
How We Live with Loss
Edited by Beth French and Kate Moreton
Foreword by Hussain Manawer
ISBN 978 1 78775 921 3
eISBN 978 1 78775 922 0

The Healthy Coping Colouring Book and Journal
Creative Activities to Help Manage Stress, Anxiety and Other Big Feelings
Pooky Knightsmith
Illustrated by Emily Hamilton
ISBN 978 1 78592 139 1
eISBN 978 1 78450 405 2

DBT for Everyone
A Guide to the Perks, Pitfalls, and Possibilities of DBT for Better Mental Health
Kate Sherman and Michelle Henderson
ISBN 978 1 83997 588 2
eISBN 978 1 83997 589 9
Audio ISBN 978 1 39981 632 8

Not Alone in NICU

A COMPASSIONATE COMPANION FOR PARENTS OF A BABY IN NEONATAL CARE

Rebecca Chilvers

Foreword by Kelly Phizacklea

Illustrated by Alice Jordan

Jessica Kingsley Publishers
London and Philadelphia

First published in Great Britain in 2026 by Jessica Kingsley Publishers
An imprint of John Murray Press

1

Front cover image source: Davy Evans

Content Warning: This book mentions the loss of loved ones, including children, miscarriage, mental health difficulties, and medical procedures.

A CIP catalogue record for this title is available from the British Library and the Library of Congress

ISBN 978 1 78775 885 8
eISBN 978 1 78775 886 5

Printed and bound by CPI Group (UK) Ltd, Croydon, CR0 4YY

Jessica Kingsley Publishers' policy is to use papers that are natural, renewable and recyclable products and made from wood grown in sustainable forests. The logging and manufacturing processes are expected to conform to the environmental regulations of the country of origin.

Jessica Kingsley Publishers
Carmelite House
50 Victoria Embankment
London EC4Y 0DZ

www.jkp.com

John Murray Press
Part of Hodder & Stoughton Limited
An Hachette UK Company

The authorised representative in the EEA is Hachette Ireland, 8 Castlecourt Centre, Dublin 15, D15 XTP3, Ireland (email: info@hbgi.ie)

This book is dedicated to my three beautiful boys – Rafael, Nicolai and Lucien – who have taught me so much about being a mother and how to live wholeheartedly.

Acknowledgements

As this book says many times and in many ways, relationships make things that seem impossible, possible. There are many people who have been a huge influence on this book at different times. My first thanks goes to my family who have been supportive and encouraging me to keep going throughout the process. With special thanks to my mum Pamela Chilvers who proofread the first draft so brilliantly. I am indebted to Ruth Butterworth, Davy Evans and Anita D'Urso for providing not only professional advice and opinions on the manuscript, but also unwavering love and friendship through all the waves – day and night. Huge thanks to Davy Evans for creating the tenderness and flows of compassion in the cover image. Thank you also to NeoLeaP and my East of England Neonatal Operational Delivery Network (ODN) team for believing in me and the project, and to the Parent Advisory Group for all your wisdom and insight.

I'd also like to thank the neonatal team at Evelina London Children's Hospital who taught me so much, and who inspired me by their dedication and commitment to the families they cared for, and each other – Elaine Wood, Alex Phillips, Patrick Desmonde and Aisling Phillips in particular, who had a vision for what neonatal care for families could look like long before much became standard practice.

There are many other friends and colleagues I am lucky to know and be part of the journey with – all have given me so much in different ways – with a special mention to Joanna Cottingham, Jenny Thomson, Marianna Murin, Danya Glaser, Jane Gilmour, Michelle Cree, Loveday Langton, Alice Jordan, Nikki Roberts, Fiona Challacombe, Laura Bridle, Cathy Green, Katie Sabin, Perina Holness and Laura Gilkinson.

My final thanks are to all the families I have met during my work as a clinical psychologist in neonatal care – you are my 'why' and you have been my greatest teachers.

Contents

WRITTEN AND PRACTICAL EXERCISES

EXERCISE RECORDINGS

Foreword

Kelly Phizacklea

As a veteran neonatal parent myself and within my roles to represent and support neonatal families, I always say that no one plans on their baby needing neonatal care. Whether you knew an admission to NICU would be required from your 12-week scan, or going into pre-term labour at 24 weeks, or your baby needing additional care after being born full term, needing to enter the world of neonatal care can come as a shock. Something that you hadn't initially planned for, because although 1 in 7 babies in the UK will require a neonatal care admission, we don't tend to consider that it will be our baby. In this book Rebecca recognises throughout the shock and range of other emotions that you may experience along your journey. She explains that you may have never considered being here, and you may feel alone, but you are not. I can agree with this statement as you have joined a large and supportive community of families, each with different experiences but a connection that binds us together.

When you arrive on the neonatal unit it can feel like a surreal experience and may feel that life is put on hold. However, life does still continue outside of the neonatal unit, and this can be challenging for families to manage other commitments such as childcare, work, finances, etc. This book highlights how you can seek help from those around you with both emotional and logistical support.

I know from personal experience how challenging it can be to feel like a parent whilst your baby is receiving care on the neonatal unit. Rebecca has identified this and provides guidance on how you can support the development of your relationship with your baby, recognising that you are the most important people to them.

Rebecca acknowledges the neonatal experience for what it is – a long, hard, traumatic journey that affects the whole family and can continue to impact long-term. Often, those around us sadly believe that once we are home from the neonatal unit, that our journey is complete. We know that for many families the impact of having a baby born early or sick will continue whether this be affecting parental mental health, caring for a child with additional or complex needs, coming to terms with an unexpected diagnosis, facing a future different to what was originally planned for, or sadly returning home without their baby.

The book has been constructed into manageable chapters, defined by particular themes, enabling the reader to select the material they would like to read, at the right time for them. In addition to useful signposting for additional resources, there are numerous activities to engage with that shall be personally beneficial.

Rebecca has utilised her many years of obtaining expertise and experience from working with and supporting families to produce this supportive resource – a compassionate companion throughout what can be an isolating and anxiety inducing journey.

Kelly Phizaklea

Please note that all quotes, parents' stories and examples are fictional. No real names or people have been used in this book.

All exercises are the author's own except those that state they are adapted, and this is indicated in the text, in a footnote.

Preface

Welcome. I'm so glad that you've found this book and that you're here. You may have picked it up because your baby has just been admitted to a neonatal unit, or you might be revisiting your experiences and trying to make sense of them some time later.

Having a baby in neonatal care is hard. It can be a long and traumatic experience that affects you and the whole family. For many it's one of the most difficult things they have been through in their lives. It's also an experience that you share with many other parents – on average three children in every school class will have spent some time in a neonatal unit as a baby.[1]

When I started working in neonatal care, I was one of only a handful of psychological professionals based on a unit in the UK. Conversations about mental health and the psychological impact of neonatal care on the whole family were growing, and yet support for babies, families and the dedicated teams that look after them was very limited. This is starting to change, but there's still a long way to go before everyone who needs support can receive it.

The motivation for this book came from wanting something accessible for every parent to help them during their baby's time in hospital. Having met with hundreds of parents for many thousands of hours who have been through this journey, I have learnt many things that have helped them along their way. I hope to share their wisdom with you.

No one ever expects or wishes to be part of this group of parents, but you will find that there is a large and supportive community of people who have been where you're at and who know how it feels. There will also be many you meet during your stay who know the reality in different ways of what it's like to be in hospital with a baby. So if you are struggling, know that whilst you may feel alone, *you are not alone.*

1 See www.bliss.org.uk/research-campaigns/neonatal-care-statistics/statistics-about-neonatal-care

Introduction

When your baby is admitted to hospital all at once, much of life is put on hold but also moves at a frighteningly quick pace. It's a time of huge emotional upheaval, full of almost every emotion and state – prolonged uncertainty, powerlessness, fear, exhaustion, shock, grief and sadness, to name but a few. In the course of a day, or even an hour, you may find yourself feeling very differently whilst also trying to support and stay close to your baby and others you love. The task can feel daunting, but you've already made a start.

This book is a guide to getting through and parenting in these most extreme circumstances. It will help you to look after yourself and your baby and to find your way through what can be an overwhelming time for everyone in the family. It hopes to meet you wherever you're at, and to be a compassionate companion alongside as you go through the neonatal journey.

Although everyone's experience is different and unique, there are similarities that join parents who have walked this road together, whilst their babies are in hospital as well as long into the future. Travelling with you are also the stories and voices of parents who have been in your shoes, and you will learn about their experiences in each chapter.

HOW TO USE THIS BOOK

The book is divided into three main parts, reflecting the different stages of the process you will be going through as the parent of a baby in neonatal care. In the first chapter I write about how you can get through those first bewildering days and weeks. I then move on to how you can make sense of what's happening and the challenges you might face. In the last chapter I talk about what happens towards the end of your time in hospital, preparing you for the transition to leaving the neonatal unit and going home. I've also included a chapter to help support you if your baby's life is expected to be short or if you're preparing to be with them at the end of their life.

To help you find your way through each stage of the book, in each chapter you'll find:

- Key information in boxes
- Bullet point lists of useful tips, key information and first steps to help
- Some helpful illustrations for some of the key ideas
- Links to further resources you can find online.

I've included exercises in each chapter, which are those I have found most useful and helpful in my work with families in hospitals over the years. Some are written tasks to help you explore your thoughts and experiences; others may be more practical in nature. symbol ✓ next to them to show that they are available to download from www.jkp.com/catalogue/book/9781787758858. There is space for you to write in the book itself, or you may want to find a notebook to set aside to journal as you make your way through. The exercises can be found wherever you see this icon:

Others are recordings you can listen to (with accompanying text if you prefer just to read), designed to help you manage anxiety, develop resources in your mind to support you through challenges and also mindfully connect with your baby. You can download these recordings via the QR codes next to this icon:

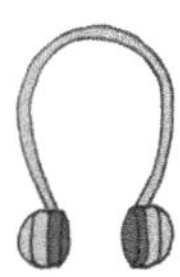

At certain points I have given you a choice as to whether you'd like to read about an issue in more depth or skip a section to get straight to steps to help. These points are marked by this icon:

OUTLINE OF CHAPTERS

When you're feeling overwhelmed, exhausted and frightened, it can be hard to know where to start. **Chapter 1** focuses on the first few days and weeks on the neonatal unit. This may be all you read to begin with, as you become more familiar with a new and unknown environment step by step. Even though neonatal units are full of high-tech equipment, they are staffed with people just like you, many of whom may also be parents, and all are committed to looking after your baby and the whole family. This chapter will help you to find your feet, recognize and understand what you are feeling, and put some initial plans into place to help manage at a time when it can be hard to know what to do next.

Chapter 2 explores the emotions you may be feeling and the kinds of experiences that are common for parents in more depth. We'll take some time to understand together how your previous life experiences can shape how you feel and impact your experience during your baby's time on the unit. We'll look at reactions to extreme stress and trauma so that you can understand what is happening in your mind and body when things feel frightening, out of your control and confusing. We'll also think about some of the more hidden and specific emotional challenges that arise on the neonatal unit that can be harder to talk about, such as shame, anger and jealousy. Each section will introduce you to ways to help yourself as well as sharing some parents' stories. You will find out more about compassionate mind techniques, and how we can use a simple model of how the brain works to help you understand how you feel and what can help. We'll come back to the principles of the compassionate mind again and again, throughout the book.

Chapter 3 is a short chapter dedicated to nurturing your close relationships, and working out how they can be supportive and helpful during your stay in hospital. These relationships are important as they help us to manage difficult situations, but they can come under strain. This chapter focuses on looking after relationships with your partner, wider family and friends, as well as some issues that may arise if you are on your own with a baby in neonatal care.

Whether or not you knew that your baby was going to be on a neonatal unit, it is not the start in life that parents have in mind when they plan for a family. Even though it may not feel like it all the time, you are the most important person to love and care for your baby – but how do you do that in this new and strange environment alongside your neonatal team? The next few chapters (Chapters 4–6) help you to find your way to being a parent whilst your baby is in neonatal care, to reflect on your parenting journey and what matters to you, and how to develop and nurture your connection to your baby.

Chapter 4 guides you through how to care for your baby through Family Integrated Care (FiCare), a model of care on neonatal units that centres you as a parent as the most important person for your baby. It will take you through how you can become involved in caring for your baby even when they are very unwell, building relationships with the care team, and planning your baby's care each day. It will also help you to manage 'parent-led ward rounds', have helpful conversations and make decisions with the team about your baby's care. At the end of this chapter a number of common questions from parents are answered, and there's a focus on developing your parenting roles.

Chapter 5 looks at the process of becoming a parent when your baby is in hospital and your path to this point so far. Through a series of exercises and parents' stories it will help you explore where your journey to parenthood began and previous experiences that may impact how you feel about being a parent. It also highlights some of the losses and changes that can happen along this journey when your baby is premature or unwell, and how you can begin to build on what matters, even while your baby is in neonatal care.

Chapter 6 is about building a relationship with your baby, which can feel particularly hard for many reasons when they are in a neonatal unit. It explores what we understand by 'bonding' and the many barriers there are in neonatal care to feeling close and connected to your baby – none of which are your fault. It introduces some core principles of starting to build a connection with your baby, and ways you can start to do this at the right pace for you. It includes how you can look after yourself so you can be a regulating presence for them, feeding your baby, kangaroo care, giving a voice to your baby and spending time with your baby as a family.

As well as looking after your new baby, you may have other children to care for. It's a common worry for neonatal parents wondering how to meet the needs of all their children, both practically and emotionally. It can often feel as if it is impossible to be in the right place at the right time. **Chapter 7** will help you identify what your children need and how to address those needs according to their age and your family circumstances. It will equip you to help your children understand and manage their emotions, develop a relationship with their baby and become involved in their care as well as take a compassionate approach to yourself as you juggle many needs and priorities.

During your neonatal stay you will have many important conversations and be involved in decision making as well as facing some challenging situations that are specific to the neonatal environment. **Chapter 8** will guide you through having these sometimes daunting conversations with your neonatal team – what to expect and how to prepare for them, and how to join in decision making that is guided by what matters to you as a parent and aligns with your values.

Chapter 9 addresses some of the many specific challenges of being in a neonatal unit and the experiences you may go through with your baby (such as the need for surgery, helping your baby with painful procedures) and events that can be distressing, such as when there is a medical emergency. Each section explores the challenges you may encounter and how they can feel, followed by a series of steps to help.

Chapter 10 looks at coping with and adjusting to a medical diagnosis or ongoing difficulties for your baby. Whilst there is much that medicine can achieve for your baby, and advances are being made all the time, sometimes there are limits to what can be done or changed. Your baby may have been born with a genetic difference that affects them or have a condition for which there is currently no treatment or cure. This chapter addresses what it's like when you receive this kind of information and how to plan a way forward when your future may be very different to the one you had originally planned for.

There is little more devastating than the news that your baby, or one or more of your babies (if you've had a multiple pregnancy), is not expected to live long and to go through the experience of their death. Whilst it can feel like you need so much more time than you have, there is much to think about for you and your baby when your time together is short. If this is your experience, **Chapter 11** compassionately walks you through some of the ways you can make the time you have with your baby as special and as right for you and the family as it can be, and it will also help you to think about your wishes when your child is dying and after their death. It recognizes that however long your baby's life is or was, they will always be a loved and cherished member of the family. It helps you to think about how to keep their memory alive as well as looking after yourself in your grief, and also those around you. This chapter also includes a section on when one of your babies is part of a multiple pregnancy, recognizing the particular challenges of going through an agonizing loss at the same time as continuing to parent your other babies.

After many weeks or months in hospital, facing going home brings with it a range of emotions. Whilst you can be desperate to leave hospital and be in your own surroundings, adjustment to life outside the hospital can be significant, whether it's from neonatal care directly or via a stay on a paediatric ward. **Chapter 12** focuses on helping you to plan for going home whatever that may look like. It also talks about how you might be feeling once you're there, and how you can start to make sense of your neonatal journey. It will help you to draw together, start to process and consolidate your experiences and those of your baby, and to think about what help and support you need going forwards. It will be a space to reflect and find creative ways to mark milestones and changes, as well as considering opportunities for personal growth.

The section on **final thoughts and next steps** draws everything together at the end of the book, reflecting on what you've been through, the main themes and threads of the book, and a moment to face forwards to the future.

CHAPTER 1

Getting through the first few weeks

Welcome to you and your baby as you start a new chapter as a family. You will have already been through quite a journey as you arrive here. A neonatal unit is a place most parents don't expect to be part of that journey, and when you first come through the doors it can feel like a very bewildering and frightening world. Even if you visited the unit whilst pregnant, for many it feels a different place when it's your own baby in the incubator. Whilst we will think in detail about the many emotional challenges on the way in this book, for now it's important to remember that everything you feel is valid, important and understandable.

If you are feeling very overwhelmed right now you can read this first chapter just on its own. It will support you to put some basic things into place straightaway to help you adjust and cope. The first few weeks on a neonatal unit are often described as 'a blur' or 'totally overwhelming', so be gentle on yourself as you read the information in this chapter. No one expects you to adapt or know what to do straightaway. Take your time, and little by little you will start to find a way through.

WHAT IS A NEONATAL UNIT?

A neonatal unit is a specialist ward in a hospital that looks after babies who have been born too soon (premature) or who are unwell and need medical care.

'Neonate' is one way of describing a baby who has been born recently, and there may be several reasons why a baby has been admitted to hospital.

Some babies who come to the neonatal unit stay for a short time and are then well enough to go home. For others the treatment they need can take many weeks or even months. All the babies in the unit are in the best place to get this treatment in an environment that is designed to help babies just like yours, with a team of professionals who specialize in their care.

> When people talk about 'levels' or types of care, they mean the type of neonatal care your baby needs to help them best with their medical needs, ranging from neonatal intensive care (referred to as NICU provided in Level 3 units) to special care (provided in all neonatal units and exclusively in Level 1 units). Babies can and do move between units, sometimes more than once.[1]

You might be on a unit that can look after your baby throughout their journey, from NICU to discharge from hospital, or they might move to a different hospital as they progress to be looked after in a local neonatal unit (LNU) before going home.

If your baby is born at a hospital whose neonatal unit doesn't have the specialist level of care they need, they will be transferred to a hospital that does. This can mean you may have to travel to a different city or region with your baby, which can bring a lot of additional stress, as you may have to adjust to unfamiliar surroundings. It can be hard not knowing where to shop for basics, park your car or see people you know.

As well as being away from friends and family, not having the medical professionals around you who have become familiar in your pregnancy can be difficult. It can also be very distressing for your baby to be moved to another hospital when you have not yet recovered from their birth or aren't yet well enough to be with them straightaway. Many of the exercises in this chapter will help you to manage the distress that comes from these challenges and to focus on what you need.

> Remember that at this early stage doctors will be making many decisions to support the best possible outcome for your baby.

Seeing your baby surrounded by medical equipment on a busy unit can be shocking and distressing at first. A range of machines and equipment helps them with breathing, feeding, maintaining their temperature and giving medicine as well as

1 See www.bliss.org.uk/parents/in-hospital/about-neonatal-care/how-does-neonatal-care-work

monitoring vital signs such as heart rate, breathing and the amount of oxygen in their blood. They might be in a closed incubator that closely controls their environment, where you put your hands through portholes to touch them, or an open incubator/heated cot that still provides support whilst your baby is easier to touch and be close to. Ask the nurse looking after your baby to take you through everything that's attached to them, from their head to their toes, at your own pace, giving you plenty of time to ask questions.

It can be helpful to learn what all the sounds and visuals on the monitors mean. This includes what you expect to hear routinely and what alarms may sound in your baby's space and throughout the unit. Knowing this information will make it easier in time to shift your focus towards your baby as their surroundings become more familiar and you know the meaning of what you're hearing. You'll notice that whilst the unit tries to keep the noise and light levels low, it can feel loud, chaotic and overwhelming at first whilst you adjust to the environment and learn what you can 'filter out'.

Unlike the experience you may have had visiting or being a patient in a hospital as an adult, where there are many regulations and limitations, neonatal units have an important philosophy of care: *parents are not visitors*. It is important that you are welcome at any time of the day or night to be with your baby, whenever you wish. Babies and families are at the heart of everything a neonatal unit does.

WHO ARE ALL THE PEOPLE ON THE UNIT?

Lots of people are involved in caring for your baby. They will be there because they have specialist skills and an interest in caring for babies just like yours. If you think about your baby in the centre of a circle, around them are a set of visible people (the ones you interact with and meet straightaway, such as doctors and nurses, family support teams), and many others who might be involved in their care in less direct ways, or you may meet at different times or for different reasons during your stay (e.g., nursery nurses, pharmacists, therapists, surgeons, feeding supporters).[2] You will see some of the ways these professionals can help you and your baby at different times throughout the book.

2 You can find a full list of professionals you may encounter on the neonatal ward on the Bliss website: www.bliss.org.uk/parents/in-hospital/about-neonatal-care/neonatal-staff-and-what-they-do

Nurses and doctors

Nurses and doctors provide the majority of your baby's day-to-day care. They usually work 12-hour shifts, allowing your baby to receive the same level of care at night as during the day. Between each shift there is a 'handover' where all the critical information about the care of your baby from the last 12 hours is given to the team taking over.

You will meet many nurses and doctors, and this can be particularly distressing when you are anxious about your baby and in need of familiarity. You will often find that the same nurse might be allocated to your baby for a few days in a row, which can give you a chance to get to know them. Depending on the size of the unit, you may also find that after a few weeks you start to recognize people, and they may be more likely to rotate in specific areas of the unit, such as intensive care. If you are staying more than a few weeks, the team will quickly get to know you.

Psychological professionals

Psychological professionals such as clinical psychologists, psychotherapists and counsellors work on units to help parents manage the psychological and emotional impact of a neonatal admission as well as thinking about the needs of the babies. They also support the neonatal team to care for you and your family's needs.

Whilst this book is designed to help you with some of the emotional and psychological challenges that arise when you have a baby in neonatal care, it isn't a substitute for the role of a psychological professional who can understand your specific needs in depth and work to support you throughout your baby's admission. Ask your neonatal team who is available to you and how you can contact them.

WHAT YOU MIGHT BE FEELING, AND IDENTIFYING YOUR BASIC NEEDS

Having a baby in neonatal care is commonly a time of emotional and physical strain and exhaustion that takes its toll. You may still be in pain from procedures or surgery and taking medication that can make you feel drowsy or not quite yourself. You may feel like nothing seems real or you may be in shock, anxious and unable to rest or feel calm. The challenges and tasks of adjusting to being on a neonatal unit are significant.

Normally when we feel like this we recognize the need for recuperation and recovery, giving ourselves the time and resources to do so. If you have had a baby before, you might recall being on the sofa in your pyjamas for a few weeks afterwards, suspending the rules of 'normal life' as you slowly gather the confidence and energy to venture out of the house or get back into your normal routine.

In contrast, when your baby is transferred to neonatal care, everything can happen very quickly. You may have been at their side as within a few hours you are trying to take in so much that is new and frightening, to work out what the situation is and doing your best to support and comfort your baby. You may be far away from home, had to travel suddenly to a new city or be separated from your family or other children. It's a lot to know how to process or take in straightaway. As a consequence, parents often feel the first few days and weeks on the unit are overwhelming.

ALLOWING TIME FOR PHYSICAL RECOVERY AND REST FROM BIRTH

It's important to remember that you, or your partner, have just given birth, and that it takes time to recover from this experience physically as well as emotionally, even whilst your focus and that of the neonatal team may be largely on your baby. Sometimes it can feel like an impossible demand to be up, dressed and looking after your baby when you are exhausted, in pain and may be unwell yourself.

What to do if you are in pain or unwell yourself

Ask your neonatal team what's in place to assist you with your own recovery from birth and what check-ups you can expect. Let them know if you are in a lot of pain, feel unwell or need a consultation. If your baby has been transferred to a different hospital after birth, it's essential that your neonatal and midwifery team ensure you have access to follow-up care where you are, and that your health visitor knows that you are in a different hospital.

Your baby's neonatal nurse will help you to arrange yourself so you are as comfortable as you can be at your baby's side. Extra cushions, reclining chairs and ways to hold your baby that don't cause discomfort can be worked out together.

If you are prone to self-criticism or find it hard to attend to your needs, remember that your body has been through a lot of demands, and it deserves an opportunity to heal and recover. You are not taking any focus away from your baby by also looking after yourself.

What to do if you are not getting enough sleep

Sleep is important to prioritize as lack of sleep is likely to leave you more emotionally overwhelmed and unable to cope, as well as having an impact on how you think and react. However, achieving longer periods of sleep is difficult due to high levels of anxiety and stress and an uncomfortable and busy environment on the unit. Whilst parents are advised to go home and sleep, for many the separation from their baby can mean that it is very difficult to do so. Increasingly units welcome parents to sleep next to their babies or have beds available nearby on the unit. Others have specific free parent accommodation that is near to the hospital, and may also be able to provide facilities for the whole family if parents have other children. There is often a waiting list, however, so it's helpful to make the team aware of your preferences and needs for accommodation as soon as possible.

To help with rest and sleep:

- Rest, when you can, next to your baby, particularly when they are sleeping or having a more settled period. Most units have 'quiet times' when there will be less happening in terms of procedures and visits from professionals.
- Block out the noise of the unit with headphones and use an eye mask when needed. You can agree with your baby's nurse when they should wake you and how.
- Request a reclining chair if available, raise your feet up, and cover yourself in a comforting blanket.
- Discuss plans for pumping ('expressing') milk or other tasks that may be disrupting longer periods of sleep, and how the needs of you and your baby can be considered.

If you leave the unit to sleep it can be helpful to talk through any worries with your baby's nurse beforehand, such as when and how they can contact you if needed, what's likely to happen to your baby when you are gone, and what to expect when you return. Naming what is worrying you and planning what can help with those worries can reduce anxiety and makes your needs clearer for the team.

UNDERSTANDING FEELING OVERWHELMED AND YOUR EMOTIONAL CAPACITY

We all have a certain capacity for dealing with the events that happen in our lives, the stresses and strains and responsibilities we carry, and the emotions they leave us with. You can imagine you are like a container that fills up with things over time. When the container isn't too full, there is some space to deal with things that come your way. They can be hard, but you don't feel overwhelmed by them. But at times, when the container is full to the brim, it takes very little to feel you cannot cope, and you can experience all sorts of overwhelming emotions.

You can see from Taylor's container that it's already full. A change of nurse after three days was enough for her to feel suddenly overwhelmed, as her capacity to hold all her emotions and experiences was exceeded.

The contents of Taylor's container

'WHAT AM I HOLDING?' IMAGINING YOURSELF AS A CONTAINER

Here is a container for you to complete for yourself. Think about what you have in your container and how much space it takes up for you emotionally. What you put in your container may be events and situations that are happening now or that may have happened very recently, but they can also be things from the past that have a longer-term impact.

What I am holding (the contents of my container)

This exercise may help you to see how much you are dealing with, alongside what is happening to your baby. Most parents who take the time to reflect on this are surprised by just how much they have been holding, often over a very long period of time – and how 'close to the edge' they feel. You might have experienced several events that have left you feeling overwhelmed already. You can begin to help yourself by taking action to bring the level in the container down, even if it's only a little, to give you a bit more capacity or space to deal with what's happening. This might be by:

- Problem solving specific issues with the help of your family, friends and neonatal team – how to rest and recover post birth whilst being with your baby, for example
- Finding out information – think about what would be helpful to know and who around you can signpost you to it
- Adding in nurturing and soothing things that you can do for yourself to help reduce distress

- Working out what you can acknowledge is hard or needs doing but that can be left to one side for now.

When faced with a crisis situation there are many things that have to be put to one side, even though they're important, as Max's story shows:

> Max was really worried about his business's financial situation, which had been a huge strain during the pregnancy. Although this was important and mattered, he realized that he couldn't continue to give it so much thought and time whilst his baby was in a critical condition. He allowed himself to take this out of his container and put it aside, so that he could focus on what was ahead of him, letting his colleagues know he would come back to them in a month's time.

REDUCING WHAT YOU'RE HOLDING IN YOUR CONTAINER

Have a look at what's in your container and list anything that you acknowledge is there but that can be put to one side for now:

....

....

....

....

....

....

Make a list of what's in your container that needs *immediate* attention. This may be practical worries, concerns about care or emotional distress:

....

....

....

....

....

....

We will now think together about how you can start to think about these needs.

THINKING ABOUT YOUR NEEDS RIGHT AT THIS MOMENT

Neonatal care teams know how hard it is for parents, especially when their baby has just been admitted, and will be trying to meet your needs as best they can based on what they know is helpful to everybody. However, there will also be needs that are more specific to you and your family.

As you thought about what is filling up your capacity in the 'Imagining yourself as a container' exercise, you might have started to think about what your needs are in relation to each item. Let the team know if they can help you directly or signpost you to appropriate help and support. It won't mean that they are spending any less time caring for your baby if they are also thinking about you – neonatal care is about looking after the whole family.

First needs

First needs are often practical in nature, such as making sure you have adequate pain relief, some cushions on your chair to be able to sit or lie next to your baby, a place to rest or some comfortable clothes to put on. You may also need the neonatal team to help you address specific anxieties or questions that are at the forefront of your mind. For example, you may want to know if your baby feels comfortable or in pain, what the equipment around them is for, or what it means.

Connections to one person

At times of very heightened stress a lot of our emotional needs are met by connections we build with other people who can help us feel safe and calm when we are afraid and worried. Having consistent contact with one person over the first few days can help, as someone familiar in the unfamiliar. This will often be a neonatal nurse who looks after your baby for a few days in a row, or a member of a family support team. The following exercise will help you to think about your needs – physical, practical and emotional – in the first few days.

'WHAT I NEED'

Think about what you need right now to help you in these first few days (bearing in mind that these needs will evolve and change during your time on the unit) to help with everything you've identified. This exercise breaks these down into different areas. You may wish to do this for yourself and then think about what you might need as a couple or as a family. Keep this list nearby and add to it as things come to you throughout the day.

'What I need physically', *for example, pain relief, help with moving, help with finding a comfortable sitting position to see my baby, sleep and rest, food/drink, help with expressing and breast soreness.*

....

....

....

....

'What I need practically', *for example, someone to look after my dogs, someone to inform work and friends of the situation, tops I can wear to hold my baby skin to skin, maternity and breast pads, mobile phone charger/credit, help with expressing equipment and timings and a map of nearby amenities.*

....

....

....

....

'What I need emotionally', *for example, time with my baby without too many visitors, open conversations with my partner and family and people around me on the unit who help me feel calm, confident and safe.*

....

....

....

....

'What I need from my partner' (you can discuss this together and think about how you can meet each other's needs), *for example, lots of holding and hugs, reassurance, encouragement and support when talking to the consultants.*

....

....

....

....

'What I need in relation to my baby', *for example, time to be with my baby without other demands, cuddles or close touch when I can, time to talk and sing to them, time when I know they are more stable so I can wholly relax when I'm with them and minimal separation.*

....

....

....

....

Note: You may never have asked yourself what you need before, and thinking about yourself in this way may be new. You may also be thinking, 'How do I know what I need? I have never been in this situation before!' Whilst it may be true that this situation is new, there may be similarities with other difficult times in your life. If you can, write something for each area – you are then making a great start.

Here is an example of how Rosie identified her needs in the first few days.

Rosie struggled to remember her first few days on the unit, and it felt like they had all merged into one. She hadn't slept properly for five days and was finding it hard to keep going, although she was scared to go home and sleep away from her baby.

When thinking about what she needed to help her manage at that moment, she identified rest as something really important, and the team worked with her to help her find a way to get comfortable whilst next to her baby on the unit.

Rosie felt very anxious each time the consultant came to speak with her as she felt like they were going to give her bad news. To meet her emotional need at that time, she identified a nurse who could put things in a way she understood and who was calm and containing.

Dave, Rosie's partner, was trying to be supportive, but she experienced his enthusiasm to help as 'fussing', which, in turn, made her feel 'on edge'. By explaining this to him, and that he was doing enough by being by her side, they were able to find some calm time together in the nursery.

Rosie felt most connected to her baby when she was touching her. Although she wasn't yet able to hold her, being shown how to give her a cuddle with her hands in the incubator enabled Rosie to feel that connection when she needed it, even with all the medical equipment around her.

SETTING EXPECTATIONS OF YOURSELF AND OTHERS

We all hold multiple expectations of how we might behave or cope in traumatic or stressful situations, imagining we need to adapt or 'manage' straightaway. In fact, being able to come to the unit and function with some first tasks – perhaps spending time with your baby, managing to eat something, rest and start expressing milk – is an incredible achievement. Over time you will find yourself adjusting, and some things will become easier and more familiar. Be gentle and compassionate when all is distressing and new.

Here is a list of things that parents often report in the first few days of being on a neonatal unit:

- Feeling tearful or crying a lot
- Feeling overwhelmed and afraid
- Finding information and language difficult to understand
- Feeling unable to plan or think ahead, or worrying about the future constantly
- Feeling in shock or like events aren't real
- Feeling alone or lost
- Being unsure or unable to communicate with family or friends
- Feeling watched or monitored by staff
- Not feeling like a parent
- Feeling devastated to be separated from their baby
- Feeling like everyone else is coping or doing things better
- Experiencing 'sensory overload' from all the new sights, smells and sounds.

Finding a compassionate voice inside you that acknowledges your distress and wishes to help you find ways to lessen it will help during your baby's admission. We will talk about how you can develop a more compassionate approach to yourself and your challenges throughout the book. For now, you could ask yourself some of the following questions when you might be setting some unrealistic expectations of yourself:

- If my best friend or a dear family member were sitting here with me, would they have the same expectations?

- Would I expect the same of a friend if they told me they were in the same situation?
- Would I talk to my children like that if they were distressed or finding something difficult?
- Is it helping me by being so harsh to myself right now?

If you can't find a compassionate voice for yourself just yet, think about whether there's someone in your life who can bring this compassion to you. This may be a partner, friend, parent or a grandparent.

It's okay not to have all the answers or to feel like you can make sense of all your emotions. Sometimes one person to start with who can hear you and sit with your situation and feelings can make a big difference.

BUILDING A SUPPORT NETWORK

Many people struggle with the idea of asking for and receiving support from others even when they would happily offer it themselves. Take a moment to notice what it brings up for you when you think about asking for help, and what beliefs you hold about it. Maybe you hold beliefs about being independent or not relying on people. Perhaps you have been let down or mistreated by those you have confided in or trusted to help you. Whether it's professional support or support from friends and family, whilst asking for help may not feel straightforward or easy, it's important to consider who around you can help and how, through a very challenging time.

To do this you can think of *types* of help and support, and *who* in your network can provide them. We go to different people in our lives for different reasons, for different things and at different times. For now, think about who you need around you for the next few weeks.

Note: It is also important to consider who you may *not* wish to have around you, particularly if there are people in your life who you find difficult or who are not able to nurture and support you. This doesn't necessarily mean you need them to keep this distance forever, but perhaps you can 'pause' their involvement until you feel able and ready to have them involved in your new baby's life.

MAPPING OUT A SUPPORT NETWORK

In the centre of the page is you. In each box are some types or areas of support to help get you started, and a space to write the names of people in your network who can provide this for you as well as a box to add others who are also important to you.

People who can provide a range of practical support, *for example, ensuring bills are paid, collecting and washing clothing, organizing childcare, cooking or delivering food, liaising with my employers, driving me to and from the hospital and feeding pets.*

People who can help me with information gathering, *for example, finding out about maternity and paternity pay/rights, researching support groups for parents whose children have a similar issue and working out financial benefits or assistance.*

People who can share information and manage my network, *for example, being the spokesperson on the phone and through social media, giving weekly updates and updating more distant relatives or acquaintances.*

People who can provide support relating to my baby's condition, *for example, explaining what's happening in a way I can understand, talking me through what equipment or treatment they need and explaining plans and the reason for a particular approach.*

Me

People who can provide emotional support, *for example, listening to what is happening without judgement, validating my experiences, encouraging me, sitting with me and keeping me company, being in the hospital even if they can't come to the unit if I need them and helping me find ways to cope.*

Other key areas and people who can support me in each of these:

WAYS TO HELP IMMEDIATELY WHEN EMOTIONS FEEL UNMANAGEABLE

When anxiety or panic overwhelms us, the thinking parts of our brain shut down and we struggle to organize our thoughts, know what to do next or even find the words to express ourselves. It's useful to concentrate on bringing our mind and our bodies back into a state where they can function and help us. Here are some ways to do this using a 'Soothing breathing rhythm' or 'Dropping anchor'.

SOOTHING BREATHING RHYTHM

When we are highly anxious our breathing becomes shallow and rapid. We can feel like we can't get enough air and we might start to have thoughts that something dreadful will happen. Our body's threat system has become activated and is flooding our system with adrenaline. To apply the physiological 'brakes' and bring ourselves back to a calmer place, we can use a simple breathing method.

Sit up straight in your chair, with your feet firmly on the floor. Bring your shoulders back so that your chest is open and not constricted. You may wish to close your eyes or choose a fixed point to lower your gaze onto. Bring your attention to your breathing and notice as the air comes in and out of your body. Try to breathe in through your nose and out through your mouth.

At this moment focus most on your 'out' breath – and see if you can hear a noise as the air escapes from your body – just blow it out through your mouth. Then breathe in again through your nose, try to pause for a brief moment and then breathe out again through your mouth.

Sometimes it's helpful to imagine blowing a feather further and further away from your body or imagine blowing a colour that represents your distress out of your body. See if you can push the imaginary feather a little further away from you each time you breathe out.

Continue with this breathing for a few minutes.

If you find your attention moving back to thoughts or things happening around you, just gently bring your attention back to your breath for now. You may notice that your heart rate begins to slow and that your breathing becomes steadier. Your body may feel heavier or change in other ways as it becomes less tense and on 'high alert'.

When you're ready, gently open your eyes and bring your attention back to your surroundings.

'DROPPING ANCHOR'[3]

When we are completely overwhelmed by our emotions, we can find it hard to think, be unable to stop crying, or feel so panicked we experience lots of unpleasant physical sensations such as a rapid heart rate, feeling faint or like things around us are unreal or terrifying. Doctor and psychotherapist Russ Harris describes this as like being in an 'emotional storm'. What we can do to help at this moment is to 'drop anchor' – that is, whilst the storm rages around us we can find a way to keep ourselves steady in that storm. It doesn't make the storm and everything that we are affected by go away, but it helps us to not get swept up entirely in it at that moment.

Acknowledge that you are experiencing overwhelming emotions in this moment. Push your feet hard into the floor, push your fingertips together or stretch your arms.

Acknowledge the pain you are feeling in the present and also notice there is a body around that pain, a body you can move and control. Whilst you are noticing all the parts of your body, press your feet into the floor...

Now look around where you are and notice five things you can see. Say them to yourself as you see each one.

Bring your awareness to three things you can hear and mentally note each one.

Notice there are painful thoughts and feelings, and notice your body in the chair. Move it and stretch it. Also notice there is a room around you. Then come back to what you are doing.

You may find yourself needing to do this several times as emotions come like waves. Keep anchoring yourself by using this brief exercise as much as you need.

PLAN FOR VERY SMALL WINDOWS OF TIME

When we panic or feel totally overwhelmed, we can start to worry about how we are going to get through the next day or even the next couple of hours. We can also find ourselves having thoughts that go a long time into the future – How will I pay my mortgage? What about my job? How will my child cope at primary school? How will I survive this? Notice what happens when you start to think ahead too far – it can often make us feel worse.

When this happens, it can be helpful to shorten the time window that you're dealing with into something more manageable. *This means you may be coping hour*

3 'Dropping Anchor' script copyright Russ Harris (2016). www.actmindfully.com.au/upimages/Dropping_ anchor_script.pd

by hour to start with. Plan how you are going to get through the next hour only. It may look something like Anna's plan.

ANNA'S PLAN FOR THE FIRST HOUR OF DAY 3 ON THE UNIT

Take a brief walk around the block before I come onto the unit.

Make a hot comforting drink in the unit kitchen to have whilst pumping breast milk for my baby.

Do a nappy change with the nurse and talk to them about my baby and how they've been overnight.

Look through messages of encouragement from friends on my phone.

Hug my partner.

Engage in my 'Soothing breathing rhythm' each time I feel panicky.

If you find your thoughts wandering or panic rising, try and bring yourself gently back to what is next on your list. When you have completed that hour, you've done so well. Now plan the next one.

You may want to ask your baby's nurse if they can help you as they will have ideas about what you could be doing with your baby at first, including what you can do with their support and guidance. *Focus on what you can do*, rather than those things that you may not be able to do or solve yet.

✓ ENHANCED COPING STATEMENTS/CARDS

If you are struggling to hold hope or find a way through the next moment, it may be hard to hold onto anything positive or comforting. Sometimes we don't even remember information that may offer a different perspective.

Making coping statements/cards either physically or on your phone is a way to remind yourself of important facts or encouragement of others when you can't recall them on your own.

Step one: Ideally with a partner or friend, make a list of anything that has been said to you about your baby or situation that has been helpful. Also include anything anyone has said to you about yourself that has been encouraging or made you feel better, even for a moment.

....

....

....

Step two: Imagine the tone of voice you need these statements to be spoken to you in right at this moment. You might want to use the voice of someone real in your life, or the voice of an imagined perfectly soothing and wise person.

Step three: If you find it is more effective to listen to recordings of these statements and you have a person who can do this for you, you could store them as a recording or video on your phone.

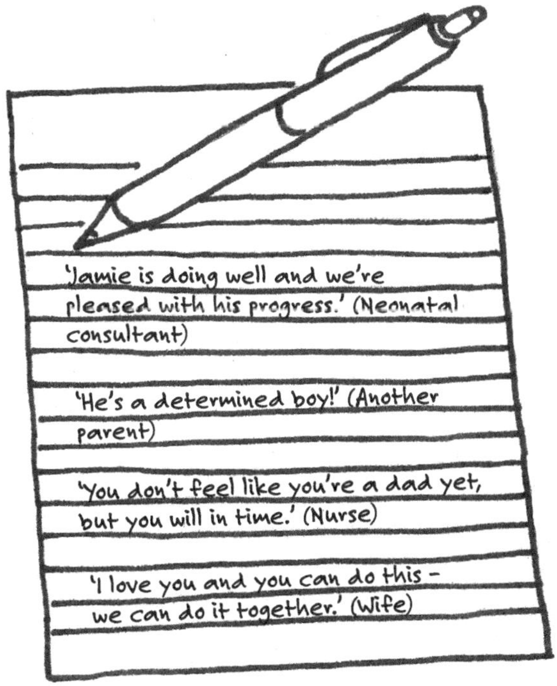

John's coping cards

John found it most helpful to imagine the voice and loving face of his grandmother when he looked through these statements. Hearing her voice say them in his mind changed how he felt emotionally, from being panicked to feeling more soothed and reassured, which enabled him to move on to the plans he'd made for the morning.

✓ DRAWING ON WHAT HAS HELPED YOU IN A CRISIS BEFORE

Whilst the situation may be different, we often forget that there are things we have learnt about coping in a crisis from earlier in our lives. You are an expert in yourself and you know yourself best. Think about what can help. It doesn't have to be something for the long term; it can just be something that can get you through right now. You may have already put some of these things into practice without thinking about it.

Look back to hard times in your life and what has got you through, and make a list of those things here. Make time to put some of these things into your day, building them into your routine:

....

....

....

....

....

....

DEVELOPING A ROUTINE ON THE UNIT

Having a routine and some shape to your day and weeks can help things feel more predictable and containing. At the start you won't know what a day on a neonatal unit looks like, but as you see what is happening with your baby and talk to the team and other parents, you will begin to have more of an idea of what is involved. Of course, the environment has a degree of uncertainty about it, as days do not always go to a plan, but having a basic structure is a helpful starting point. You might find that you're able to start being involved in caring for your baby bit by bit, even though this can feel daunting at first (see Chapter 4). It can also help you make time for elements of the day that are less focused on your baby's medical care or physical needs, such as incorporating a bedtime routine.

Your neonatal unit's daily routine

Your neonatal unit's day will have its own 'rhythm', for example, having times for procedures, treatments and ward rounds and other 'quiet times' when your baby can rest and have uninterrupted time with you. As well as thinking about what your baby's day is like, it's also important to think about building in parts of your day to nurture and look after yourself even if they are short, such as allowing 10–15 minutes outside to get some fresh air and walk through the park, a trip to get a fresh coffee, or having a shower and changing your clothes.

Your baby's routine

You may find it easier to take a break when your baby is asleep and settled, or wait until you are confident to leave them in the care of their nurse. We wouldn't normally expect ourselves to leave our children with someone we don't know, and it can feel the same when we are on the unit. Take time to get to know your nurse and help them to help you feel confident and safe. Sometimes agreeing when they will call you and letting them know how your baby likes to be soothed and comforted can help you manage a short period apart.

MAPPING OUT A ROUTINE

Start to map out a routine based on a list of what is most important for you and your baby. List the most important things here:

1. ....
2. ....
3. ....
4. ....
5. ....

Discuss and share your plans with your baby's team so they can work with you to put in place what's possible at this moment in time and what you'd like to be involved in straightaway. For example, if you would like to do the first nappy change of the day, shared planning means they can wait until you come in in the morning rather than doing it before you get there. If you would like to hold your baby skin to skin, this might need a bit of planning to make sure the right staff are present to support you and your baby. (You can find more details about planning your day around the needs of your baby and yourself in Chapter 4.)

MANAGING SEPARATION FROM YOUR BABY

The sudden change from being pregnant and constantly with your baby to being apart when they're in hospital can feel devastating for many parents. Whilst every effort will be made to keep you and your baby together, there will be times when you're apart, often due to necessity. For example, you may need to spend time with your other children, sleep and eat, which may not be possible beside your baby, or you may need to travel a long way to and from the hospital. If you are the parent of twins or triplets, you might find that your babies are in different hospitals or different parts of the unit, which means you may spend longer periods apart from them.

If you are struggling with separation from your baby, here are some ways to manage and keep connected to them:

- Remind yourself you are doing your best for your baby. You are their parent at all times, even when you aren't with them.

- Find ways to stay physically connected to them. You can use 'bonding squares' to help. These are small pieces of fabric or knitting that are used to help connect you and your baby and are soothing for you both through the sense of smell. One square goes in your bra or down your top against your skin, so that it smells of you over time, and another is placed with your baby, which will start to smell of them. When you exchange the squares, you can both benefit from the smell of each other, which can be soothing and connecting. You can also think about ways of connecting through touch, such as having items of your baby's clothing (if they are able to wear clothing), as well as looking at photos and videos. You may wish to set some time aside to look at photos without other distractions, so that you can focus your attention solely on your baby.

- When you are with your baby, spend a moment taking in the whole sense of them as a person, using all your senses (what you can see, smell, hear, touch and even taste). Scan their body from head to foot, and notice how you feel in your body when you are close to them. When you are apart, reconnect with this state memory by imagining how it feels to be with them, sense by sense.

- Ask the team to keep you updated with messages and videos of your baby (see 'Keeping a diary and using a shared diary with the neonatal team' for some creative ideas to tailor this to your needs).

- Find symbolic ways to connect you with your baby. This may be by having particular objects that in some way represent them or your connection, or pieces of music, poems or prayers that give you a feeling of togetherness. You may wish to leave a photo of you both together with your baby as well as having one for yourself.

- Read stories to your baby that address ideas and themes that are important to you, such as love across distance. Talk to your baby about how you feel about them when you can't be there. You may want to record yourself talking or singing to your baby so that this can be played to them when you're apart. Explore with your neonatal team what technology they have available to facilitate this.

- Remind yourself that this separation is temporary and will come to an end. One day you can tell your baby the story of how much you longed to be with them and how much they were loved, even when you were apart.

MANAGING PUMPING (EXPRESSING) BREAST MILK FOR YOUR BABY

Whilst you may have been told expressing milk is 'the one thing you can do for your baby', particularly when they are very unwell, it's often a difficult and emotionally charged task. Your body is still recovering from birth, and there are many practical, physical and emotional factors that can make expressing a challenge, *none of which are your fault*. If you're planning to express milk, here are some first general principles to help. Remember that many nurses have specialist expertise in helping you in this area, and some units also have lactation consultants who can offer you one-to-one advice and support:

- Compassionately reduce the pressure and expectations on yourself, even if you feel them acutely from others. You are doing the best to make a start wherever you're at.

- Spend some time intentionally bringing your body and mind into a place to express. This can range from being in the right physical environment (beside your baby, chatting to supportive others or on your own) to allowing yourself time to engage in soothing breathing/imagery exercises to settle your body before starting, and reducing your anxiety and stress even a little (see the 'Soothing breathing rhythm' exercise). For some mothers, expressing whilst they are looking at their phone or distracting themselves can be easier at first – it's okay to do what works for you at different points in time.

- It's natural to compare, but try and resist comparison with others when you can. There are many reasons why others may have different amounts of milk to you, and it doesn't mean your efforts are in any way inferior or less valuable. Your baby will benefit from everything you are able to give them.
- Talk to your partner, family and team about what's possible within your routine and commitments. Whilst you will be advised to express very regularly, it's imperative that the whole picture is considered (such as the impact on your sleep). Specialists on your unit will be able to advise you further.
- Professionals should always ask before touching your body, if this is required, to support you with expressing. If this touch is difficult or distressing in any way, or there is something about the process of expressing that is troubling, let them, or another member of the team such as a psychological professional know so that the right support can be provided quickly.

PERSONALIZING YOUR BABY'S SPACE AND FINDING POCKETS OF 'NORMAL' IN HOSPITAL

This space is our home for now, and the only home she has known so far.

SAM, NICU MUM OF BABY KRYSTAL, BORN AT 27 WEEKS

It can feel like many of the things you would have liked to do for your baby have been changed or taken from you when your baby is admitted to hospital, particularly if they are in intensive care. You will have had plans and dreams for how you wanted this time to be and what you wanted your baby to experience in their very earliest days.

It may seem like there is little you can do in the hospital to make it feel like your child's space or for anything to feel 'normal' in a highly medicalized environment. At the same time, you yourself will be spending a huge amount of time in hospital away from your home at a time when you need safety and familiarity. For both you and your baby it's important for the neonatal team to understand that the space around your baby is in many ways an intimate and personal space that is acting as a temporary home. Working out how to occupy this space together is important, and done well can mean it feels both flexible and protected. There are places within this space that are private (such as your baby's drawers or bedside cabinet), and there may be times when you can use screens to physically shield the space from other families and healthcare staff.

For every parent it's important that their baby is seen as a unique person and not simply as a collection of medical problems to be fixed. A baby's identity and personality develop over time, and it can start with something as simple as their name. There may be a story, memory of someone or a particular meaning associated with their name that you'd like to share with others. In many hospitals each baby is given a name sign to personalize, which also includes the names of their parents. When you personalize this sign, think about what you'd like to include that is already part of your baby's story and history, as well as who they are in the context of their family.

Let's look at baby Tetsu's story:

> Tetsu had been referred to affectionately as the 'jumping bean' during pregnancy as she was very active, so her parents drew this on her name sign. The meaning of her name – 'strong as iron' – was also important to share, and was a positive focus of discussions during ward rounds. The parents took the sign home for her brothers and sisters to draw on themselves, so that the whole family was represented and could watch over Tetsu until they were all together at home. Aya, Tetsu's mum, spent time colouring in the sign at her cot side, which she found calming and a different way of 'doing something' for Tetsu.

When considering how to more broadly personalize and normalize your baby's cot space, think about what is important to you and your family as well as what reflects your style and personalities. Are there pictures of you or any siblings you can safely place in or near the incubator, any soft toys that have been brought for them they can have nearby, or particular music or sounds they can listen to?

As they grow and get well, there will be less equipment and more scope to add in things that are meaningful to you. It's important to keep what you've created in any transitions or moves (both within the unit and hospitals) (see 'Moving between different areas of the unit' in Chapter 9 for more).

Let's look at what Johannas's family put in place for him in the NICU, and how this continued to be important as he got older:

> Johannas came to the unit very poorly, and there were many nights when his parents described keeping a vigil at the side of the incubator despite being told to rest. They were a religious family who believed that God was watching over

Johannas even when they had to step away or go home. In their family they had many symbols that represented being watched over by God or angels. They were given a small angel who could be placed over Johannas's incubator – an important recognition of their belief that gave them a sense of peace in the middle of a busy intensive care unit. When he was older, they placed the same angel on his bedside table, as a reminder of what he had come through and the continued importance of God's presence in their family.

Small changes such as using your own blankets from home as an incubator cover or doing washing with your own familiar detergent rather than placing items in the hospital laundry can bring moments of familiarity and homeliness, as well as organizing equipment and supplies for your baby to help with the flow of their day. Plans to read particular books, sing certain songs and a range of traditions you might have shared with your other children or planned for your new baby can be incorporated into the neonatal environment and may feel more 'normal' than activities that are focused on medical care.

A sense of normality can also come from the everyday chats with the team, keeping some of your routines from life before the neonatal unit (such as catching up with friends on the phone, buying the newspaper) or 'top and tailing' your day with regular routines and tasks (such as the school run, cooking dinner for your other children or helping with homework). Normality can be grounding at a time of rapid change, both for you and your family (see Chapter 7 for more). Take a moment to think about how you can bring this into your days and weeks where you can.

DISCOVERING AND CONNECTING WITH YOUR BABY

Some parents fall in love with their babies straightaway, feeling an intense connection from the moment they are born. For many others this is not the case, particularly when their baby has been born early or is sick. There can be a lot of shame or worry about not feeling connected to your baby, and this is often amplified by messages from the media and others. Common misconceptions include there being something wrong if you don't feel a 'rush of love' straightaway, or that perhaps you've missed a critical window of opportunity you'll never be able to recover. In fact, feeling a bond with your baby is something that develops over time for many, and we will talk about this process in greater depth in Chapter 6 of this book.

Here we are going to focus on how you can start the process of connecting with your baby with an acknowledgement that it's often challenging or can feel a 'risky' thing to do emotionally. If you're able to do something small every day, even if you don't feel an overwhelming change straightaway, you have made the first step.

FIRST STEPS TO HELP

- Acknowledge where you feel you are with the connection to your baby, and that it's okay to feel the way you do, whatever it is. Remind yourself that feelings are likely to change gradually and are often linked to factors outside your control (such as how medically stable your baby is, how sedated they are or what physical barriers, such as incubators, there are around them).
- Spend some time watching your baby, and see if you can look past the medical equipment for a few moments, finding perhaps a small part of them to focus on, such as their hands or eyes. Remind yourself that underneath all that equipment they are a real little person waiting to develop and change – there is a lot they can't show you yet.
- Hold them if you can, either skin to skin or using your hands around them (also called 'containment holding'), and just notice how you feel. Does that feeling change at all, day by day? What kind of things lead to a change, even if it's fleeting? How does your baby respond to you?
- Use 'bonding squares' to help with connection, which also aid with bonding and milk production at a biological level through the sense of smell.
- Start to become involved in your baby's care when you feel able. There are many ways to do this. Ask your nurse to help you to notice how they respond to your presence if it's not obvious straightaway. Feeding your baby can sometimes be a powerful way to start to feel connected to them, particularly when they are able to move to the breast and/or bottle.

Remember that simply being alongside your baby when they need you is building your relationship with them.

CELEBRATING AND MARKING SMALL STEPS AND MILESTONES, AND MEMORY MAKING

The baby world is often full of talk and marking of milestones – from firsts to new developments. Many parents enjoy celebrating these with their baby, but find that the milestones families mark with babies outside the neonatal unit are vastly different to those in hospital. It can be helpful to begin to think about the ways you want to mark new milestones in neonatal care. These can be related to:

- Changes in medical care (e.g., moving from a closed incubator to an open cot, a change to the type of breathing support)
- Baby care and parenting (e.g., first bath, first cuddle, first breast or bottle feed)
- Facts and figures (e.g., weight gain, days in hospital)
- Development (e.g., starting to look at things, grasping a finger, smiling)
- Significant transitions (e.g., moving to a different level of care or going home).

Many parents also enjoy using cards (or other creative ideas such as coloured beads, charms or buttons) to mark things such as bravery, getting through surgery or days when someone significant came to visit. Marking these milestones helps as a reminder of progress and the small but significant steps your baby is making, which are helpful to keep track of, particularly when there are difficult days or it feels like there are few positives.

A number of local and national neonatal charities and organizations produce beautiful milestone cards, and many units will have some available for use. You might wish to use these when taking a photo of a significant moment, file them in a diary or use them as a visual aid to remind yourself of progress. If you would like to make your own or add to existing cards, this can be a mindful and helpful activity at cot side – you will find most units have a craft trolley available with supplies. Siblings and your wider family may also enjoy contributing to these and personalizing them, helping you to include elements that are significant and important to you.

> Stuart, a long-time fan of racing cars, designed cards with different vehicles for his son Kian that reflected something of the milestone itself (e.g., a picture of a roofless sports car when he moved into an open cot from an incubator). When he left the neonatal unit, Stuart put all the cards in a frame as a visual map of Kian's journey, with Kian racing over the finish line at the end.

Many parents have a special box or folder for memory making. As well as milestone markers, these can hold items such as first clothes, medical memorabilia, things they use each day, dummies and clean nappies of various sizes and locks of hair. They can also include messages and cards from friends and family and significant things you have been sent or had made for your baby.

There are other memory-making activities that many units offer, such as making hand and footprints of your baby alone, or with your handprints altogether as a family. Think about how you would like to use photos – you might wish to include certain people in these, include objects for scale that can show you over time how your baby has grown, or take photos of your baby with special gifts or connecting items (such as matching teddies) from a sibling.

KEEPING A DIARY AND USING A SHARED DIARY WITH THE NEONATAL TEAM

Diaries can be a helpful way to process events, put words or drawings on paper that reflect experiences or simply a way to record the 'landscape' of the neonatal stay. Consider what you'd like to record in a diary and how you want to do it. You may wish to use it as a scrapbook, including photos and some smaller objects from the unit, or simply a written account just for your reference.

If you prefer a premade structure, many NICU journals are available to purchase that have the format of a baby book (which you can search for online, as well as online neonatal journey apps). You may also wish to use a journal or diary to record specific information for a particular purpose.

Let's look at how this helped Lydia:

Lydia found it hard to see her baby in pain, and began to feel that all her days were filled with painful procedures and distress. At night she couldn't recall anything else about her baby's day, feeling low and anxious as a result. Using a diary, she reserved a special section for recording times when her daughter was settled and content. She made notes describing how her baby showed her she was settled (taking a photo to accompany her description) and how long this period lasted. This specific information helped her to balance her thoughts and perception at nighttime, reducing worry, and became a valuable record of her daughter's development and progress later on.

You could invite the neonatal team to contribute to your memory making or a family diary by writing messages to your baby at different stages of their stay. This can include their own memories of your baby (e.g., of when they first arrived on the unit or what they have enjoyed or noticed about your baby, such as glimpses of their personality).

Shared diaries can range from those that are open for contributions from the neonatal team on paper by the cot side to the use of electronic diaries through your baby's electronic notes systems (such as Baby Diary in BadgerNet) or secure video diary systems (such as vCreate). Many units have a shared diary system set up as it often helps improve communication and trust as well as making care feel more personal. You may wish to tailor some aspects of this to meet your needs.

Here are some things to consider when setting up a shared diary system:

- Would you like to hear about progress or general comments in the voice of your baby or in the voice of their nurse? (e.g., 'Hi mummy, I had a good rest last night and I can't wait to see you this morning' or 'Kane had a good rest overnight and was settled').
- What would you like them to include or exclude?
- Would it be a helpful place to raise concerns or questions?
- Are there any phrases or words you would like them to avoid or use more of? (e.g., you might prefer technical terms, or wish them to avoid phrases such as 'grumpy' or 'fussy').
- What would you like the staff to call you when writing in the diary?
- How would you like them to use photos and videos?

If you are struggling with particular worries such as overnight separation, discuss with your neonatal team whether they could help by sending a diary update overnight, bearing in mind what's realistic and possible for the neonatal team to facilitate at the time.

SUPPORTING EACH OTHER IN THE EARLY DAYS, IF YOU HAVE A PARTNER

The shock and exhaustion of the first few days and weeks in neonatal care can take its toll on the closest relationships. Whilst you are in the same situation, overall it's important to remember that there can be many differences in your individual experiences. You may well have had different experiences of the birth and your baby, come from different backgrounds, hold particular beliefs that shape how you are feeling or have different coping styles. Allowing each other to be where you're at and supporting emotions and responses even when they are different from yours is important, as well as recognizing when there are different expectations and hopes for your baby.

This is illustrated in Drake's story, where a conversation about what was really going on for him allowed his partner to understand his reaction was one of fear, not rejection or lack of interest:

> Drake struggled after the arrival of his baby Gina who was born at term but was in distress during labour and delivered under general anaesthetic. His partner had no memory of the events around the actual birth, but Drake was troubled by images of her being rushed into theatre, the look of panic on the midwife's face, and the wait

to see if his baby and partner were okay, which had felt like hours, even though it was only a few minutes. At the time he thought they would both die and he would lose everyone he loved.

Drake found it very hard to come to the hospital, finding reasons to be 'getting on with the practical stuff'. His partner felt abandoned and distraught, thinking he wasn't interested in her or Gina. One evening, when he dropped her off at the hospital to see Gina, Drake began to sweat heavily and found it hard to breathe in the carpark. He told her that just seeing the building made him feel an overwhelming sense of panic and fear. By talking together and with the team they found ways to help him approach his new baby and feel more comfortable on the unit gradually, without any pressure.

When Drake was ready to come into the hospital, he did so in a way that helped him feel safe and supported. His partner felt reassured that the change in Drake was not a reflection of him not wanting to be with her or Gina, but instead a response to a traumatic and terrifying experience.

FIRST STEPS TO HELP

- Try to make time to talk and listen to each other every day, even if it's just 10 minutes, to check in on how each other is doing. You can make a set time for this to help cement it into your routine – having a cup of cocoa in the hospital cafeteria before going home or talking on the way to the station, for example.
- Find ways to spend time together and connect with each other that have worked well for you before and help you feel more emotionally and physically regulated, for example, physical closeness and supportive touch, playing games such as cards or solving puzzles for short periods, cooking food together or watching a favourite movie.
- If your relationship feels under strain, spend a moment thinking about what you love about each other and what you're like when not under such difficult circumstances.
- Be realistic and open about your expectations and hopes of each other.

(We will look at the impact on close relationships, including those with your own parents and friends, in more detail in Chapter 3.)

COMMUNICATING WITH THE MEDICAL TEAM AND COPING WITH 'INFORMATION OVERLOAD'

Some of your thoughts or memories about hospitals may conjure up images of remote consultants you rarely meet, and decisions and discussions about you or your family taking place behind closed doors. Neonatal units have a difficult philosophy and 'feel', where regular communication with the whole team is encouraged and welcome. It can be difficult to navigate, however, as when we are overwhelmed, stressed and anxious it's hard to think. This section aims to give you some first ideas to help with conversations and digesting information about your baby (you can read about this in more detail in Chapter 4).

You'll develop preferences over time for how you would like the staff on the unit to communicate with you. Some of the following might be useful to consider when the doctors have asked for a meeting or to start a discussion as part of a ward round or check-in. Remember that communication on the neonatal unit is a collaborative process:

- Tell the doctor if you feel too overwhelmed or anxious to take in what they are saying, and ask them to help you. You might also have your own ways of helping 'dial down' your anxiety to allow you to be in a place to be able to hear what is being said (or look back to 'Ways to help immediately when emotions feel unmanageable' for ideas).
- Ask them to give you some idea of what you may be talking about – are you meeting for a general update or is there new information? Is a decision required? This will help you to be mentally and practically prepared.
- Take some control over what information is given to you and when, such as asking the team to wait until someone who can support you is present.
- Make a note yourself or ask a team member to write down for you three to four main points or headlines from your discussion that you can come back to when you are ready.
- Ask your baby's nurse to be present so they can hear the same information and talk it through with you in your own time.
- Remember that it's okay to ask questions, and no question is a 'silly question'. You can ask the same question as many times as you need.
- Work with your baby's doctor and give feedback so they pitch the discussion at the right level – this may include taking out medical 'jargon', or speaking about research or more technical aspects, if you find this helpful.

You will find that a lot of information is available, and you may already have a collection of leaflets, links, websites and posters to refer to. You will probably only be able to take on board some of that information at any one time, especially in the first few weeks. You can ask your neonatal team to filter some of the information for you, and to tell you what they think you need to know right now and what you can come back to in the future.

Over time you will start to learn the more technical language that is used on the unit, alongside becoming more familiar with what the numbers and sounds from the monitors mean. Be gentle with your expectations of how much there is to learn and take in, and that it isn't possible to know everything straightaway.

When you feel ready to know more, there are many routes to acquiring information. Ask your neonatal team where you can find accurate and reliable resources online, and look out for parent education sessions on your unit. (For more information on what your unit might provide, see Chapter 4.)

COMMUNICATION WITH EMPLOYERS AND MANAGING WORK COMMITMENTS

As you can often find yourself in a neonatal unit unexpectedly, you may be wondering how to let your employer know what has happened, and how to ensure you have the time you need with your baby. You may also be thinking about how you are going to return to work and manage the challenge of being away from the hospital.

If you have given birth and you are entitled to maternity leave, it will begin when your baby is born. Some employers are more flexible around maternity and parental leave, and parents of babies requiring neonatal care who meet specific criteria are entitled to up to 12 weeks of extra leave and pay. Ask your neonatal unit for details.

As a partner, be honest about whether you feel able to return to work and when. If you don't feel able to return, talk to your GP who may be able to support additional time off, or your employer may be able to offer compassionate leave. You can also ask your neonatal team if they can write a letter supporting your time on the neonatal unit or any special considerations (such as being able to work from the hospital or leave early) that would be helpful for you.

If you need to return to work, you may wish to consider the following:

- Think about what you feel able to do and who you feel able to see. You may not feel able to return to your normal duties or you may find it hard to be people-facing. You may find the possibility of having to answer questions about your baby or how you are coping too much to deal with. Equally, you may find the presence of supportive colleagues and a different focus helpful. Sometimes letting key people know information by email can be a way of controlling the situation and letting your colleagues know what would be helpful.

- Be gentle with your expectations of yourself. View the first few days as a trial to see how it feels, without making any longer-term commitments.
- If you have a sympathetic manager, consider sharing more detailed information with them and how they might help you in the workplace. Remember, most people don't have experience or knowledge of neonatal care, so it can be helpful to explain the reality of your situation and what it means day to day.
- If you are self-employed, consider how much you would feel comfortable sharing with your clients about your situation so they understand that your response times, capacity and availability may be altered for a period.
- Plan for potentially challenging times in the working day. Events can change rapidly on the unit, but also how you feel emotionally is likely to vary from day to day or even hour to hour. For example:

Sam arranged with his team that he could 'get some air' for 15 minutes when feeling anxious without having to explain to anyone at the time.

Harry's employer relaxed their policy on personal mobiles on the shop floor so he could receive regular updates and photos from his partner and the medical team.

If your employer is not being flexible around your needs, ask a member of the neonatal team in a family support role to advocate for you. Bliss (a neonatal charity) also has information on its website that helps with financial considerations and legal rights around work, whether this is whilst you are on the neonatal unit or afterwards. You can find this information on their website (see 'Resources' at the end of this chapter), or contact them directly for advice via email.[4]

You may also find needing the support of other people in your family requires them to take time away from work. Encourage them to ask for help from the neonatal unit if needed to assist with their requests, or ask them to signpost you to additional resources.

SUMMARY

The first few weeks on the neonatal unit are a challenging and difficult time for every family. You are finding ways to cope in sometimes unimaginable circumstances and

4 Bliss email: hello@bliss.org.uk

without a clear map of what the journey is ahead of you. By trying some of the exercises in this chapter you will have made a start in finding a way to cope and draw on the support you need, but this is an ongoing process. You may wish to return to some of these exercises again as needs change over time. In the next chapter we will be exploring the emotional impact of the neonatal unit in more depth, and exploring some ways to manage difficult feelings, thoughts and responses.

RESOURCES

You will have been given some information local to your neonatal unit on arrival, and there are multiple resources that may be helpful to you. At times the number of resources themselves can be overwhelming, so here are some places to start.

Somewhere to find more information

Bliss is a well-established charity for babies born premature or sick. A variety of support is available, from email to peer support and groups, and there is also a wealth of information on its website, including a short series of films that introduce you to the neonatal unit step by step: www.bliss.org.uk

Something to watch

Small Wonders (part of Best Beginnings) is a series of 12 'bite-sized' films about neonatal care, including 'First hours', 'Holding your baby' and 'Your time in hospital', available on YouTube, on the Baby Buddy app, or direct from the website: www.bestbeginnings.org.uk/small-wonders

Something to listen to

Unexpected Beginnings is a series of podcasts about life on the neonatal unit covering issues such as 'Mental health', 'Practical ways to bond with your child' and 'When your baby needs surgery'. It is available on Spotify, Apple Podcasts and other platforms.

Something to read

Listening to Babies in the Neonatal Unit: A Guide for Parents and Practitioners is a brief guide on how to support your baby on the neonatal unit and understand how they are communicating with you. It is available for free from the Brazelton Centre UK: www.brazelton.co.uk/wp-content/uploads/2022/06/Listening-to-Babies-in-the-Neonatal-Unit-Guide.pdf

CHAPTER 2

The emotional impact of the neonatal experience

HOW IT CAN FEEL AND WHAT CAN HELP

HOW IT FEELS IN THE FIRST FEW WEEKS

The first few weeks in neonatal care are a time of physical and emotional exhaustion, huge adjustment and finding your feet in a new world. Anxiety and vigilance, shock, bewilderment and feeling overwhelmed are common. There are also many differences between individuals emotionally that are important to recognize. Often what those around you see is a very small part of you (like the tip of an iceberg) and underneath are all of your life experiences, thoughts, feelings, beliefs and parts of you that have formed over time. What's under the surface influences how you interact with what's happening in your life right now, bringing huge variation in how you'll experience and make sense of your neonatal journey.

Adding another layer to how you're feeling may also be expectations on how you 'should' be from those around you. Perhaps you've heard people say that you '*should* be delighted' or that you '*should* be grateful'. Maybe you have also felt pressure that you '*should* fall in love with your baby straightaway' or that you '*must* be strong for your baby'. You may even be questioning yourself and thinking 'I *should* know how to cope with this'. In fact we don't often know what to do when faced with something so overwhelming and different. Like putting up a tent in a storm, you're trying to find ways to cope as the gale rages around you whilst facing uncertainty about when the weather will change.

You may also feel that there isn't much space to have feelings or reactions when you're surrounded by people or you may be concerned that they might judge you. You don't need to suffer in silence through fear or shame.

In this chapter we will think about the common emotional reactions to a neonatal experience and how they *make sense*, both in terms of what's happening to you and your baby now, and in light of what you've experienced before in your life. We'll also look at some ways to help in the here and now when you're struggling with these big emotions, and how you can foster a compassionate approach to distress. Remember that as a parent, you need a type of intensive care of your own.

'TUNING IN' TO WHAT YOU ARE FEELING

Sometimes it's hard to know what we're really feeling, particularly if you're not someone used to thinking or talking about your feelings. When you ask yourself 'How do I feel?' you might find yourself responding 'I feel absolutely awful/overwhelmed/unlike myself'. You might feel everything at once or nothing at all, being quite numb or distant from what's going on. Some parents describe being in a big cloud of emotion, where it's hard to see or do anything. Others report that they feel like a ball in a pinball machine, being thrown from one place to the next without warning.

Often simply noticing and naming emotions can be calming and containing. If you can't find the words, you might want to focus on what's happening in your body first and what that might tell you.

NOTICING AND NAMING EMOTIONS

Think of some words to describe how you are feeling at the moment, *for example, I feel really overwhelmed. I'm terrified all the time, angry at everyone around me trying to help, powerless to do anything, guilty that I can't be there for my partner or my other children, so tired, so empty. At the same time I'm excited to see my baby and so pleased I can be here for her.*

My words/experience:

....

....

....

....

Think about experiences in your body that are linked to your feelings, *for example, I feel sick, I feel exhausted so much my chest hurts, my pain post birth recovery gets worse when I'm feeling all this, I sometimes can't breathe, my heart races and then I feel unwell – a bit like things are surreal or far away.*

....

....

....

....

My experiences in my body:

....

....

....

....

As you go through your list you might start to make connections between some of the things you are feeling and what's happening around you. These kinds of connections can be helpful in terms of making sense of feelings that might seem at first like they 'come out of nowhere' or are hard to make sense of initially. Some of our emotions might be easier to identify (such as fear). Others might be more complicated as they involve judgements or particular thoughts about ourselves (such as guilt or shame), or arise from being in certain states (such as a state of uncertainty or powerlessness). You'll notice that it's common to feel many different things, often at the same time. Some of the feelings can be a response to what's happening in the here and now, but others can arise, or be more intense or difficult as a result of what has happened to you before (both in the recent as well as the more distant past).

WE ARE SHAPED BY OUR EXPERIENCES

What we experience in our lives shapes who we become and how we think, feel and behave in different situations. Whilst you have something in common with the person sitting next to you in the nursery, even this neonatal experience will not be entirely the same as it will have arisen from different circumstances, and your baby and your family will be facing their own unique challenges and triumphs – you are in the same storm, but not in the same boat.

You and your neighbour may have come from very different backgrounds, had different experiences of being loved or cared for, grown up with varying levels of uncertainty and unpredictability, or be going through your very first time of something traumatic and frightening. And it's not only your experiences but also the way you understand these and deal with them that will be shaped by many things – such as whether you've had access to people who can care for you. Our experiences play a part in how our brains develop and how we respond to stress. We can also shape our responses over time by developing new ways of relating to and managing our distress.

Let's meet three typical parents on the neonatal unit, Sam, Diego and Liz, to understand their different situations:

Sam had struggled with anxiety since being a small child. Her worries were often to do with what might happen in the future, and she would find herself worrying about everything – her job, what might happen to her parents, and how she was perceived by her friends. As a result of her worry, she suffered from chronic stomach pain and struggled to 'wind down' to sleep. Sam tried to manage her worries around pregnancy by planning everything in great detail, so she felt more in control. When her baby needed a neonatal admission due to seizures, something she could not have foreseen or planned for, she felt overwhelmed by a state of uncertainty and powerlessness, which, in turn, led her to feel intense anxiety and panic. Her previous coping strategies didn't work in this new situation, and understandably she felt rapidly unable to manage.

Before his baby was born Diego had suffered from depression for many years, after the death of his parents. He'd wished that a baby would give him a sense of purpose and hope in a world that felt like it had lost meaning. When his baby was born extremely premature, Diego was flooded with feelings of hopelessness and thoughts that nothing good would ever happen to him. Whilst the staff on the unit rallied around to help him feel involved, he wanted to withdraw and 'sit out the wait', feeling like everything was on hold until he knew what was ahead of him.

Liz had grown up in a close family and was raising two children when she became pregnant again. The pregnancy was a shock, but she began to adjust to the idea of another child, and started to enjoy thinking ahead and planning. Whilst out with her husband at just over 23 weeks she began to go into labour. The events around the delivery were extremely traumatic, leaving Liz struggling with flashbacks and a pervasive sense that the world she thought was safe wasn't anymore. Liz began to feel very low and fearful, constantly on the lookout for danger, and terrified something serious could happen again.

WHAT'S IMPORTANT IN UNDERSTANDING YOUR OWN LIFE EXPERIENCES?

As you read these stories, think about the similarities and differences in your own life experiences that are important in understanding where you are emotionally. Make a note of those that come to the forefront of your mind, and notice how they may have shaped you over time, including how they have shaped your thinking about yourself and others:

....

....

....

....

....

....

....

....

....

....

....

If you would like to understand more about emotions and how they operate, read this next section for some more detail. If you would like to skip to what can help straightaway, skip to 'Emotional challenges and first steps to help'.

EMOTIONS AND YOUR BRAIN: UNDERSTANDING EMOTIONAL EXPERIENCES IN NEONATAL CARE

A neonatal admission is full of many things that cause stress and distress, from events that make you fearful about your baby's survival to significant worries about the long-term implications of their experience. For some parents this can feel so unfamiliar and distressing that they describe it like they're 'losing their mind', which can be a terrifying feeling.

It can be helpful to understand a bit about what your mind is doing and how it's organizing itself to make sense of what's happening. Your emotions serve a *function*, telling you when something is important and indicating what you might need. Whilst emotions are complex and there are many ways to understand them, here we will think about three main emotion systems that are helpful to get to know briefly, each of which organizes our behaviour to help us survive as a species, based on the work of psychologist Paul Gilbert.[1]

The threat and self-protection system

Our threat and self-protection system ('threat system') is designed to rapidly respond to threat to ourselves or others we care about and to protect us. These responses are fast because when we perceive danger, it's critical for our survival that we act as soon as possible. Many of the emotions we can experience along the neonatal journey (such as anxiety, anger and fear) are activated responding to threats we see around us, threats we have experienced in the past that still feel very current in our minds, or threats linked to what we fear might happen in the future. Because our brain takes the approach of 'better safe than sorry' in terms of survival, if we are experiencing periods of time that are high in threat, then we have evolved to have heightened attention to things around us that are cues of danger (such as raised voices, alarms or rapid movement). You might notice how much you are sensitive to these right now.

When we are in a 'high threat' we have survival responses designed to protect us known as the '5 fs' – fight, flight, freeze, fawn and faint. At times more than one response can occur or they can change rapidly (such as feeling very angry, and then shutdown and numb). When we enter this survival mode, we also lose the ability to think clearly or logically, to find the words and to manage our emotions, and these responses are not in our conscious control.

Let's take a closer look at what they feel like, both physically and emotionally, and the kinds of situations in which you might encounter them:

- Fight: In 'fight' mode, your body is preparing for physical activity (such as defending yourself or your baby) by releasing hormones into your blood stream, which result in an increased heart rate, the shutting down of digestion and changes in the way your body functions, such as being more alert. If you have found yourself feeling angry or shouting at those around you or wanting to push people away from carrying out a painful procedure with your baby, this could be an example of your *fight* response.

1 See www.compassionatemind.co.uk

- Flight: In 'flight' mode, your body is also preparing for physical activity, in this case running away from danger. You may have experienced wanting to get away from the hospital or wanting to remove yourself from the room your baby is in. This doesn't mean you don't care – it's a response to fear.

- Freeze: In 'freeze' mode, people often describe feeling so terrified they cannot move, like a 'rabbit in the headlights'. Fundamentally it is another way of increasing our chances of survival, but it can mean that we respond in ways that can be hard to understand initially – such as being unable to walk across the operating theatre to comfort your partner or being unable to go through the door of the NICU.

- Fawn: The 'fawn' response to threat is less well known and involves trying to act in ways that reduce our danger, mostly from other people. You may find yourself trying to give the 'right' answer to doctors or nurses, or feel unable to voice a concern if things are worrying you.

- Faint: When we can't escape a threat our heart rate decreases and we can feel faint. We may also find it hard to speak or think, and our body releases endorphins to numb pain, and dynorphins, which can lead to us feeling detached from our body and dissociated. You might feel like you are watching yourself from the ceiling as you're with your baby, or that everything around you is unreal or like being in a dream.

Activation of our threat system is often linked to events, particularly on the neonatal journey, but it can also be activated from within our own minds when we start to think about what has happened to us or what might happen to us, such as:

- Self-criticism and judgement – feeling like you've done something wrong or not feeling like a good enough parent, for example
- Feelings of guilt and shame
- The process of worry when thinking about things that could happen in the future
- Thinking about things that have happened over and over, without any sense of resolution or relief.

For most of us, even though our lives and situations can be extremely challenging and distressing, they aren't solely about responding to threats in order to survive. We have two other systems – one that helps us to pursue resources and experiences that are important to our survival (the *drive system*), and one that allows us to rest and recover, connect with others and feel peace and calm (the *soothing system*). These 'positive' emotion systems are important as they can help to regulate our threat system and calm some of the overwhelming emotions it produces. We will be finding ways to activate these systems to help manage distress in this chapter and throughout the book.

The drive system

Our drive system gives us positive and pleasurable feelings that motivate us to seek and desire things that we want, and contact with people and experiences we find rewarding. These things ultimately help our survival and that of our loved ones. For example, you may have felt excitement when you first found out that you were pregnant, and this may have led you to put plans in place, buy things for your baby or start getting the house ready. As you are getting to know your baby on the unit you may be motivated by what you're able to do for them as a parent and how they respond to you. You might notice that the response of your baby (or others) to your efforts gives you pleasure and a sense of achievement. So this system helps you to move towards doing more of what is important to you, and as it feels good, you're more likely to do it again.

Our drive system can be 'trumped' by our threat system, however, meaning that positive emotions can be 'switched off' very quickly. This is often the case in neonatal care, where some of the joy and excitement that often comes with having a new baby is reduced or absent. You might also notice that after a medical emergency or an alarm sounding continuously you find it hard to engage again with your baby. Understanding this as an evolved response and a way of your brain trying to protect you from threat can help reduce some of the judgement and criticism that can be present when moving into or out of a state of threat activation, often numerous times a day.

We can also experience difficulties when we are not able to meet our goals or wishes, which initially activates our threat system, often leading to anger, anxiety and frustration, for example, not being able to hold or feed your baby when you've planned for this and imagined it for a long time.

The soothing system

Our soothing system brings us into a state of feeling safe, calm and connected to others. It is linked to the production of endorphins and oxytocin and the activation of our parasympathetic nervous system, which is sometimes referred to as our 'rest and digest' system, promoting rest, recovery and the conservation of energy. For example, you will see in wildlife documentaries that after a lion has given up chasing a zebra, the zebra will graze and eat grass – their soothing system is activated and they can gather energy and recover from the terror of the chase. Zebras have the advantage of not having parts of their brain that can think about what has just happened or worry about it happening again, and so we face a uniquely human challenge in moving into our soothing system and away from threat, particularly when we are experiencing a lot of difficult events and circumstances.

More than just an absence of drive or threat we can experience a sense of safeness and soothing from within us (a general feeling of peace and contentment) or from being connected with others (where we are physically and mentally calmed by their kindness, affection and soothing behaviour). Like your baby, we're all wired to need care, affection and connection with others throughout our lives. When we are with people who we feel safe with, are warm and kind to us, this helps us to become more regulated and calmed if we are distressed. This system plays a key role in helping create and respond to caring relationships, including building an attachment bond between you and your baby. When our soothing system is activated, we are able to think, explore and engage with the world differently, and it plays an important role in helping us to manage when our threat system is triggered. We will focus on how we can activate your soothing system to help you in various ways in this chapter.

EMOTIONAL CHALLENGES AND FIRST STEPS TO HELP

Ideally our emotion systems are all in balance, which means that we can move between them flexibly as needed and we don't spend significantly more time in one over another. However, being in neonatal care often means they are not in balance, and you will spend large amounts of time in 'threat mode'. Previous life experiences can play a significant role in how activated our emotion systems are. Sometimes dramatic changes that can occur post birth as a result of hormonal changes also lead to big differences in a sense of threat or the ability to feel soothed, calm and connected.

Our emotional experiences tend to be 'messy' in that they often don't fit neatly into categories and are a product of many things. This section covers some of the common reactions and challenges, recognizing that this is by no means an exhaustive list.

Whilst you may have experienced these reactions and challenges before in your life, our task together in this chapter is to: (1) understand what they look like for you right now; (2) understand how your mind and body organize around emotions; and (3) find ways to decrease threat where possible and build your positive emotion systems, particularly the soothing system.

In each of the following there is a 'First steps to help' summary. Whilst different starting points are listed under different experiences, many will be applicable across categories, and you will begin to notice which are the most helpful or resonate most with you. At the end of this chapter there will be a broader focus on building your soothing system and compassionate mind to approach all your distress.

Prolonged and extreme stress

We all thrive on certainty and predictability, usually coping with some stress in response to the pressures and difficulties that happen in everyday life. In neonatal care you are in circumstances and situations that are far out of the 'everyday' – high uncertainty, powerlessness, lack of control and lack of safety, which continues for prolonged periods and can be overwhelming. This has led many to describe the neonatal unit as an environment of 'toxic stress' for everyone. This toxic stress activates threat for long periods, overriding and 'turning off' positive emotions. When we are under this level of stress our 'window' in which to operate carrying out everyday tasks and having the capacity for things is narrowed. As a result you may notice your threat responses are activated much more easily than usual – for example, being very quickly panicked, feeling irritable (feeling on a 'short fuse') and unable to cope.

FIRST STEPS TO HELP

- Look back at some of the first steps to reduce stress and demands in Chapter 1. Refresh your plans regularly, particularly at times of rapid change. What works one day may not the next.
- Attend to your body's basic needs such as rest, exercise (when this is safe to resume), eating and drinking regularly. If exercise has been a significant part of how you cope with stress, think about how to factor this into your routine on the unit where you might find lengthy sitting challenging. Start small with periods when you can incorporate movement and time outside the hospital

in the outdoors, if you can't return immediately to your preferred method of exercise.

- Seek anchors and moments of safety throughout your day, even if they are short, including people, places and activities. This could be connecting with other parents over tea and coffee, making things for your baby that involve a degree of concentration and focus, or putting in small moments of self-care and comfort around certain points of your day, such as mealtimes.
- Minimize threat where possible. Everywhere you look there will be something that is likely to activate your threat system. Whilst some of these are unavoidable, take a look at what you can change, even a little, such as focusing only on your baby in the nursery or reducing exposure to distressing conversations involving other families.
- Start to create elements of predictability, control and routine in your days where you can (see Chapter 4).
- Look at different ways to activate your soothing system in this chapter (see 'Finding ways to a more soothed, safe and connected state').

Traumatic events and experiences

Having a baby in neonatal care often follows a traumatic birth, and there can be many other traumatic events you might experience in the course of a neonatal admission over a long period of time. Traumatic events, by definition, overwhelm our ability to cope. Suddenly giving birth or having to deliver in ways you were not expecting to can lead to feelings of shock and a sense of disbelief, such as 'this can't be happening' or 'this can't be real'. Events may have moved very quickly around you, and many parents describe how they can feel quite emotionally numb, or like they are watching events from afar, as if they are in a movie or a dream. You may experience the same feelings when you see your baby for the first time in the unit. For many parents the speed at which things have changed, from a normal day into having a baby in hospital, can be hard to process, particularly at first.

When these things have happened to you, or continue to happen, you may feel chronically unsafe and constantly scared of what might happen next. The longed-for need for a signal to be able to 'stand down' might be a long time coming. There is also a lack of time, space and the usual signals of safety that are more easily accessed at home. Whilst what has happened or is happening to you might be familiar or expected by health professionals, validating the reality of your own experience is important. What matters is how you experienced events and their impact.

A range of reactions can happen afterwards in the short and longer term, after and during trauma. There are often differences in responses between people who have been through the same event, for example, you and your partner or supporting parent.

Whilst this section will focus mostly on the impact of trauma associated with your maternity and neonatal experience, it's also important to acknowledge that, for many, the impact of trauma throughout their lives is significant and complex, often occurring in the context of relationships. There are many ways that this interacts with what's happening in the present or more recent past. You may find yourself making connections as you read through this section, perhaps in terms of how you've coped with traumatic experiences before, or your previous experiences of events that are similar to those that are happening now.

Here is a list of common responses to traumatic events. Some can resolve in time, whereas you may need more help for others:

- You experience 'flashbacks' of events (where you feel like it's happening again or right now), or find it comes into your mind when you're not trying to think about it. This can include re-experiencing physical sensations that you felt at the time, and other sensory memories like smell and sound. These activate your threat system, even if there's no current danger.
- You have nightmares about what has happened or they may be related to what's happened in some way.
- You experience intense distress when faced with reminders of what has happened (which can also show up in physical reactions, such as a racing heart, sweating and feeling sick).
- You try to avoid thoughts, memories and feelings about or actual reminders of what happened (such as people and places). This can be really hard if you're in the same hospital or feeling like your baby is a reminder.
- You feel 'on guard' (hypervigilance). You might be extremely sensitive to alarms or changes in the expressions on nurses'/doctors' faces.
- You are easily startled or jumpy as part of being 'on edge'.
- You find it hard to concentrate or focus.
- You have difficulties going to or staying asleep.
- You might notice an impact on how you are thinking and feeling – feeling that the world is not a safe place or blaming yourself for what happened, for example.

- You may feel detached from yourself or others, such as feeling far away/cut-off or watching yourself from a distance.
- Your memory and sense of time might be affected. You may find it hard to put events in sequence or make sense of them. You may also find it hard to know the difference between what has happened in the past and what is happening in the here and now, or have gaps in your memory. These things happen due to changes in the way memories are stored during trauma.

These experiences can be really hard to manage on the unit where there are often constant reminders of what has happened, and an environment that is very stressful and high in continued threat. There's little time to process or make sense of events that have happened to you and your baby, or to feel safe in the here and now. Both the trauma responses to previous events and the environment and circumstances that you are in now can contribute to not feeling safe.

To help yourself, it's important to focus on both, bearing in mind that some of your reactions may not change until you are able to work with them from a greater place of overall safety. You may need professional help to recover from your traumatic experiences, but there are also things you can do to help yourself.

FIRST STEPS TO HELP

- Connect as soon as possible with your support network and those around you whose presence feels helpful. Close and supportive relationships act as a 'buffer' and help to reduce the impact of traumatic events.
- If you feel able, talk to people who feel safe around you about what has happened, or try to write it down and piece together the sequence so that it has a beginning, a middle and an end. Whilst you are in hospital, as well as family members you also have professionals around you who can help you fill in gaps in your memory and understanding, and who can help you make sense of things. If you don't feel able to talk about every part of what has happened, that's okay – it's important not to put any pressure on yourself, and to go at your own pace.
- Let those around you know what things you are finding hard as a result of a traumatic experience so they can be sensitive to your needs, such as not asking you to recount your birth experience at every ward round, giving you choice and control where possible on the unit and helping you to build trust in the system and healthcare professionals little by little.
- If you are struggling with feeling like events are happening again, if you feel

the emotional and physical impact in a way that's overwhelming or feel disconnected from your surroundings in an unhelpful way, you can help connect back to the here and now using grounding techniques, such as the exercise that follows. You can try these on your own, or you may want to do them with someone who can help support you.

5-4-3-2-1 GROUNDING TECHNIQUE

This exercise can be used anytime and anywhere, to help to ground you in the present moment.

Begin with a few cycles of your 'Soothing breathing rhythm', and then bring your focus very deliberately to:

5 things you can see: Look around you. Can you find and name five things that you see in your immediate environment? Describe to yourself objects, textures, colours and shapes.

4 things you can touch or feel: This may be the feeling of your clothes on your skin or your baby's warm body. Describe to yourself what they feel like, the temperature or the sensation.

3 things you can hear: Listen carefully to what's around you. Describe to yourself the sounds, the pitch or the volume.

2 things you can smell: Gently inhale through your nose as you notice the smells around you. Describe the qualities of the scent, such as the smell of your baby or the smell of cleaning fluids in the nursery.

1 thing you can taste: Open and close your mouth or swallow and note the various tastes you notice. You may wish to introduce a taste such as a strong mint to orientate you back to the present.

Establish relative safety where you can (see 'anchors of safety'), reduce further threat inputs and work on connecting with emotion state memories that enhance safety and calm (see 'Connecting with memories of feeling safe, connected and regulated (and other helpful "state" memories)').

MAKE YOUR OWN CALMING KIT

Having a physical collection of objects with you that help you to connect to feelings of calm and connection with others can be very helpful. Think about your five senses and what object provides something either directly or indirectly that works best to increase your sense of comfort, familiarity and calm. Put these objects into a kit for yourself that contains everything you need and can easily travel with you. Jot down some ideas under each sense below, and then see the example of Taz's calming kit that he took to NICU and also to the parent accommodation so he could use it at night when he felt particularly vulnerable.

Sight:

....

....

Touch:

....

....

Sound:

....

....

Smell:

....

....

Taste:

....

....

Sight: A picture of my wife and child at a family reunion by the sea.

Touch: A special stone that was given to me by my grandfather that represents bravery.

Sound: The soundtrack from my honeymoon, which always helps me feel centred and connected with that happiness.

Smell: My baby's bonding squares and my wife's perfume, particularly when we are apart.

Taste: Hot chocolate, which also has good memories from when I was a child.

Taz's calming kit

In time, and sometimes with appropriate professional support, being able to process the trauma in particular ways will alleviate symptoms and they will have less of an impact on your life day to day. However, there is huge individual variation in when this takes place, and for many it only becomes possible after their baby is home from hospital.

Difficulties getting to sleep

Difficulties with sleep can be associated with trauma, but more broadly with any stressful experience. Even short periods with little sleep can have a significant impact on how you might feel, both physically and emotionally. Difficulties getting to sleep can have many causes. Ask yourself what makes this difficult, for example, is it fears about what might happen when you close your eyes? Worries about your baby's safety? Difficulties physically and mentally winding down? It may be a combination of factors.

FIRST STEPS TO HELP

- Explore if you're able to sleep and rest next to your baby or near to them on the unit. Tell the team when you would like to be woken up to attend to your baby.
- If you are away from the unit, request a call or video of your baby to see that they are settled.
- Remind yourself of the facts about who is looking after your baby and watching over them whilst you rest. Be clear about when they will call you, e.g., emergencies only or when certain things happen that you have agreed between you.
- Allow yourself a chunk of time between pumping (expressing) milk so you can relax into rest without thinking of when the next alarm will sound. You can seek advice on patterns of pumping to allow more sleep from unit staff.
- Connect with a safe and soothing mental image or space or other soothing techniques or activities to help your body and mind come into a more restful state.
- Use smells, sounds and anything sensory that allows you to feel soothed and connected to your baby.

Difficulties with frequent waking

You may not know the moment of waking where your baby is and need to be reminded where they are and that they're safe. If you are waking often due to nightmares related to your own safety (e.g., not being able to move all your body when you're having a caesarean section) then it can be helpful to remind yourself or ask another person to remind you of your ability now to move your body around as you need to.

FIRST STEPS TO HELP

- Keep items next to your bed or space that help you feel safe or have an element of the here and now, e.g., a photo of your baby accompanied by a bonding square, to have a sense of their smell, or other items from your calming kit.
- Orientate to your environment – remind yourself where you are, and that right now, at this moment in time, there is no emergency. If you are experiencing any physical sensations such as feeling frozen or numb, engage in some gentle movement or touch to bring your body into a more regulated state.
- Call the unit if you need to talk to someone who's able to check in on your baby. Ask them to describe what your baby is doing and how they are. You might also want to know who's in the room caring for them.

- If your unit has a baby diary system where you can receive real-time messages, ask for more frequent messages written by the team from your baby during periods of high anxiety and disrupted sleep.

Managing nightmares

Nightmares can be extremely frightening whenever they occur. They might be about things that are happening to you now or have happened in the past. It can make it very hard for sleep to be restorative if you are troubled by nightmares, and for many parents, it can make them afraid to sleep.

FIRST STEPS TO HELP

- Before you go to sleep remind yourself of things in the here and now that are true, e.g., 'We both survived the birth, I am safe in my own home, I have control over my body.'
- Use grounding and soothing techniques to help you if you wake up during or after a nightmare. Try to ensure you are orientated to the present before falling back to sleep.
- Consult a psychological professional to support you with a range of other approaches that can be effective in managing nightmares if they persistently cause distress and disrupt sleep.

Anxiety, panic and intrusive thoughts

Anxiety and panic can feel like constant companions due to the nature of the environment, keeping your threat system constantly active. Feeling some anxiety can be useful in that it tells us something important and leads us to act to protect our own or another's safety, but at times it can be disabling. First fears in neonatal care often centre around survival and change over time to reflect new challenges, transitions and uncertainties.

It's common to move between levels of anxiety day to day or even hour to hour. Changes might arise from things that are happening to your baby or in the nursery and/or from changes within yourself, such as what you're thinking about or focusing on. It can be helpful to start to get to know your own anxiety so you can build a picture of what you might need to help and when.

Anxiety changes how we think (including *what* we think and *how* we think). One example is the experience of distressing and disturbing thoughts or images that come into your mind suddenly (intrusive thoughts). These might be about things happening to your baby such as dropping them, a nurse, doctor or you harming them, or there being an accident or serious event. These thoughts are very common in neonatal care where your threat system is constantly activated. They don't mean the things you imagine are any more likely to happen because you've thought them, or reflect anything about you as a person for having them, but they can be alarming and distressing when they occur.

Jane's experience is one that's common in neonatal care:

> Jane found that when she was sitting next to her baby in the nursery, she had many intrusive thoughts about a doctor hurting her baby, the monitors stopping working, dropping her baby or her baby becoming suffocated in the crook of her arm when holding him. These thoughts became more intense when she felt less confident in the team looking after her baby, but she felt she couldn't mention them to anyone. She began to wonder what was wrong with her and what all these thoughts meant.

An activated threat system also changes how we feel, what we pay attention to (in our environment and inside our minds and bodies), how we act as well as what we can remember. These factors all interact with one another, so that the way we think might start to change how our body feels (e.g., *thinking* 'I can't cope with any of this', leading to *feeling* short of breath and faint), or what we *remember* starts to impact how we *feel* (e.g., only remembering the things the doctor was worried about rather than the progress your baby has made, leading to feelings of dread or fear). Take a moment to notice how this may play out for you.

Anxiety fluctuates in severity, and panic is a particularly intense and acute anxiety state that can come on very quickly and feel terrifying. Some people experience what's referred to as a panic attack where they feel in sudden danger and have physical symptoms such as a racing heart, rapid breathing, shaking, differences in temperature, dizziness and nausea, and typically thoughts that something catastrophic is happening or about to happen. Whilst you may be able to identify a trigger for panic (such as some difficult news about your baby), you might also experience a panic attack without a specific trigger in the context of already elevated and prolonged anxiety.

At first you may feel at the mercy of your threat system as it attempts to help you survive. This is likely to change to varying degrees over time as you adapt to what's happening around you – for example, you may find that you don't startle and feel afraid when you hear an alarm after it has sounded multiple times. However, there may be many events that remain frightening, or new occurrences that leave you overwhelmed with anxiety or fear. Sometimes all you can do is focus on recovery from these events and engaging your soothing system to bring you back to a more balanced and regulated state in time.

There are many approaches to helping with anxiety and there is no 'one size fits all', given the many ways it can manifest, reasons it arises and what keeps it going. Some approaches can be helpful at one point in time, and you may have to change or tweak these as things change. Flexibility and being able to review what's useful is key, as well as sticking with some things to give them a try, even if they don't work immediately.

FIRST STEPS TO HELP

- Remember that you are in a situation where anxiety is an understandable response to a lot of what is happening to you and your baby.
- Recognize that your brain is trying to help you and ultimately protect you by being in a 'better safe than sorry' mode by default. Be compassionate towards yourself in these very difficult circumstances, and remember that it isn't a weakness, fault or inability to be 'strong' when you feel anxious.
- Think about helping yourself in two ways – *proactive approaches* (things you can put in place ahead of hitting a point of crisis or extreme distress) and *reactive approaches* (things you can put in place if you find yourself there already).

Proactive approaches

BEGINNING TO NOTICE PATTERNS

Notice when you are moving into a more anxious mindset, and what changes for you first. This may be physical sensations, thoughts or emotions, or a change in how you start to view what is happening around you. The better you become at spotting these changes, the easier you can put things into place to help prevent distress escalating.

Notice perhaps when you are in a calmer place any loops or cycles that you get stuck in when you feel anxious. It can also be helpful to identify the triggers for entering a loop, such as a particular event, conversation or feeling.

Here are some examples of the loops or cycles that can emerge:

Thinking 'I am powerless to do anything in this situation' > feeling fearful > feeling more powerless and out of control as your threat system becomes progressively more activated.

Add some of the loops or cycles you might find yourself in here:

....

....

....

....

....

....

Identify particularly vulnerable times for anxiety in the course of your day, and problem solve how to manage these yourself and with others. Here are some examples:

Time/event that is likely to increase anxiety	What helps
Periods when my baby's oxygen levels are dropping (often referred to as 'desatting') and regularly setting off the alarms – feeling terrified of what's going on, what I should do and how someone is going to help – should I help?	• *The nurse to clearly and calmly tell me what is happening and what she is going to do to help, step by step, also letting me know when I can assist and when I need to step back.* • *To recognize that this is likely to set off thoughts and images that are distressing of something terrible happening to my baby, but that these thoughts don't mean this will happen or make something bad more likely.* • *To remind myself that whilst this is scary, it's common, and the team know what to do.* • *To take time to recover and connect with my baby once they have settled.*
Leaving the unit to get a snack, use the bathroom or get some fresh air. Worried that if I step away something will happen as I won't be 'on watch'.	• *When I can, choose a time to pop out when my baby is calm and settled.* • *Collect information to remind myself that they are not more likely to have an incident when I step outside for a few minutes than if I was here, even if it can feel like the risk is increased.* • *Work towards leaving them gradually – moving from a few steps away from the incubator to standing at the door, and then build up to stepping out of the nursery. Make a note of what happens.*

Think about your own examples and what you can put in place. Sometimes these may involve very small changes or modifications to what already happens (such as someone talking you through continuously and calmly what the neonatal team are doing or looking out for during a procedure). Here are some questions to help you find some solutions and aid with planning:

- What made this situation easier to cope with/less anxiety provoking before? (Look for 'key ingredients', whether these are people, actions or other things)

  ....

  ....

- What do I know about myself and how anxiety works for me that I can bring to this situation and let others know?

  ....

  ....

- When do I find my anxiety perhaps in the same circumstances is reduced? What is different then, and what can I learn from that?

  ....

  ....

Reactive approaches

The 'Dropping anchor' exercise from Chapter 1 can be helpful if you feel in a moment of overwhelming anxiety. It is often helpful to pay attention to calming and regulating your body first before trying to move to something that is more reliant on your thinking brain. 'Finding ways to a more soothed, safe and connected state' will look more at other methods to soothe and regulate. Splashing your face with cold water or a quick cool temperature change on your skin can help your mind and body to move through distress and regulate your emotions in a moment of intensity.

If you find yourself having a lot of distressing or intrusive thoughts racing through your mind, it can also be helpful to change the way you *relate* to those thoughts, particularly if you are finding that they are so overwhelming they get in the way of doing things that are important to you, which was the case for Kayden:

> Kayden found that even though the neonatal team reassured him that his son was doing well and they were happy with his progress, he kept experiencing thoughts such as 'There's something they are going to miss, he's just a second away from an emergency' that were causing him great distress and making it difficult to engage

with his son. For Kayden, being able to see that these were thoughts and not immediate facts was helpful, but he still struggled with their impact.

Approaches that help us to relate differently to thoughts can be helpful in this circumstance. Try the following exercise if you find your mind is racing with a lot of distressing thoughts. Often this exercise helps create distance between you and your thoughts, and it lessens their impact. You can change the imagery as you see fit, for example, cars going past on a busy road or clouds floating in the sky – think about what might work for you.

'LEAVES ON A STREAM'

Take a moment to engage with your soothing and calm breathing rhythm and imagine that you are sitting by the side of a stream on the bank in the sunshine. As you are sitting there, imagine that leaves are floating past you as you sit – you can see them coming, be right across from you and then pass by down in the water.

As you sit watching the leaves floating by, notice the thoughts that are flooding into your mind one after another. As you have each thought, imagine placing it on the leaf, and then watching it float past you and into the distance. If other thoughts or images come thick and fast, just place each one of them on the leaf and let them go.

Notice what is happening as you do this over time. If you find yourself thinking 'I'm not doing this right', just place that thought on a leaf and watch it travel away from you.

Sadness, depression and despair

Sadness can feel like a heaviness or darkness that's always there, or it can come in waves. At times the waves or weight might feel difficult, but bearable. At other times it can break like a tidal wave over everything, leaving little perspective or sense of anything hopeful or good.

Sadness can come from many places in the neonatal journey. Sudden hormonal changes that come after birth are associated with feelings of sadness, anxiety and being more sensitive to criticism. You may find that sadness arises from feelings of loss, difficulties in relationships, isolation and loneliness, feeling hopeless, helpless and defeated. It may also arise from the ways you might relate to yourself (e.g., being very self-critical, not feeling good enough or feeling like you've failed your baby in some way) and the meaning you make of what's happening. You may be struggling with difficult thoughts and beliefs that affect how you feel. Beliefs such as 'I'll never feel any better', 'I'm a terrible parent' and 'I'll never cope with this situation' are common when mood is low, and they can make it hard to see a way forward.

It's important to validate how you are really feeling, and to recognize that it's not a fault or deficit in you but something understandable that needs care and attention to begin the process of helping you feel better.

Let's look at Lola's story as an example:

> Lola had been through a recent breakup from her baby's father after she became pregnant, and had been feeling hurt and distressed at being abandoned by someone she thought cared about her and their unborn child. He rarely asked how she was feeling, and didn't come and see her when she went into hospital with preterm prelabour rupture of membranes (PPROM). Her days on bed rest were lonely, and she felt as if no one cared about her. When her baby was born and transferred to the neonatal unit, the team were supportive and positive about her baby's outcome, but she couldn't feel the same. She spent many hours crying and withdrawing from life on the unit, describing her sadness as like a heavy cloak that covered her whole body with darkness.

Some of the things that happened to Lola are experiences that understandably result in low mood. Once our minds are operating through this lens, much like anxiety or anger it starts to change how they organize – changing how we think, what we pay attention to and the kinds of memories that come into our minds. These feelings are on a spectrum, and if you move towards the end of the spectrum where your mood becomes depressed, this state is as much a physical as a mental one.

When your mood is depressed you may feel a loss of connection to others and your surroundings, feel hopeless about the future, find it hard to think or reason in a balanced way or feel in a 'fog', very sad and tearful, or you may have periods when you find you feel nothing or you feel numb. Things that might usually motivate you or give you joy, such as your new baby or a thoughtful gift, may not have that effect (as your drive system becomes less active). Your soothing system that helps you to feel calm, content and connected also dampens, making it hard to draw comfort and reassurance from others. You may also find that your sleep, appetite and concentration is affected, and these changes to basic functions can themselves worsen how you feel.

When you're in this state your mind may bring up memories of similar times you've felt this way in the past and it can feel frightening to connect with these again – you might be worried about what it could mean and how you will cope, particularly when so much is being asked of you on the unit. You may also be feeling scared if this feeling is new and you've never experienced anything like it before. Either way, know that you are not alone. One day this feeling will come to an end, but it is important that you don't ignore it.

'What if I don't feel I can keep myself safe?'

Sometimes low mood can worsen to a place of hopelessness and despair where you have thoughts about harming yourself or ending your life. If you are experiencing these kinds of thoughts, you are not alone (even if you feel painfully alone and disconnected), *but it's important to seek the help of a health professional such as a psychological professional on your unit, a member of the neonatal team or your GP as soon as possible*. Let your partner or loved ones know how you really feel so they can help you to get the help you need and keep you safe (e.g., 'I don't feel there's a way out and this feeling is frightening', 'I've been having thoughts that I'd be better off dead/you'd all be better off if I wasn't here'). It can be hard to put these feelings into words and they might be shocking at first to those who love and care about you. Remember that even if it doesn't feel like it, you and your safety are important and your partner or loved ones will want to help. They will also be able to provide useful information for others about how you are when you feel your normal self and what's different.

If you feel you can't keep yourself safe or start to feel like you might act on these thoughts, it's important to find help immediately via emergency services such as A&E. These are often available in the same hospital that is looking after your baby – and open 24 hours. If you do seek help in A&E, remember to tell them that you have a baby in the neonatal unit so they can be mindful of your situation (both in understanding it emotionally, and also what you might need practically). Some parents find it helpful to contact the Samaritans who offer a range of ways to talk to you – by phone, online chat or text.[2] Also remember that you won't feel like this forever, even though your mind may be trying to rob you of hope and a future.

2 See www.samaritans.org

FIRST STEPS TO HELP

- Gently let yourself know that the sadness and hurt you're experiencing makes sense given what you've been through, and that there is a way to understand what you're feeling and thinking. This understanding might come in time rather than all springing into place straightaway – give yourself time to put the pieces together.
- Notice any part of you that seeks to shut down feelings, minimize them or tell yourself to 'buck up'. Sometimes we think that these voices are what we need, but a compassionate inner voice that really sees your distress and wants to help you will be much more beneficial to you in the long run.
- Think about whether you're adding a second layer to your struggles by your own self-criticism or judgement. The idea of 'clean' and 'dirty' pain from Acceptance and Commitment Therapy (ACT) can be helpful here. 'Clean' pain refers to emotions such as sadness that come from the hurtful and difficult events that happen to us, and there may be many of these before and during your baby's time in neonatal care. 'Dirty' pain refers to distress that comes from our thoughts, evaluation and meaning we make about what has happened to us, such as 'I should have gone to the doctor sooner', 'If only I wasn't so weak and unable to cope with this situation' – these are the ways our threat system becomes activated from our own thinking. Take a moment to reflect on your own sadness and what it's made up of. Do you notice a mixture of 'clean' and 'dirty' pain? If you find you are experiencing a lot of 'dirty' pain, consider developing a more compassionate response to your harsh inner voice (see the next point).
- Think about what response you really need to your sadness and struggle, and what the perfectly compassionate response would look like. Try out the exercise 'Creating a compassionate companion to help at times of distress and difficulty' to help provide the emotional experience and response you need when you're feeling sad or depressed (and all the distressing feelings and thoughts that come with it), or facing any other emotional challenge. When you go through any of the exercises in this book, if you find it hard to be compassionate or non-critical with yourself, take a moment to revisit being in the company and wisdom of this compassionate being, and think about how they may act and speak towards you, validating your distress and being wholly focused on caring for you and helping you feel better.
- Consider making some small changes to address some of the 'loops' or 'cycles' you can get caught up in when you are sad and low that can make you feel

worse. Withdrawing from others (such as supportive adults and even your baby), for example, can have the unintended consequence of moving you away from the very relationships that play a part in you feeling more connected and 'alive' in time.

- Some of your basic needs, such as sleeping, eating and drinking, which may be disrupted by feeling low, can also worsen your mood if they become difficult to maintain. Gently explore with yourself and others how you can look after these physical needs with the wellbeing of all of you in mind. You may need to start small, such as eating very small amounts rather than meals or building up sleep and rest next to your baby. Whilst each step can feel enormous when you're feeling low, they will be nurturing your recovery.
- Notice small glimmers of feeling better, more connected or even small moments of joy. Moments of connection are particularly important as disconnection from others can fuel a sense of isolation and loneliness, even when surrounded by people. Keep a note of these moments in your diary to come back to.
- Seek help straightaway if you feel your low mood has moved into something that feels frightening or is impossible to overcome. Others around you will hold hope for you when you don't have it yourself, and find you the right support.

Self-blame and shame

Many parents blame themselves for what's happened to their baby, and it can feel devastating. Blame comes from many places – from feeling responsible, like you're the one who's always wrong in a situation, guilty that you did something (e.g., kept going to the gym when pregnant) or didn't do something (e.g., alert the midwife sooner when things didn't seem right) – seeing things that weren't or couldn't be in your control as your personal responsibility. Sometimes the list of things you hold the blame for can feel endless, even when others give the clear message that there was nothing you could have done any other way.

It can be easy to have 'hindsight' bias when looking back at things you may wish you'd done differently. Hindsight bias refers to the conviction we should or could have known what the outcome was going to be and therefore done something different at the time of an event, *based on what we know now*. You may find yourself thinking 'If only I'd done X then things would have worked out alright'. You may also find yourself applying this same reasoning to the actions of others, discounting the uncertainty and unpredictability probably present at the time. As you learn more about your baby and their needs during your neonatal stay it can be empowering, but it can also lead to looking at situations for which you had no knowledge in the past in a blaming and self-critical way. The 'if onlys' mount up and can cause all sorts of distress.

For others from certain backgrounds and experiences the position of self-blame is a default. You may have been in an environment where you blamed yourself for what happened to you or others as a way of making sense of the senseless (such as others being cruel, neglectful or hurtful). *At times it can be hard to come to terms with the fact that there are many things that can happen to us and those we care about that are out of our control.*

FIRST STEPS TO HELP

- Self-blame can arise as a way of making sense of a situation that gives us a feeling that it is controllable in some way. Whilst this serves a function, in reality babies are often born premature for unknown reasons, or require neonatal care after a series of events or processes that are not possible to foresee. In these situations, finding ways to cope with feelings of loss of control and helplessness might be more helpful.
- Think about whether what you blame yourself for is something you could have realistically known about *at the time it happened* (e.g., without the benefit of hindsight). Also think about what other factors were present at the time that might have meant you acted differently, such as 'I didn't raise the alarm because I could see the midwives were already run off their feet', 'I ignored the bleeding because every time I'd been to the clinic about it before they told me it was nothing to worry about'.
- Recognize if high self-criticism or the views of other people around you are contributing to how you feel. Ask yourself if those who share their views with you that make you feel to blame are acting with helpful or unhelpful intentions. Often blame from others comes from a lack of knowledge or inaccurate beliefs around pregnancy and childbirth.
- In cases where you've learnt something new, remember that this knowledge could be useful in avoiding the same outcome in the future, even though it can't change the past.

Shame is also common in neonatal care where you feel that *you yourself* are wrong, bad or deficient in some way. Shame often arises in situations where there's a profound fear about what others may think of you, and that this may result in harsh judgement or even exclusion from a group or relationship. Shame is distressing and overwhelming. In an evolutionary context, back when we lived in harsh climates, the consequences of being excluded from our tribe or social group were severe or even fatal. There are many similarities in the brain between areas that show physical pain and the emotional experience of rejection that can help us to understand the often all-encompassing reality and distress of this state.

Whilst others usually help us regulate our emotional states, shame usually causes us to withdraw from others, and therefore has a secondary consequence of isolation and aloneness. Shame can arise for many reasons in the neonatal journey. Sometimes it comes from thinking about things that you may have done or not done before the baby arrived, or from thoughts and feelings, for example, not feeling like you are connected or love your baby, not wanting to or feeling repelled by the idea of breastfeeding, being jealous of other families or glad that it wasn't your baby who died, or other feelings and thoughts that are in some way 'unspeakable' or 'unshareable'. These can weigh heavily and cause significant distress, and are often described by parents as feelings 'with nowhere to go'.

Let's look at the experiences of Katy and Paul to understand how shame and self-blame can show up in the neonatal context:

Katy found it extremely hard to speak to the doctors when they asked her questions about when she sought medical attention in her pregnancy. She was flooded with images of the morning she started feeling unwell, which was after a weekend away with her partner where they had had sex often. She wasn't able to ask the questions she wanted to know the answers to, and started to blame herself, thinking she had done something that had caused her baby harm. Talking to another mother on the unit who had been upset because she had 'done everything right and was still here', Katy felt worse as she feared she had done something wrong, which meant she was a careless, reckless woman. When people asked her what was wrong she became tearful and frozen, telling others there was nothing they could do to help her.

Paul became friends with another father on the unit and they regularly went for coffee to catch up and support one another. His friend's baby was doing well but developed a sudden illness and tragically died. Paul was deeply upset for his friend, but also felt relieved that his baby was okay. He felt ashamed of his relief and happiness for his own child, and thought that this meant he was a selfish and dreadful person.

Finding a compassion voice to respond to shame

FIRST STEPS TO HELP

- Begin to find the words to describe what is driving these feelings for you – this could be thoughts, a feeling or actions. Start writing in a locked file on your phone or notebook – you don't have to show this to anyone. Sometimes the very act of putting something unspeakable into words can lessen the intensity of the emotional impact.
- Take steps to reduce isolation, as shame thrives on silence and secrecy. Keeping things hidden takes us away from sources of help and support and being able to share our 'common humanity', where we are connected and understood by others. If the idea of opening up to someone feels too difficult straightaway, you might want to start reading about others who have had a similar experience. Reading about what has happened to others can help what's happened to you feel less shameful or rare. Over time you may build up confidence to hear from other parents on the unit in person or online. A well-facilitated peer support group on your unit might provide an opportunity for this as well as online chatrooms and forums. If you have a psychological professional on your unit, consider talking to them about your feelings of shame. They will keep what you say confidential, which means that only you and them will know what you've spoken about.

- Imagine how you might respond to a friend in the same circumstances as you. This can help you to realize that the harsh judgement or blame you may be anticipating is not something that you would apply to others. Indeed, there can often be a sense of relief and closeness that comes from recognizing we often share similar thoughts, feelings and experiences.
- Cultivate a more compassionate response to your distress within yourself. When we feel shame, it's often met with a hostile or critical response within ourselves, which causes further distress. You can also use the 'Creating a compassionate companion to help at times of distress and difficulty' exercise to work with feelings of shame, which originates from Compassion Focused Therapy (CFT) that is particularly effective for people who struggle with shame and self-criticism.

Anger

Anger can sometimes be difficult to acknowledge to ourselves, and it can also be difficult for those around us. You may have received messages from your family or healthcare providers that anger is unacceptable, unjustified or 'won't get you anywhere'. The messaging around anger can lead it to be unexpressed, turned inward or for it to come out in ways that feel uncontrollable or towards people you love and care for.

In truth, there are many reasons to feel angry on the neonatal journey and the impact is often cumulative. You may feel:

- Angry about being in hospital with your baby after all you've been through in your life so far
- Anger from a sense of injustice and helplessness
- Angry about the outcome for your baby
- Angry about being uncared for or treated poorly by your medical team, your family or others
- Anger due to the frustration of being in a system that can feel impossible to influence or change
- Anger at being unable to be a parent in the way you'd like to be for your baby
- Angry that no one around you understands how you feel or knows how to help.

Take a moment to think about what belongs on your list when you think about your feelings of anger. Whilst there are many significant events or situations you may have endured that have made you feel angry, it's often a smaller thing that can act as the 'final straw' after a long period of suppressing or holding in feelings.

This means that sometimes anger is expressed towards people who may not have been the main cause or even have knowledge of what's happened to you and your baby, leading to confusion, hurt and difficulties in that relationship.

If you cast your mind back to where we talked about threat responses, whilst anger can arise from many causes (such as hurt, helplessness and humiliation), it's a threat system emotion and it serves a function – usually to protect ourselves and others. It can change our behaviour, thoughts and feelings in the same way as other emotions such as fear. When we feel angry, we often want to approach the issue (linked to our 'fight' response) to resolve it or protect ourselves and fend off danger. For example, you might feel angry when you see a doctor carry out a procedure on your baby that causes them pain or when no one comes to silence an alarm.

You might also notice feelings of anger towards healthcare professionals you don't know well (think of all the new faces and names) in the personal and intimate space around your baby. Not only can this stem from feeling they are in some way taking your rightful place as a parent, but it also has biological roots. Research has shown that oxytocin, a hormone heavily involved in processes around childbirth, feeding and feelings of closeness to others, can also have the effect of producing more aggression towards those we don't see as being part of our 'group'. On a neonatal unit you are in a situation where you're constantly surrounded by those who are not part of your group – relative strangers who are involved in keeping your baby alive. Many parents describe a mix of feelings towards staff on the unit – that they are grateful for what they are doing, but also often angry or resentful they have to be there and have so much control about what happens to their baby.

Your previous experiences will play a part in your relationship and response to anger. It might be difficult to express anger towards others and it may come with anxiety (if your early life experience has taught you anger can result in harsh punishment or is in some way socially unacceptable and leads to rejection, for example). Anger can give way to sadness and despair as your 'fight' response shifts to 'faint' or collapse. Many parents find themselves feeling angry, and then desperately hopeless and helpless. For others, anger and irritability can become dominant and the main response to the constant threats in the neonatal environment. This can start to have unintended consequences, such as getting in the way of helpful relationships with the neonatal team, or even with your baby.

Let's look at Piotr's story:

Piotr arrived on the neonatal unit in a state of high threat and agitation. He had been awake for over two days without rest, and despite his efforts to raise the alarm during his wife's labour, no one had come to attend to her. Circumstances changed quickly, and by the time she had been rushed into theatre, their baby had been without oxygen for many minutes. Piotr screamed at the team to do something, watching helplessly as they resuscitated baby Jan. He felt he had failed his partner, but he also felt livid that they had been left unattended when he had called for help. Piotr could not trust the neonatal team to act in Jan's best interests, suspicious of each procedure and intervention, and unwilling to talk with the consultants. When Jan had a significant desaturation, he became so distressed and angry that the unit called security, telling him his behaviour was unacceptable. He felt no one was able to listen to what he had to say, and the team began to avoid interactions with him. Piotr felt the only way to communicate with the team was by a series of formal complaints, and he felt increasingly emotionally alone. His wife felt that his anger meant there was no space for enjoying time with Jan or for being a new father. She wanted to help, but found herself unable to talk to Piotr about anything related to the birth or Jan's admission.

Piotr's experience highlights how important it can be to address emotional needs as they arise, and to recognize that an elevated threat response to danger isn't the same in everyone. Piotr's anger was cumulative after a series of events where he felt helpless to prevent harm and trust that healthcare professionals could act to help when they needed to. Piotr's mistrust and anger towards the team at delivery understandably transferred to those in the neonatal unit, his stance of suspicion a survival response of 'better safe than sorry'. Because Piotr's threat response was dominant it made it hard to connect with his partner or baby, and put a strain on his relationship at a time when he needed the support of his wife and the unit staff.

FIRST STEPS TO HELP

- Name and validate your experiences of anger. Start to be curious about where it has come from – experiences of injustice, mistakes, feeling unheard or ignored, feeling trapped or helpless, resentment, jealousy, for example. For some anger comes from longstanding hurt and pain, such as a feeling of being let down or actively hurt by others, oppressive or abusive experiences in systems or issues relating to becoming a parent when perhaps you yourself had a difficult experience of being parented. Like other emotions you might find anger is mixed with anxiety, shame and grief, etc.
- In a moment of anger recognize you are mounting a threat response with poor access to your 'thinking brain' that allows you to thoughtfully work out

the situation you are in or to access a sense of perspective. Some describe this as being emotionally hijacked or 'seeing red'. It can be helpful to press a mental 'pause' button when you find yourself here, and to engage in ways to calm your threat response to give you space to think, and to consider your needs and your actions. You may need others to help you to do this, at least initially – think with them about how they can do this without further adding to feelings of anger in that moment.

- Bring a compassionate stance to your anger – it may be that it's understandable given what you've been through, and that it shows an emotional need rather than a shortcoming.
- Work with the team and those around you to reduce triggers for anger such as poor communication or sharing of information. It can be worth taking the time to make a plan with the team around particular pressure points, such as what to do if no one is picking up the phone when you call for an update.
- Find ways to channel your anger into action that can help alleviate distress. If there are specific things you've experienced in the hospital setting that need to be addressed, find out what is available to you. You can start by raising a concern with a senior member of staff on the shift (usually the nurse in charge), which can be escalated on the unit if needed. If you feel this is not sufficient or the issues you are struggling with happened in another department or hospital, you can contact the Patient Advice and Liaison Service (PALS). Sometimes these are difficult discussions to have and there are mediation teams to facilitate in some hospitals. This can be particularly helpful when you are facing a longer stay and the issues raised are about care or people within a team.

Grief and loss

Experiences of grief and loss are never far away on the neonatal unit. Ask any parent and they will share losses that may have occurred along their pregnancy journey, previous deaths of babies or close family members, or those that may have happened during their current neonatal stay, such as the loss of a baby from a multiple pregnancy. For many the process of grieving for these losses is still ongoing and the impact cumulative. You might feel it's risky to imagine or hope for a different outcome, feel cut-off or detached from the enormity of your grief, or that you are in some way not allowed or don't have a right to grieve or feel the way you do (sometimes called *disenfranchised grief*).

Whilst loss is often linked to death, there are multiple other losses that aren't always immediately visible or obvious to others that cause significant distress and pain:

- Loss of your imagined pregnancy and/or birth
- Loss of the life you imagined after your baby was born
- Loss of time together as a family, time to see your other children develop and grow or be present at important events
- A multitude of everyday losses that happen due to your baby being unwell and in hospital
- Broader losses such as loss of certainty, personal and/or parental identity and hope.

Take a moment to think about the losses you have experienced at this stage in your journey. Whilst we will take a look in more detail at some of these losses and responses to them throughout the book, here it is important that they are recognized and acknowledged as part of what you hold emotionally, for what has happened, is happening, or in anticipation of what you might lose in the future.

Loss of your own parent when having a baby

One of the losses that can be particularly difficult and painful when becoming a parent or having another child is the loss of your own parent through death or another type of absence.

Let's meet Karen who faced this situation when her daughter was born:

> Karen was looking forward to the birth of her baby, but was still struggling with grief following the loss of her mother six months before her daughter's birth. Whilst there was so much excitement about the new arrival in her family, she felt like people were suggesting that her new baby would be a 'fix' to the grief she felt so acutely – for the loss of her mother and the loss of her in the specific life stage of becoming a mother herself. When her baby was found to have a heart anomaly and spent several months in the neonatal unit, Karen felt like all the joy she could muster in an already difficult situation had been stolen, and the sadness and loneliness of her situation became increasingly distressing.

For Karen, the death of her mother meant that she felt the acute loss of her presence when she needed it in such a difficult situation, and also felt like the imagined shared experience in this period of transition to being a mother herself was irreplaceably stolen away. For other parents whose family relationships have been difficult or even abusive, the transition to parenthood can bring up a different type of loss and grief – for the imagined parent who is still alive, for the loss of what they need but cannot have, and the recognition and felt sense of the absence of a loving parent when they themselves were babies.

Having a baby in neonatal care when you've experienced the loss of a previous baby

Many parents have experienced previous pregnancy loss or the death of babies in maternity or neonatal care. It can be difficult to allow hope for a different outcome when the worst possible outcome has already been a reality.

Sometimes when a new baby arrives after a loss it can be hard to separate them from the baby you may have known and loved before, as we can see in Shelia's story:

> Shelia's first baby Maddie died after three weeks in NICU, 18 months before she found herself on NICU again with her new baby girl, Katie. Whilst the team tried to reassure Shelia that the situation with Katie was very different to the difficulties faced by Maddie, she found herself terrified history would repeat itself. She also saw many similarities between Maddie and Katie that were painful reminders of what she had lost, and that triggered moments of unbearable grief. She found it hard to know how to love Katie at the same time as feeling so much loss for her sister Maddie.

Loss and grief can become more complex when they are combined with self-blame or even a sense that you might have deserved what has happened to you. The stories we tell ourselves about our losses and grief, the expectations of ourselves and others and the ways in which we turn towards it or move away are part of how we live through and with grief and loss in our lives.

Experiences of grief and loss and how they manifest are different for each person and there is not one way or a 'right' way to approach it. Here are some starting points to think about in relation to your own life and internal world, as you turn towards really difficult feelings.

FIRST STEPS TO HELP

- Validate your losses in all their forms in your life at this point. Take a moment to jot them down or talk to someone you are close to about how much loss you are holding on to and trying to make sense of. Try to give your experiences of loss space without rushing to 'fix' them (or others rushing to 'fix').
- Practise being alongside that part of you that is grieving and feeling hurt by loss. Ask yourself, what does that part of you need? How can you meet those needs where you are now? You may consider using some of the emotional resources (see 'Connecting to emotional resources') to help you at a

particularly difficult moment of loss and grief, such as courage or unlimited physical and emotional comfort.

- Notice if there is a critical part of you that comes with unhelpful judgements or expectation, such as 'You should be getting over it by now' or 'Life's tough, you just have to move on!' Acknowledge that this critical voice may be trying to help you in some way, but remember, it won't be helpful in the long run.
- Limit your time around those who minimize, invalidate or ignore your losses, particularly whilst you are still in hospital. Look for those who can provide the kind of emotional connection and company that honours your losses and supports you.

(You can find more help with loss and grief when you are facing or have experienced the death of a baby in Chapter 11.)

In the rest of this chapter is a practical series of exercises to help you move into a more soothed and safe state and to access your compassionate mind to help with all the challenges you're facing. You might find some exercises more helpful than others at different times. Take time to find what works for you and when.

FINDING WAYS TO A MORE SOOTHED, SAFE AND CONNECTED STATE

Being in a constant state of threat takes its toll on your body and mind. It also makes it harder to do some of the things you may need or want to do whilst your baby is in hospital. As well as reducing a sense of threat where possible, it's important to build and grow a sense of safety and connection to others.

In Chapter 1 we used a breathing exercise called 'Soothing breathing rhythm' to help us to do this. It's important to use this exercise not only when you are feeling very anxious, but also proactively, each day, to help it become easier to use and engage when you need it. It can be helpful to use 'Soothing breathing rhythm' when you wake up (in the morning or during the night, as this can often be a 'spike' of anxiety), as you are arriving at the hospital and coming onto the unit, and when you are holding or interacting with your baby. If you find yourself becoming very anxious before speaking with a nurse or doctor, you could quite deliberately direct your focus to your breathing, grounding your body (e.g., by bringing your focus to your feet firmly on the floor and your body supported by your chair) as they approach the cot space.

Just as our body's responses influence our thoughts, the images and thoughts in our mind influence what we experience and feel in our body. A simple example is imagining eating your favourite food. As you imagine that, your body will start to produce saliva and stomach acid in anticipation of eating. What is key is that there is no actual food, but this image has created a change in your body's response. Because of this incredible effect, you can use imagery to help when you're experiencing more distressing emotional states – to reduce a sense of threat and to enhance feelings of safety, connection and calm.

You can help your body to move into a more relaxed and regulated state using the following techniques that make use of imagery, connecting with your senses and your body. Take some time to try them and work out which ones work most effectively for you. These recordings are available via the QR codes below, and you may wish to save them on your phone to listen to them at cot side.

PROGRESSIVE MUSCLE RELAXATION

You can use this when you find it very difficult to relax and your body is tense, stiff or unable to be still and settled. It can be helpful to do this when you are going to be spending a period of time doing skin to skin with your baby, or as you plan to go to sleep.

Take a moment to find a place to take a seat, placing your feet firmly on the floor about a shoulder width apart. Bring your shoulders back and open your chest allowing plenty of space to breathe slowly and calmly, focusing first on your out-breath and moving into your soothing breathing rhythm.

Notice a sense of stilling and stability in your body. We are going to make our way slowly from the top of your body to the bottom with the aim of reducing the tension and stress you are holding.

Bring your attention to your face and notice all of the tension you may be holding around your eyes, your mouth and anywhere else you can sense it.

Quite deliberately tense your muscles in all those places for a few seconds, and then exhale, letting the tension flow out of your face and away from your body.

Move the focus of attention to your neck and your shoulders. Notice if there is any pain or discomfort in your neck, or any tightening or heaviness in your shoulders. Whatever the sensation you're holding onto, again tense this area, bringing your shoulders up to your ears and then let them go with an out-breath. If you have a particular colour or texture associated with this tension, imagine it flowing and dissipating into the air around you.

Then move your attention to the middle of your body around your chest and stomach. You may be tender here from birth, feeding or expressing as well as tense.

Just notice what your body is holding. And when you're ready, tense the muscles in this area of your body, and then after a few seconds let them go.

If it's too painful or difficult to do this in this specific area, imagine breathing the sensations in your body out directly from this space.

As you move your attention down to the top of your thighs and your legs, continue to notice what this part of your body holds – perhaps it's tense but also tired from carrying your weight and standing a lot of the day. Perhaps your legs feel numb or disconnected from your body in a moment of anxiety.

Tense these muscles, reconnecting to any part of this area that feels separate from you if needed, and then relax.

Finally move your attention to your lower legs and your feet. Notice if they are weary, sore or aching. Wiggle your toes and then tense them with your calves, next letting go and imagining that tension travelling down through your feet and into the floor.

Connecting with memories of feeling safe, connected and regulated (and other helpful 'state' memories)

We can use a memory of a time in our lives when we have felt safe, calm and connected to others to help us when we are struggling. To do this, spend a few moments scanning your mental library of images and experiences that have given you this feeling. You may need to try a few out before deciding on one that best represents this state. Once you have found a scene or experience in your mind, try to connect each one of your senses with this experience, one by one:

- What you feel in terms of touch or sensation (this might be the sense of a caring and calm body next to yours – people and animals are popular choices, or the sensation of a particular place such as water or sand)
- What you can hear (this may be someone speaking to you or just a soothing sound)
- What you can see (this may be someone's face or your surroundings)
- What you can smell and taste (this may be perfume, the cooking of a comforting food or a smell associated with a particular place).

Notice what changes in your body as you connect with this memory. Notice what changes to how you feel emotionally.

You can also use memories of other emotional states to help meet your needs at this moment in time. For example, thinking of a time that you felt brave, in control, or felt you mattered deeply to another person. The archive of state memories you build can be a valuable resource for different times in your neonatal journey to help you to manage and have what you need emotionally.

CONNECTING TO EMOTIONAL RESOURCES

Take a moment to make a note of what you feel you need in terms of connection to an emotional state, and when you might use it as a resource to help you. Add your own notes after the example.

Situation	Emotional state memory resource
Feeling anxious and ignored in the nursery – no one around to talk to.	*Connecting to a time when I felt cared for and special with my grandma. Feeling the warmth of her presence and the smell of her kitchen.*

'LIGHT STREAM' MEDITATION[3]

This can help when you feel you are holding emotions in your body that you would like to release or lessen. It can also be helpful when you are feeling overwhelmed by something very difficult and it feels like you are loaded with painful feelings, thoughts and sensations. This exercise can be particularly helpful at nighttime when you are looking

3 Based on work by Francine Shapiro (2001).

to bring your body and mind into a more settled state so that it can rest (see 'What to do if you are not getting enough sleep' in Chapter 1).

Take a moment to close your eyes and come fully into your body, and your own internal space. Allow yourself to filter out some of the sounds and chatter around you, and gift yourself your full attention for this moment.

As you focus into your body, concentrate on any upsetting body sensations or feelings that you are holding.

Ask yourself, if they had a shape what would that be?... If they had a size or texture what would that look like?... If they had a colour or temperature what would that be right now?'...

Take time to really identify these attributes, without any pressure to know the answer to all of them – some people only have a couple that really match what they're feeling. Once you have a sense of them, imagine a healing light that is coming down from above you – give this light a colour and temperature that for you is associated with a sense of healing, compassion and calm. Imagine that this light is flowing into your body down from the top of your head and is able to direct its flow, so it's channelled straight into the part of you that needs its attention and healing presence.

Just notice how it feels to be filling your body with this light, vibrating and gathering around the shape of your distress, coming to each part of your body that holds it in turn. Notice as you let the light come into your body what happens to the shape over time. Allow yourself to stay with the light stream until the shape has become smaller or gone completely.

Now bring the light to every part of your body, starting at your feet, up through the centre and into your face.

SAFE PLACE IMAGERY

This can help when your body is stuck in a 'high alert' state. It is a short exercise you can do anywhere that allows you to have a felt sense of safety within your own mind and body. There is a strong link between what we imagine in our minds and our physiological state. Some people create several safe places from a library in their mind, others just one. For some it is key to have people in this safe space, and for others it is a location where they experience a soothed state on their own. Some choose to include their baby, and again, for others, this doesn't help to make the place feel safe whilst there is still uncertainty and fear around the situation. What is key is that the *felt sense* of this place is safety.

Find somewhere comfortable to sit and take a few moments to find a posture where you feel grounded and secure. Engage in your soothing breathing rhythm, allowing your breathing and your body to slow down a little.

Notice the air coming in and out of your body, feeling the air coming in through your nose and out through your mouth. Spend a few moments to settle into this rhythm.

When you're ready, bring to mind an image of a place that you feel is safe, soothing or calming in some way. This may be somewhere you have been before, or a place that you create in your mind just for you. This may take a few moments, and you may want to try out a number of places before you find one that feels right.

When you have an image in your mind, spend a few moments being with it. Notice what you can see first in your safe place. You may notice certain colours, objects or people. You may notice how the light falls or what time of day it is. Take time to look around you.

Now notice whether you can hear anything in this place – first pay attention to the sounds you can hear close to you...and now those that you can hear in the distance. Notice if you can smell anything around you – this may be the smell of herbs, earthy smells or those that you remember from a safe person or place in your past.

Now notice what you can feel and touch in this safe place. You might notice the breeze on your face or warm sand beneath your body.

You may find your mind wandering away from this place for a few seconds. Just notice when it goes, and then gently return your attention to the part of your safe place that is most important. Imagine that the place itself takes joy in you being here. Even if it's fleeting, try to create an emotional connection to this place.

Remember this safe place is your creation and really welcomes you and wants you to be here, offering you safeness and rest. When you are in your safe place, allow your body to relax. When you are ready, take a picture in your mind of this safe place, somewhere you can always return to and will always welcome you.

Identifying others who can help you move into a soothed, safe and regulated state

Thinking back to the section on the soothing system you might remember that we talked about the importance of others in helping create a sense of safeness, being cared for and contained. You may notice that there are certain people who have these qualities for you – it might be their tone of voice, their posture, their ability to tune in to you, validate your experiences and understand what you need. Be curious for a moment about how you know you are experiencing this sense of connection and safety with another person. Once you have a sense of this for yourself, make a list of people you can seek out at times of distress as well as have as much contact time as possible with during your time on the unit.

Magda found the reception staff a particularly reassuring presence on the unit. They were there throughout her day – to greet her when she arrived and also to drop by to talk to at difficult moments. She found that even knowing they were there helped her to feel more regulated during her long stay.

IDENTIFYING PEOPLE AROUND YOU WHO HELP YOU FEEL CONTAINED AND CALM

Have a look at Mary's example. You can add your own examples below Mary's.

Person	Where and when can I see them?	How do they help?
Mary	*She's the unit cleaner, there every day on the corridors and by the lockers.*	*She always says hello with a big smile, she talks to me about her grown-up children and normal life. She helps me to feel calm and sometimes makes me laugh. The fact that she seeks me out and asks about baby Josh helps me to feel seen and cared for.*

CONNECTING WITH YOUR COMPASSIONATE MIND

We can use '"Light stream" meditation' and 'Safe place imagery' from the previous section to help us move into a more soothed state so that we aren't always responding from our threat mind. It is also particularly helpful to engage with our compassionate mind, a state of mind that allows us to (1) tune in and validate the suffering and struggles we are having at this moment in time and (2) that is motivated to help make them better and decrease our distress. We thought about this together briefly in Chapter 1 and earlier in this chapter, and now we're going to look at it in a little more detail here.

You may already have thoughts about what you'd consider are compassionate qualities. Here are some core qualities that are key:

- Wisdom – having a perspective, insight and knowledge about what you're going through, gained through experience in life and perhaps experiences that are similar to your own
- A deep commitment to help you – a desire to help you cope with suffering and relieve pain
- Acceptance of you as you are and not judging you in any way
- Strength and courage – being able to engage with your distress, not be overwhelmed by it or shy away from it, enduring it with you
- Warmth, kindness and openness – caring for you in a genuinely supportive and committed way.

Many people find it hard to access these qualities directly within themselves, and find it easier to imagine another person or being they can interact with in their minds to help. To help you to develop a companion for you who is perfectly compassionate, take some time to work through the following exercise. This will be worth the investment for your neonatal journey, as there will be many times when you might need to connect with this compassionate presence and have a sense that they are beside you.

CREATING A COMPASSIONATE COMPANION TO HELP AT TIMES OF DISTRESS AND DIFFICULTY[4]

The aim of this exercise is to create a sense of inner soothing and security via a perfectly compassionate companion who embodies all the qualities you would need from someone totally focused on your welfare.

Think about the *qualities* that this person needs to have. In addition to compassionate qualities just highlighted, add other qualities here that matter to you:

....

....

....

4 This exercise has been modified from Deborah Lee (2012).

Other important qualities:

....

....

....

....

....

Think about what your compassionate companion would look like. Describe their physical appearance, thinking about how old they are, whether they might be a person, or perhaps an animal. Would they have a certain smell or a certain 'felt sense' that is unique to their presence? What would their voice sound like (soothing, calm, low or high, familiar)? You can be creative here, but take the time to really elaborate the image so that it feels as vivid as possible. If you have artistic talents, you may even wish to draw them in your journal or on a blank piece of paper:

....

....

....

....

....

....

Think about where you would like your compassionate companion to be. They can be anywhere. You may wish to meet with them in a specific place that represents safety and calm, or you may wish them to be alongside you wherever you are. Take a moment to map this out:

....

....

....

....

....

....

How would they respond to your distress and experiences? When you are struggling with what is happening, memories or difficult emotions, what would your compassionate companion offer you by way of comfort? What might they do first? And then, what would they do next? What would they say to you? Jot down some of their actions and what they might say, including how they might say it (think about their tone of voice, emphasis and overall delivery):

....

....

....

....

....

....

Once you have a good sense of your compassionate companion, take time to develop all the aspects listed above for yourself. You might want to start by spending a few minutes each day in their company. Notice what it feels like to be there with someone who profoundly understands you and what you are going through and wants to be with you and to ease your suffering. Notice if any critical elements creep in, and gently guide yourself back to focusing on their qualities as a perfectly compassionate and non-judging figure (who may also wish to help with that critical part of you).

If you face challenges ahead in your week, consider how it might feel to imagine your compassionate companion being alongside you, or being someone to go to before and afterwards – always there, and always ready to greet you.

Bringing our compassionate mind to difficulty and suffering

When we come to look at the thoughts and experiences we're having that are causing us great distress and suffering, we can bring our compassionate mind to these, which may help us to gently look at them and respond to them differently. Catastrophic thoughts are very common and understandable in the context of the neonatal unit, as Darren relates:

> Darren found himself thinking about something terrible happening to his baby every time he saw a doctor approach him or he had a procedure that led to overwhelming anxiety. His threat system had no trouble in generating hundreds of thoughts throughout the day, and as this happened his attention became more focused on possible danger. Darren started to practise connecting with a more

compassionate mind, leaning heavily on the experience of a teacher at school who had cared for and advised him through some difficult experiences in his teens, and who was a good fit for his compassionate companion. He wrote down the thoughts that proved particularly distressing, and then imagined what his teacher would say in response – both what he might say, and also how he might say it from a position of caring for Darren and wanting the very best for him:

Darren's thoughts	Compassionate response
The doctor is coming to tell me he can't do anything more for my baby.	*It's understandable you are feeling so scared when you see a doctor; sometimes they have to deliver bad news and your threat mind is telling you that when they approach you it's going to be bad. It's hard to suffer continuously with this fear, particularly as you're so exhausted. Perhaps it's helpful to remember that they also come to see how your baby's doing, give you updates, which include his progress, and carry out procedures and tests to take care of him.*
My baby is experiencing endless pain and I'm powerless to stop it.	*It's so hard to see your baby in pain – any parent would find that difficult because you care about them so deeply. Remember, too, that there were moments today when you weren't powerless – recall when you placed your hands around your son's body to let him know you were there when he was uncomfortable earlier. Even though you can't take all the pain away all the time, many times you can make it so much better.*

ENGAGING WITH YOUR COMPASSIONATE MIND

Take a moment to identify some of the thoughts you are experiencing, engage with your compassionate mind, and then see if you can write a compassionate response:

My thoughts	Compassionate response

Developing a compassionate mind takes practice, and if you've had few experiences of compassion, warmth and empathy, it can be particularly challenging. Whilst it's easy to feel disheartened if it's difficult, remember that it's something you can practise as you're going through the neonatal journey with yourself and others who are important to you.

SUMMARY

Whilst you are attending to your baby's physical and emotional needs, it's also important to attend to yours when your baby is in neonatal care. In this chapter we have thought about some of the ways in which distress can show up in our minds and bodies, and how an understanding of this can help you take the first steps to reduce your suffering. We have focused on starting to develop and nurture a compassionate mind, and how this approach can help with many of the challenges you face. You may have found that this chapter has started a process for you in terms of understanding yourself in the context of your own life and experience. You may choose to take this process forward through seeking help from a psychological professional, now or in the future. So much of neonatal care is about relationships – with your baby, with your partner and with the team – but the longest relationship you have is with yourself – so make time to nurture it.

RESOURCES

Somewhere to find more information

The **Canopie app** is full of Compassionate Mind resources to help neonatal parents through their journey, and can be downloaded via the QR code.

Something to watch

'No one plans on their baby needing neonatal care' by **Kelly Phizacklea** is a heartfelt poem with real photographs from families who have experienced the neonatal journey. View and listen to this on YouTube: www.youtube.com/watch?v=xIA5xFvPRUo

Something to listen to

'Sharing experience of birth trauma and the Neonatal Intensive Care Unit', a **London Health Podcast**, features parents talking openly about some of their experiences, the impact on their mental health and what helped them. It is available across platforms via: www.transformationpartners.nhs.uk/perinatal-mental-health-podcasts/perinatal-mental-health-podcast-2-transcript

Something to read

Miracles and Shining Stars: A Collective of Voices from the Neonatal Ward, edited by **Charlotte Burkett and Vicky Mather-Willis**, is a collection of poems written by everyone affected by a neonatal journey – from grandparents to hospital consultants.

See also:

The Compassionate Mind: A New Approach to the Challenges of Life, by **Paul Gilbert** (2009).

Eye Movement Desensitization and Reprocessing: Basic Principles, Protocols, and Procedures, by **Francine Shapiro** (2001).

The Compassionate Mind Approach to Recovering from Trauma: Using Compassion Focused Therapy, by **Deborah Lee with Sophie James** (2012).

CHAPTER 3

Close relationships and the neonatal journey

SUPPORTING ONE ANOTHER AND FINDING SUPPORT FROM OTHERS WHEN YOU'RE ON YOUR OWN

Nourishing and looking after close relationships is important as they can help buffer the impact of traumatic and stressful situations and help us to cope better. Supportive partners, family members and close friends who provide a compassionate and soothing presence help us to 'dial down' the sense of threat. However, these relationships can also come under pressure from the stress of a neonatal admission. This short chapter will look at some of the challenges for these three different types of relationship, and also help you think about your needs if you're on your own.

RELATIONSHIPS WITH YOUR PARTNER

Intimate relationships can be helpful and joyful as well as challenging and hard. You may have already gone through some challenges before your baby arrived in neonatal care, and the stress and pressure of an admission can make these more pronounced.

It's key to recognize that not only are you managing a change in your role when you become a parent (or a change in your role as you move into parenting a baby in hospital if you already have other children), you are also navigating that relationship *between* you both, as a couple under high emotional distress, uncertainty and exhaustion.

Some common challenges for couples when their baby is in neonatal care include:

- Breakdown of communication or re-emergence of unhelpful communication patterns from the past

- Reduced space and capacity to think about what's happening from each other's perspective; psychological distress may make it even harder to understand each other's behaviour or reactions
- Differences in coping strategies between you – whilst your ways of coping will make sense to you, they might be difficult for your partner to understand or manage, for example, one of you may cope by avoiding medical information and the other by wanting to know all the details
- Spending lengthy periods apart with little private space when you're together by your baby's side
- Differences in emotional and physical needs – for physical contact/intimacy, a need to talk things through, for example – which may cause distress and tension
- Differences in views about the care of your baby – from everyday decisions to those that concern long-term outcomes, which can cause conflict and distress
- Parenting roles not feeling equal – for example, one of you may be spending a lot more time with your baby than the other – which can lead to feelings of exclusion, jealousy and inadequacy that can play out within a relationship. You may also find that the neonatal team develop a closer relationship with whoever is there more often, which brings difficulties of its own.

Let's meet a couple who were finding their relationship coming under a lot of strain three weeks into their baby's admission:

Tyler and Matthew's baby girl Rose was born with a congenital heart defect, which they knew about from pregnancy. They had both previously struggled with depression and had felt like their lives were settling and improving when they found out they were expecting Rose. Her condition was something that caused Tyler a lot of anxiety, and she found talking to other parents when she was pregnant and on the unit very helpful. Matthew, however, found his mood getting worse over time and didn't want to speak to anyone about Rose's situation. He felt like he was being pushed out of the unit community as he didn't feel able to join any support groups, and felt uncomfortable in the kitchen and corridors as he didn't know anyone. Matthew was resentful and angry towards Tyler for sharing what he considered to be private family information with others. She, in turn, felt increasingly isolated and separate from Matthew. The situation became more difficult as they were required to make decisions about surgery together and couldn't speak without it becoming an argument.

Tyler and Matthew had come to the unit having already gone through a difficult time in their relationship. Their different ways of coping meant that whilst some of Tyler's emotional needs were met, Matthew found himself isolated and resentful. Whilst these may have resolved in time after a period of adjustment, the events with Rose meant that their need to communicate and work together became pressing.

FIRST STEPS TO HELP

- Noticing what's coming up between you and your partner and naming it is an important first step. If you tend to be avoidant around difficulty (ignoring it and hoping it goes away) or anxious about it (worrying what it would mean to raise a problem), this can be hard. Try naming what is happening to yourself emotionally first – for example, 'I am noticing a feeling of anger/insecurity' – before sharing it with each other. Remember, whilst your internal experience may feel obvious to you, your partner might not understand or know the extent of your distress without being told.
- Recognize the similarities and differences in your experiences and the meaning you make of them. Find the common ground first that can help you to know what you share, and then look for what's different. Listen carefully when your partner is explaining their perspective without interrupting, trying to correct them or invalidate what they are saying. If you can, summarizing back what they've told you can be a powerful way to show you've really listened, and gives an opportunity to clear up any misunderstandings.
- Be careful not to assume that understanding automatically leads to knowing how to help. You may need to be explicit about what your needs are in a given situation or period of time – for example, 'After the resuscitation that happened in the room earlier I am feeling very on edge and frightened. I need you to help by speaking and moving calmly and slowly and remind me our baby is doing well today.'
- Be clear about what you need physically from each other and what feels comfortable. This may be an ongoing negotiation and will be influenced by your patterns of physical intimacy and how they link to your emotional state and needs. Explore with each other what feels desirable and what feels doable, bearing in mind the need for physical recovery after birth. You may find that non-sexual ways of physically connecting with one another meet some of the need for intimacy and connection. Be careful not to put any pressure on your partner for intimacy if they aren't ready.
- Look for what you can say and do to help you feel cared for and connected

to each other. What words can you say to your partner that really help them to feel seen and cared for? Take a moment to think about what the content of your conversations is right now. If they are wholly focused on logistics or problem solving, make sure there's also space to say what each other needs to hear emotionally, for example, 'I'm here with you whatever happens today', 'I know you're struggling with not being able to feed him, but I think you're doing an amazing job'. Think about what actions you can take to show them they are cared for, and make time to do this every day, such as making sure they have sterilized expressing equipment with regular food and drink provided, arranging cushions and clothing to help them feel comfortable at cot side.

- Think about what your strengths are as a couple and how to maximize them in this new situation. These might include things such as being thoughtful about each other, being good joint problem solvers or strong in mutual encouragement. Once you've thought about them, share them with each other.
- Notice things your partner is doing and encourage them. This can include appreciation of things they might do for you, encouraging them in a new part of their parenting role (such as mastering a tube feed) or telling them how well you felt they managed a conversation with the team. Being seen and appreciated by your partner is important. You could start with aiming to notice three things each day for each other, and share them at the end of the day.
- Plan well ahead for situations you know will put extra strain on your relationship when you can, for example, when one of you returns to work. Again, an explicit conversation about both your needs in a new situation will allow you to plan around these thoughtfully, such as sending regular messages and videos to address the fear of missing a change or new development (see 'My partner isn't often able to be on the unit...' in Chapter 4).
- Make steps to repair damage and difficulties between you when they happen. All relationships have times when there's conflict, when you feel apart or are simply not being 'tuned in' or thoughtful towards each other. What matters is how you repair these times between you and move forwards. It can take courage to go back to something hard and apologize or acknowledge you have hurt someone, but this will help your relationship feel safe and emotionally open in the long run.

Whilst we have thought about ways to approach and work through some of the difficulties that can arise between partners, if you feel *afraid* or *unsafe* in your relationship, or if your partner is violent or abusive towards you, it's important to tell someone. They can make sure that you receive the appropriate help quickly, which may include planning to keep you and your baby safe and supported in hospital and when your baby is discharged.

RELATIONSHIPS WITH YOUR WIDER FAMILY

A neonatal admission affects the whole family including other children you may have, your own parents or other significant family members. (If you have other children, Chapter 7 looks in more detail at how you might support them.) It can be hard when you are aware that others in your family might be struggling to understand or process what is happening to you and your baby. You might feel in some way responsible for their struggle or that their distress should be directed elsewhere. Much like other relationships, patterns of relating and managing distress are well established in families over time.

For grandparents, the change in role from what they might have expected can be difficult and they may not know how best to support you. They may not be able to visit your baby or understand what it means to be in neonatal care. If your relationship with your parents is not straightforward or they are not involved in your life, becoming a parent yourself may evoke all sorts of new and difficult feelings for you (see Chapter 5).

FIRST STEPS TO HELP

- Be clear about what your parents or other family members can do to support you. It can be helpful for them to have specific roles or jobs on and off the unit, and to be aware of when these might be useful, such as helping to research car seats near to discharge.
- If you'd like them to have a more active role in looking after your baby, ask your unit what's possible and when – for example, are they able to spend time with your baby when you are elsewhere?
- Encourage them to seek support from others if they are finding the situation difficult, to allow their focus to be on you and your needs. The unit may be able to link them up with other grandparents or extended family on the unit.
- The change in your role in becoming a parent may bring up challenges in family relationships, such as accepting who makes decisions or who 'knows

best'. Take time to work out what your boundaries are in these relationships and how to make those clear.

- Seek help on the unit if you are struggling with family members and don't feel like you can manage this on your own. Psychological professionals and family support teams are well placed to support you.

RELATIONSHIPS WITH YOUR FRIENDS

Friendships often play a key role in emotional support, and the role of good friends who care about you cannot be underestimated. It can also be difficult to know how to maintain those friendships when your baby is in neonatal care, particularly if you're a long way from home. It can be hard if your friendship groups are based around being pregnant (such as baby classes), or if your friends don't have children of their own – there can be something isolating and disconnecting from these positions and your own when your baby is in hospital. Often even with good intentions and wishes it can feel as if friends 'don't get it'. Those who have become close through baby classes may struggle to know what to say, often sitting with their own anxiety and discomfort.

Many intense friendships are formed with other parents during their time in neonatal care. These unit friendships are formed through shared understanding, solidarity with difficulty and being present through moments of joy and sorrow. You might find that for a period your focus shifts to just interacting with these newer companions. Don't feel the pressure to have to maintain all your other relationships if this doesn't feel possible. However, if friends from outside the neonatal unit are important to keep connected with, there are some things you might consider.

FIRST STEPS TO HELP

- Allocate one friend to update your social network (this may also include family members).
- Let your friends know that whilst you may not be able to reply so often, messages and supportive contact is welcome. They may be anxious about saying the wrong thing, so you might want to tell them what kind of messages you'd benefit from at any point in time – messages of encouragement, hope or simply being alongside you, for example.
- Encourage them to do some of their own research about neonatal care so they can understand more about what's happening for you and your baby.

- Remind them that being in touch or coming to see you is particularly important during a long stay. Schedule those times in ahead and regularly.
- When you meet or talk to friends, let them know what you're comfortable talking about and what you need at that time – for example, you may find it helpful to discuss your baby but also have time to talk about other things outside of hospital. A gentle direction from you can often make meet-ups easier for everyone.
- Remember, whilst this time in your friendship might feel more 'one-sided' as you need their support, you would do the same for them if they needed you. This time won't be forever.

IF YOU'RE ON YOUR OWN

Being a single parent in the neonatal unit can be difficult when you're often surrounded by couples, and much is designed with a two-parent 'traditional' family in mind. It can also be difficult to feel like you have to explain the circumstances around your situation, whatever these may be, and it's important to find ways to let the team know how you would like this to be handled, especially if it feels sensitive, and to avoid repetitive questions. They will ask some initial questions about the circumstances around your baby's conception to understand who holds parental responsibility. You can ask that this be clearly indicated on your baby's notes along with any information that's key for the team to support you (such as whether your baby's co-parent or your ex-partner can see your baby). However your family is set up, it's important to feel that your situation is understood, and you can work with the team and those who support you outside hospital to help you manage the neonatal stay.

FIRST STEPS TO HELP

- Identify at least one other key person who can be given the same access to your baby on the unit as a partner would – this may be a parent or a close friend. It's important to think about what you'd like this person to be able to do and to discuss their role with the unit – for example, if you were unwell, what would they be able to do or decide, and what would need your input? How can the unit make sure they can be present for important discussions and decisions about your baby?
- Think about how you would like your baby's significant relationships to be

acknowledged in memory making and special events – for example, you may wish a father's day card to be made for their grandfather or another person who holds a special role in their life such as a godparent or guide parent. Let the team know about your family set-up and how they help honour and acknowledge this.

- Consider a small group of friends or family to support you throughout the admission. A family member or one individual may not be able to be with you as much as you need whilst your baby is in hospital. Identifying a small group who can actively commit to being there for you and communicate with each other can help, particularly around stress points, such as your baby needing surgery, moving between hospitals and school holidays.
- You may find that you form very close relationships with other parents on their own on the unit who can understand how you feel and the challenges you face. Often these groups of friends provide emotional and practical support during and after the hospital stay. Ask if your unit can introduce you to other parents who may be in a similar situation.
- If you have other children and little support from others, there are sometimes local or national charities (such as the Rainbow Trust[1]) that can help with everyday practicalities, including childcare. Some units may have facilities to accommodate other children whilst you spend time with your baby, and in bigger hospitals siblings can sometimes attend hospital schools if you are all a long way from home. Ask on the unit who can help you access family support as soon as possible.
- If you are worried about seeing an ex-partner whilst your baby is in hospital, discuss this with a member of the neonatal team who can advise and help you make arrangements. If you feel unsafe or scared around them, or feel they aren't safe to be around your baby, let the team know immediately and they can take steps to help, which may involve the hospital safeguarding teams.

SUMMARY

Partners, family and friends can provide essential emotional and practical support whilst you're going through a very difficult period. At the same time, relationships sometimes need extra thought during such a significant time of adjustment, where there are many new and changeable challenges and pressures. Being clear about what your needs are and how they can be met is key. Coming back to repair relations at times when communication breaks down and finding moments of

1 www.rainbowtrust.org.uk

meaningful connection with others through shared experience will help you look after the relationships that matter most to you.

RESOURCES

Somewhere to find more information

For stories, writing and advice about being a single parent on the NICU, see:

'Being a single parent on the neonatal unit – Grace's story': www.bliss.org.uk/story/graces-story

Single, pregnant, & preemie, Cardiff girl (still) juggling it all: https://single-pregnant-preemie.com

Something to watch

Watch **Rachel Marzario and Martha Sharkey**, who met in hospital during bed rest, talk about the importance and power of friendship through the NICU journey on their podcast **TODAY is a Good Day** (although be aware that this episode contains a discussion about baby loss): www.todayisagoodday.org/podcasts

Something to listen to

'Supporting your NICU grandbaby' on **Hand to Hold Podcasts** (available on Apple Podcasts, Spotify and YouTube). Listen to paediatrician **Dr Judith Ender** and a grandparent talk about how to support your child and grandchild through the NICU stay: https://open.spotify.com/episode/7hh2TJZQtNhjDcF2w3Ongz

Something to read

Resources on relationships can be found on the neonatal **Canopie app** in Section 4. Download this via the QR code.

CHAPTER 4

'Parents are not visitors'

CARING FOR YOUR BABY THROUGH FAMILY INTEGRATED CARE (FICARE)

Amongst the wires, monitors and incubators is your precious baby, even if it may not feel like it just yet. When your baby is in neonatal care it can feel as if everything about the experience of becoming a parent has been taken from you. You may feel helpless to help them, and at the worst, redundant. Alongside these painful feelings you may also feel a desire to help and an excitement to become involved, but an uncertainty in knowing how.

This chapter will introduce you to a model of care practised in neonatal units called Family Integrated Care (FiCare),[1] which centres *you* as the most important person for your baby as their primary carer. Everything that happens during your stay in neonatal care should reflect this core principle, from the way ward rounds take place and how decisions are made to what clothes your baby wears and your daily routine.

For many parents their relationship with their baby has begun in different ways before their birth – perhaps even before conception. FiCare is a way of honouring and empowering this special connection and relationship amidst the medical care and changed circumstances you find yourself in. It's a model of care that gives you more control and ways to feel empowered in a setting full of unknowns and uncertainty. It also helps reduce levels of anxiety and depression, and helps you to bond with your baby and develop confidence in parenting. Importantly it also improves outcomes for babies such as shortening their stay in hospital and reducing readmission (having to come back into hospital once you've gone home).

The majority of neonatal units in the UK practise FiCare due to the benefits for everyone. Whilst you might see some variation in the details from hospital to hospital, the core aims and guiding principles will be the same. Ultimately good

1 https://familyintegratedcare.com

FiCare is about building safe, supportive and loving relationships where as much care as possible is given by the parents. It is also about *removing the need to ask for permission* to be with or to do things with your baby as their parent.

In this chapter we will look at:

- What FiCare means for you and your baby, the members of the team who will work with you to deliver it, and what they do
- Your involvement and role in key areas of care for your baby, including their everyday care, being involved in ward rounds and decision making
- Why relationships are key to FiCare culture, and how to develop these on the unit
- Common questions and concerns and your many roles as a parent whilst your baby is in neonatal care.

WHAT DOES FICARE ACTUALLY MEAN?

It has long been recognized that:

- It's beneficial for families in all sorts of ways to be involved in the care of their baby
- Babies tend to do better when their parents are involved as much as possible in caring for them
- Having a baby in hospital impacts the whole family – on an individual, couple, immediate and extended family level – so everyone's needs should be considered.

Family-centred care looks after the needs of your baby (e.g., thinking about how to help them feel soothed and safe and support their development), your needs as parents (emotional and practical needs, and developing your confidence and skills in your parenting role) and those of the wider family (such as siblings and grandparents).

FiCare evolves the concept of family-centred care so that you, as a parent, are equipped to provide as much care as possible for your baby over time, and the neonatal team provide the support and structure around you to do this *at a pace and level that's right for you at any moment.*

A lot of information is available about how to become involved in your baby's care in a way that takes into account their stage of development and particular needs whilst receiving medical treatment. Your baby will seek you as their parent to keep them safe, and they need you to help them navigate all the things that are happening to them on the unit. It's your relationship with each other that flows and grows through all the things you do and the time you spend together.

Let's meet Claire and Petra who were unsure at first about how to be involved in caring for their twins:

> Claire and Petra wanted to help care for their baby twins from the beginning, and they were relieved to find that their twins were able to be next to each other in their incubators, meaning Claire and Petra could also be together as a couple to support each other throughout the day. Their first twin was able to be held skin to skin with support after a few days, and they spent long periods holding her with the support of the nursing team. Their second twin was less well, and the team felt that coming out of the incubator would be difficult for the baby. Claire and Petra were shown how to do 'containment holding' or 'hand cuddles', where they supported their baby to feel safe and soothed by specific touch. Whilst they felt nervous and frustrated that they couldn't pick the baby up for a full cuddle, they were encouraged that what they had learnt to do seemed to be helping the baby, even though it felt much less involved than they wished.

WAYS YOU MAY BE INVOLVED IN OR LEAD ON YOUR BABY'S CARE

Here are some of the ways you may be encouraged to be involved in caring for your baby or are involved or taking a lead on:

- Changing your baby's nappy and helping keep them clean and comfortable; these tasks are often called 'cares'
- Pumping (often called 'expressing') milk for the baby or feeding them directly
- Supporting your baby to feel safe, regulated and soothed, such as holding them skin to skin (also known as 'kangaroo care') and using particular types of touch such as 'containment holding' or 'hand cuddles'
- Reading, singing, talking and interacting with your baby
- Observing your baby's responses, reactions and ways of communicating as you get to know them, and sharing this with the team
- Personalizing your baby's space so that it feels homely and individual – for example, by putting up family pictures, important keepsakes, symbols or religious relics that represent important things to you
- Making decisions on everyday parenting tasks and preferences, such as your baby's outfit when they can first wear clothes, whether they have a dummy, or when you will do baby 'firsts' such as their first bath or first feed.

Many of these ways of being involved have significant short- and long-term benefits for your baby.

WAYS TO SUPPORT YOUR BABY IN OTHER KEY PARENTING ROLES

You will also find that you are supported in other key parenting roles, which may include:

- Starting to monitor and record your baby's progress or development
- Taking part in discussions and ward rounds (which can include leading ward rounds, ensuring that what is discussed is helpful and relevant to you)
- Advocating for your baby and making decisions with the team about their care
- Working with the team so that communication and the care you and your baby receive reflect your needs, communication styles and beliefs.

These aspects of care may not feel like being a parent in the same way, although they are all important elements of your role, and ones you will continue as your child grows up, alongside their direct care day to day. (We will think more about all the elements of becoming and being a parent in Chapter 5.)

When you are starting out on the unit, it might be tricky to have a sense of where you're at with all these many roles and tasks. It's easy to lose sight of change and progress and have the space and time to think about what you need to help with your baby's care. The following exercise invites you to consider this. You might want to add this to your neonatal diary or keep track of it on your phone. Many units have a list of FiCare elements where they might ask you to rate your confidence in certain areas or tasks (on paper or via an app), so you could add the extra information from this exercise to those to keep everything in one place.

CONFIDENCE, MEANING AND CONNECTION IN CARE

Make a note of the ways you are starting to get involved in your baby's care. Here, we are going to consider three key areas:

1. How confident do you feel doing a particular care/activity?
2. How connected do you feel to your baby during this activity?
3. What does doing this task with your baby mean to you?

These will change over time, and sometimes it may be helpful to revisit this exercise to take stock of the things that may feel different over the weeks or months. You might want to make an additional note of what you need in each area to help increase your confidence, to make the activity feel more meaningful,[2] or to help you to feel more connected to your baby.

You can see Samir's examples below. Add yours. You may want to continue this in a notebook or shared document with your neonatal team.

Area of care	How confident and connected do I feel during this activity? How does this activity have meaning for me? What do I need to increase my confidence and/or help the task feel more meaningful?
Changing nappies	*Quite confident now I know how to manage the wires. I prefer an extra pair of hands when my wife is there to help!* *It helps me feel connected when I can get a bit closer and watch her face to see how she feels. She enjoys me talking to her too – she's definitely happier when I do it than a nurse.* *This feels like it has meaning to me as it's something I would be doing if we were at home – a sense I'm able to do the basics of baby care as a dad.*
Reading stories	*Confident (when the nursery is quiet). It felt odd to start with – like my words were going into a void.* *But I put my hand on her now when I am reading, which helps us feel more connected, and I've chosen a book that's meaningful for us.* *Now it feels like I really want her to hear the words I speak because they are for her. I will read it to her when she's older too, and can really understand.*
Talking with doctors about her care and what I feel she needs	*Not so confident. I will ask for some more help with this as it always feels like I'm not the expert, that I wouldn't know. I sometimes feel I can feed back to the nurses about what she likes for her 'cares' – though sometimes I tell them things they don't know about her, which feels good! It means I can speak up for her little by little and be her voice.*

2 When using a word to describe certain interactions with your baby you may hear people use the word 'activity' or 'occupation'. Whilst these might seem to fit at certain points, there may be other moments where this feels like it doesn't quite capture the nature of what's taking place between you and your baby. You may want to experiment with the right vocabulary for you, and share this with others.

HOW THE NEONATAL UNIT WILL WORK WITH YOU TO HELP CARE FOR YOUR BABY AND SUPPORT THEM WITH THEIR SPECIFIC NEEDS

FiCare units are focused on finding ways to keep you and your baby together as much as possible. This includes everything, from having enough space to recline your chair when feeding them to having space to rest, express milk and park your car nearby. They will also be providing care that is tailored to and supportive of your baby's development, including protecting their brain, which is in a sensitive and immature phase of development if they have been born early. Staff in the hospital will always be thinking about how they can change and adjust features of the hospital environment that can be highly stressful and overwhelming for babies.

You will hear lots of terms to describe the elements of care for your baby, such as developmental, neuroprotective and trauma-informed care, which overlap with one another, all acknowledging the environment of the neonatal unit, and the experiences your baby has there are very different to that of the womb and those they would experience if they weren't unwell or in hospital. They form part of an overall approach with FiCare that takes findings from research and puts them into practice, to ensure the very best outcomes for your baby and for you.

Developmental care focuses on your baby's growth and wellbeing by ensuring *all* care is sensitive to your baby's sensory, physical and emotional needs. Occupational therapists, physiotherapists and speech and language therapists often lead on these aspects of care, alongside your baby's nurse. This approach ensures that the care given to your baby minimizes their stress, helps them feel safe and secure, and gives them a range of experiences that are beneficial for their development.

Neuroprotective care is a range of practices in caring for your baby that aim to minimize injury to their brain and ensure that they have the best neurological and developmental outcomes. It includes medical, environmental and developmental interventions.

Trauma-informed care recognizes that there are many events that can be experienced by babies and families as traumatic in neonatal care. These need to be recognized and responded to, to reduce distress in the short and longer term. It also aims to prevent traumatic experiences where possible (e.g., reducing separation between you and your baby).

Care for your baby considers:

- Supporting the relationship between you both, including reducing separation and helping you to respond to your baby sensitively and to support their development
- Your baby's environment in the neonatal unit (taking into account all their sensory needs, such as exposure to light and sound and touch); this may include looking at how care is delivered most appropriately and closely monitoring your baby's responses
- How they are positioned in the incubator and touched (aiming to reduce stress, improve how regulated your baby is and to support their brain development)
- Safeguarding their sleep (to assist with brain development and growth)
- Reducing stress and pain during procedures – by encouraging closeness with you, hearing your voice, swaddling and sucking for comfort, for example
- Ensuring their nutrition is as effective as possible, which includes ensuring they benefit from the protective properties of breastmilk (which reduces the risk of infection or severe responses to infection) and overseeing their growth (this is managed by neonatal dieticians)
- Helping your baby to navigate complex tasks such as feeding from the breast or bottle, which can require the specialist support of a neonatal speech and language therapist
- Protecting their skin, which has many functions that impact their neurodevelopment (such as relaying information about the senses to the brain).

There are plenty of resources to help you become more skilled and confident in caring for your baby when you are ready, most of which your unit will have available to you (for some suggestions, see 'Resources' at the end of this chapter). These resources incorporate what's known about developmental and neuroprotective care and the parent–infant relationship to help benefit your baby throughout their neonatal stay.

Allied health professionals (AHPs) usually oversee the delivery of this care on the unit, working with doctors and nurses, and will also be involved in helping your baby directly when needed.

Allied health professionals include:

- Speech and language therapists, who assess and support your baby's safe and positive oral feeding, swallowing and early language and communication development
- Occupational therapists, who assess and support your baby's motor, cognitive and emotional development, sensory abilities and experiences, and help support the relationship with your baby
- Physiotherapists, who help babies who may be at risk of difficulties in their development; they are specialists in assessing and providing interventions to assist with their movement, muscle tone and development within the neonatal environment
- Dieticians, who assess, diagnose and manage the nutritional needs of your baby throughout their neonatal stay, closely monitoring their growth and health, and helping the neonatal team make effective feeding decisions.

Your neonatal unit might also offer some or all of the following:

- Education sessions (either one-to-one or in a group) to help you to learn about your baby and how to support them whilst they are on the unit. One way to think about these sessions is like a neonatal baby class, which you may have been to or heard about before your baby's arrival.

- Books, leaflets and guides to help you learn, monitor and keep track of what's happening with your baby. These may also contain skills and tasks that it will be useful for you to learn and become confident in. There are also apps focused on FiCare that help you to keep a record of your baby's milestones, statistics such as growth and other key information (see 'Resources' at the end of this chapter).

- Support for you and your baby through the expertise of AHPs. These specialists are highly skilled in delivering care that enhances your baby's development, growth and wellbeing in the short and longer term.

- Support for you and your family. This may be psychological or emotional support via one-to-one sessions with a psychological professional or as part of a support group. Peer support may also be offered by veteran parents who have been through the neonatal experience and can relate to your feelings and experiences. Practical support such as help with paying bills or meeting increased costs whilst your baby is in hospital or help with childcare or transport will also be available.

- Providing what you need to care for your baby – everything from breast pumps to hire, a library of books for you to read with your baby and food and drink to keep you going.

- Providing a space and environment that feels welcoming and enables you to stay as long as you wish. When you arrive there are often people or digital guides to help you to become familiar with the unit so that it feels more comfortable.

- Ensuring there are ways for you to talk to the team about your baby's care. On a FiCare unit, it should feel safe and comfortable for you to feed back on care and what matters to you.

- Helping you to become familiar with the language used on the neonatal unit – the 'medical jargon'. This may be new words, concepts and acronyms that you might hear staff use frequently but won't be familiar to you. Don't be afraid to ask if you hear something you are unsure about and need someone to 'translate' it into simple words. There is also a very useful explanation of some of the words you might hear in the neonatal unit on the Bliss website.[3]

- Involving you in ward rounds and discussions about your baby's care as part of the care team in a way that feels empowering and comfortable.

- Being clear about how decisions are made on the unit and how and when you can be involved.

We will spend more time together thinking about building the relationship with

3 See www.bliss.org.uk/parents/in-hospital/about-neonatal-care/words-you-might-hear-on-the-neonatal-unit

your baby and your role as a parent in Chapters 5 and 6. Here, we'll think together about other key relationships on the neonatal unit that can have a significant impact.

BUILDING RELATIONSHIPS WITH OTHER PARENTS AND STAFF

As well as building a relationship with your baby, FiCare also helps you to build relationships with other parents going through similar experiences and the team who help look after your baby. Supportive relationships with others where we can feel a sense of trust, connection and safety are key to helping us manage stressful or traumatic circumstances. In neonatal care you will often find yourself spending more time with members of the neonatal team and other parents than many of your own friends or family, so these relationships can take on a new meaning. Many parents describe how they are 'thrown together' with a group of people who come from every area of life, and yet there is a sense of solidarity being in the situation together.

Often the parent kitchen or the expressing room is the place where conversations without a staff presence take place. This space is important, as a sense of being overheard or watched can make it harder to express how you are really feeling or thinking. Parents you meet who are further along in the journey may become a source of information, support and encouragement as well as parents who may be on your unit as a veteran peer supporter some years after their neonatal stay. Anyone who has been through a neonatal experience is set apart by 'getting it' in a way that reduces the need to explain, translate terms or give information, and many parents find that the friendships they make with each other on the unit become lifelong.

It is also important to acknowledge that this type of support with unknown people can be quite difficult or undesirable for some parents. If you find making new relationships difficult, or that locker side 'small talk' is a strain, this can add another layer of stress to the neonatal experience. You may be a more private person who doesn't wish to share experiences or feelings with others – which is important to respect. If you find that peer support or the company of others you don't know is difficult, perhaps consider:

- Having a few sentences to say that you can rehearse if you are engaged in a conversation or stopped in the corridor
- Wearing visible headphones at times when you wish to be uninterrupted
- Asking for a screen in the neonatal nursery for privacy/protected space
- Avoiding communal areas at busy times of the day, such as lunchtime

- Finding support via different means, such as keeping a connection with those people who are well known to you, using messaging or specific apps or organizing a rota of friends who can come and have coffee with you in the hospital canteen as regular anchors of familiarity.

What can influence your relationships with staff on the unit?

Relationships with staff on the unit are also key, and yet it's important to acknowledge that they can be influenced by many factors, such as:

- Your previous relationships and experiences with health professionals (both recent, such as during birth and maternity care, and longer term, such as experiences as a child in hospital)
- Your relationships with systems, such as the NHS or social care
- Your relationships with figures of authority, such as teachers or religious leaders
- Your relationships with parents and key adults when growing up
- Your relationships with your current and previous partners
- How confident and comfortable you feel in social situations and interactions.

These relationships and differences we have over the course of our lives can change how easy or safe it might feel to communicate, trust and find ways to be with others. Equally, positive relationship experiences in our lives can help us to feel secure and open to others in a challenging situation, make it easier to ask for and receive help, say what's on our mind and to know what we need from others.

Parents often describe a power imbalance in their relationships with healthcare professionals, which means it's harder for them to feel 'two-way' or reciprocal. Relationships also have a different timescale to those outside the neonatal context. For example, most parents would want to meet an individual who might be looking after their child beforehand and ensure that they feel that person has the qualities they need to care for their child. They may spend some time with them and their child together, and then, only when they are comfortable, leave them with that adult on their own.

In neonatal care it's often not possible to stay with your baby all the time, and therefore every parent will be making a judgement about how safe and trustworthy the nurses and doctors are who are looking after their baby. It's okay to be cautious and to feel unsure when you are in these circumstances, and to take time to get to know the person who will be caring for them in your absence, even if you don't have a choice as to who that is.

THE IMPACT OF PREVIOUS RELATIONSHIPS

THINKING ABOUT THE IMPACT OF YOUR PREVIOUS RELATIONSHIPS

Take a moment to think about how your previous relationships and experiences with others may influence how you feel and act when you meet the clinical team on the unit. Notice that you may feel differently about different people or in different contexts. You may want to jot down what you notice here:

....

....

....

....

....

Let's look at some stories from parents with different experiences, and how they can affect what happens with their relationships on the unit:

> Sarah had heard about the unit's philosophy of parents being partners in care, but she found it hard to feel this was true for her despite the staff being friendly and approachable. She'd previously had a difficult relationship with her father, who was overbearing, critical and sometimes unpredictable. It was challenging being in a position where those around her had roles of responsibility for her baby and seemed to know more about the baby than she did. Sarah found older male team members on the unit led her to feel particularly vulnerable. When she was asked to introduce her baby on ward rounds, she was unable to express her ideas, and feared being exposed for not knowing her baby as well as she thought she should. Meetings with her lead consultant began to feel more and more difficult, and she worried the team would think she didn't want information or to be involved, fearing further judgement and criticism.

Sarah's previous relationships were making it difficult to feel comfortable and form helpful relationships during her neonatal stay. Whilst it's not often possible to be able to change any of these complex feelings immediately, what can help is to acknowledge that they are there, and to think about how to manage them whilst on the unit. Sarah started to feel more safe and less fearful of being criticized with two younger nurses who were a similar age to her. Conversations and interactions about 'everyday' things helped her to learn more about the nurses as people, and after a few days they felt less threatening. The nurses were able to plan with her how they could change ward rounds so that she felt more supported. This included helping her make notes of what she wanted to ask beforehand, and a nurse there to speak on her behalf if she became more anxious. She also asked the nurses or a member of the family care team to accompany her, when they could, to meetings with the consultant. Over time Sarah felt more confident to talk with the consultant and the relationship felt more genuine and safe.

Nadia had spent most of her career in leadership roles, which required responsibility for big teams, managing people and getting tasks completed to tight deadlines. This role and set of skills felt a big part of her identity and was a huge source of pride for her. When she went into preterm labour, all of a sudden she felt she had no control over the situation or the way that people treated her. She felt no one had listened when she attended A&E, and that when she asserted that she knew something was wrong, she was labelled as 'angry' and 'rude' by staff. She arrived on the unit overwhelmed by meeting another team of people, and wanted to know who would be caring for her baby and what their qualifications were. She embraced the schedule of activities available on the unit and was keen to become involved in her son's care; however, she felt that lack of access to all the information meant she was separate to the clinical team and couldn't make informed decisions. Feeling left out of things she felt were important made it difficult to trust those looking after her baby.

Nadia had gone from a position in life where she felt she had control to a frightening sequence of events that left her feeling helpless, ignored and pushed to the side. She made every effort to do the things she understood would help her son, but feeling like she only ever had part of the picture fuelled her sense of threat. What helped Nadia was being able to share her concerns with someone who was not directly involved in her son's care. Together they made a plan focused on what would help restore a level of trust with the professionals. This included making sure updates included the information she needed to help her make sense of the situation and the allocation of a named consultant who would be a point of continuity and oversee her son's care. The consultant offered to review Nadia's baby's notes with her, and encouraged her to raise any concerns as soon as they arose. With Nadia's permission the team was also made aware of her experiences before she arrived on the unit, so they could appreciate that trust would take time.

WORKING OUT WHAT YOU NEED FROM RELATIONSHIPS WITH THE TEAM ON THE UNIT

Take a moment to consider the people around you and who your 'go to' people are. If your unit is large and you may often not see the same person, try to identify several people over time who might fulfil these roles:

- Who around me at the moment helps provide a sense of connection and safety?

  ....

  ....

  ....

- Who can help me to feel more at ease and confident in caring for my baby whilst in hospital?

  ....

  ....

  ....

- Who is a good person to go to if I have any worries or concerns or if I'm not having a good day?

  ....

  ....

  ....

- Who understands me as a person?

  ....

  ....

  ....

- Who can I feel more relaxed with and helps me feel like myself?

  ....

  ....

  ....

- Who is a good advocate and someone who can support me to say what I want to?

  ....

  ....

  ....

- Who supports and understands my spiritual and cultural needs best?

  ....

  ....

  ....

DISCUSSING AND PLANNING EVERYDAY CARE FOR YOUR BABY WITH YOUR CARE TEAM

In Chapter 1 we thought about developing a basic routine for your day and how to personalize your space on the unit. Here we are going to think in more detail about how you can plan your day with your team for your baby and for yourself. This stage is likely to come a little later, when you might be facing a longer stay. It's often helpful to go through a plan like this with a partner or friend as well as your baby's nurse. They will let you know what is possible within their shift, and how your plans can fit with what else is happening on the unit.

If you are staying for a longer time, think about planning a week at a time, with the flexibility to change when needed. If your plan involves AHPs, they will have their own pace for recommendations and changes depending on your baby's needs and progress, which they will work on together with you.

✓ THINKING ABOUT AND PLANNING NEEDS IN EVERYDAY CARE

Take a moment to think about your day on the unit and consider the following areas that will help you plan with your neonatal team.

Your baby's needs

You can think about your baby's needs in many ways as they uniquely develop as a little person, born to connect with you. First and foremost, they need contact with you to feel safe and secure, to develop and thrive. They also have a lot of work to do as they learn to breathe, grow, feed and recover from illness. Spend some time observing how they try and relate with you, and watch how this changes over time.

Your baby's behaviour is their way of communicating. They will show a number of behavioural 'cues' (which are a way of telling you something) during different activities or tasks (e.g., feeding cues or cues that show how overwhelmed, distressed or regulated and ready to interact they are). It can be helpful to make a note of their cues to share with everyone who looks after them as well as what helps (e.g., ways they are currently soothed, calmed and reassured). This means that they receive the benefit of consistent caregiving approaches when you aren't able to be with them. Update this regularly as they develop and change over time.

In the course of the day your baby may have programmes or exercises they might be doing under the instruction of an AHP or other health professional. They will need protected sleep and rest time. As they develop you can also add in their favoured activities, things they like to look at and listen to, as well as their preferences for touch and comfort.

My baby's needs:

....

....

....

....

Your needs and preferences

These can include practicalities such as when you are able to be on the unit, when you are available for the sharing of key information and ward rounds, and who you might wish to have with you for certain tasks or conversations.

Keela requested that her boyfriend was present if an important update was being given to support her and help process the information.

A key consideration over time is *when* you wish to be contacted – for example, when you want the unit to call, even if it's the middle of the night, what kind of things you are happy to happen or be decided in your absence, and when you would like to be asked if you aren't present.

Think about what your emotional needs are in the context of planning your day. Some might be easier for staff to spot and work around (such as breaks), but others might need to be made explicit (such as when you would like to spend time with your baby uninterrupted, or additional support needed at certain times of the day).

You might have additional communication needs or preferences that make a tangible difference to how the unit feels for you. For example, if you're neurodivergent, you are likely to encounter specific challenges on a neonatal unit. It's helpful to share these so that the environment and communication can be adapted or modified where possible. Specific learning difficulties such as dyslexia or language or auditory processing difficulties can also have a significant impact on how easy it is to navigate the neonatal experience, and add to distress and overwhelm if not addressed. As much as it can feel sensitive information to share, it ultimately means you are in a better position for the team to work with you when they know how to communicate, understand and help.

My needs and preferences:

....

....

....

....

What the needs are of you and your baby together, as a pair

Time for nurturing the relationship between you and your baby is important and can feel it has little space amongst all the tasks of the neonatal unit. Think here about what time you would like to spend nourishing you and your baby as a pair. This might mean scheduling when you can have uninterrupted time to get to know and 'tune in' to one another. You might want to talk with your nurse about the kind of things you can do with your baby during this protected time that are most important to you. Whilst it's not always possible to predict when your baby may need medical intervention, discussing with the team if it's possible to cluster procedures or examinations so that there are protected periods of time can be helpful.

As your baby gets better you will have more opportunities to engage in interactions that feel more actively reciprocal (two-way), but don't be discouraged if it feels a little more one-sided to start with. Your baby might find engaging with you a lot to manage alongside all the other things they're dealing with whilst in hospital, and it can take time. Even when it feels like your baby might not be aware of your presence, remember that they already know you, and the early curiosity and interest in each other is a real investment for the future (you can read more about this in Chapter 5). This time doesn't have to look like you're *doing* a lot – being attuned to your baby and responding to them is an important use of time in and of itself.

My needs together with my baby's needs:

....

....

....

....

What your needs are as a family (parenting together, involving siblings, grandparents and elders)

If you have a partner, sometimes the time you have together with your baby is very limited as you juggle the demands of family and work outside the unit. However, many parents describe this as feeling like another loss if not attended to whilst in hospital, so it can be helpful to make some time to spend all together, making memories of your earliest times as a family. If you have other children, it can also be important to have regular family time when you're all together. Consider what would be most helpful if your time as a complete family is limited, and talk to your children about what they'd like to do with their brother or sister. This can be particularly important for family milestones that you want to mark in a special way.

> Lottie's fifth birthday was an event the whole family had planned to celebrate before the early arrival of her sister Jane. By letting the unit know this was a key event, they were able to decorate the incubator to help Lottie feel like her baby sister was part of her special day.

Grandparents are also significant members of many families, and for some parents they are vital emotional and practical supports. If you have parents or other elders in your life who hold this kind of significance for you, FiCare includes them too, according to your wishes and preferences. Let your neonatal team know about how you would like them to be involved and be able to support you. The neonatal unit can be distressing and overwhelming for grandparents and other family members, and whilst their focus is likely to be on supporting you, if they would benefit from having a conversation about their own needs, charities such as Bliss[4] can help.

Our needs as a family:

....

....

4 www.bliss.org.uk

....

....

BEING INVOLVED WITH OR LEADING WARD ROUNDS

'Ward rounds' are cot side reviews that allow your baby to be assessed with a team, their treatment evaluated and plans made about care. There is usually a list of things that happen and that are recorded in your baby's notes for each ward round. If your baby is being treated in intensive care, this will happen every day, and then less frequently as the level of care they need reduces. Ward rounds tend to happen around the same time every day on a unit, although exact timings depend on what else is happening in the unit.

In days gone by, less thought was given to how to help parents feel included in this key component of care. Nowadays practices around ward rounds have changed with the aim of being more accessible and inclusive for parents. It is less common for parents to be excluded from the unit whilst they take place, and units have different ways of ensuring you can stay with your baby, whilst also protecting confidentiality and privacy.

With the advent of FiCare some units have 'parent-led ward rounds' where parents lead in updating on their baby and giving key updates and information. Although this idea can seem daunting to start with, units that practise parent-led ward rounds usually have a 'crib sheet' with some headings to provide a structure for the round, the kind of topics to cover and what you might like to ask. Like all aspects of FiCare, if you find the idea of leading a ward round to be unhelpful or anxiety provoking, you can ask the team to lead, and take part in a way that feels comfortable for you.

You might find a group of doctors intimidating or difficult to talk to at first. If so, you can ask your nurse to speak on your behalf and explain what has been said or decided. You may also feel it's hard to take in what is being talked about on a ward round – and you certainly won't be alone in not remembering it all! Feeling the need to recall a great amount of detailed information can be a particular burden as the 'holder of information' for partners.

To help reduce the pressure and aid your memory, ask your nurse or doctor to write down the key points from your ward rounds, or use a specific notebook to track rounds and medical discussions. Also remember that you can ask as many questions as you need during and after a ward round.

If it's not possible for you to attend a ward round in person, you have a number of options:

- Ask the unit if you are able to join by video call
- Give your questions to your baby's nurse who can also update you on what was discussed
- Ask for a summary of the main points when you come onto the unit, which will be recorded on your baby's notes
- Ask if it's within the unit's policies to allow a representative to come to the ward round on your behalf.

For many parents, the idea of being in a ward round without their partner, family member or close friend can feel overwhelming, particularly when critical issues are being discussed or decisions need to be made. Let the unit know who you need with you to support you, and whether it's possible to postpone a discussion until you are not alone.

CONVERSATIONS ABOUT YOUR BABY'S CARE

There are many times when a discussion about your baby's care needs to take place in a more private setting. These rooms are often referred to as 'quiet rooms' but might be referred to amongst parents as 'bad news rooms'. This can leave parents feeling fearful of the space and the meaning behind a 'quick catch-up'. The team might, in fact, have a range of reasons why they'd invite you to talk with them in another room, and these rooms may also be used by other professionals to talk to you confidentially, such as a psychological professional. Many parents prefer the privacy – not only regarding the information, but also in terms of a private emotional space away from the gaze of others.

When the team suggest a conversation in the quiet room, it can be helpful to be prepared if time allows. Some questions and points to consider include:

- Ask what the conversation is about, what it's for and for how long it might last.
- Decide what you think is important to include in the conversation and encourage the team to set an agenda together at the beginning so that there is time for what is important to you (keeping in mind your baby as a whole person and not just a set of conditions or problems, allowing time to talk about your baby's progress, for example).
- Decide who you would like with you, particularly for key conversations.
- Have questions you would like to ask written down; if there isn't time to go through them all, ask who else can help you address them.

- Take notes of the main points or ask someone else to help summarize them, particularly if you find it tricky to talk and write at the same time.
- Decide together when you can follow up any issues raised in the meeting and when the person leading the conversation is on shift; most parents have a preference for continuity with one or a small group of people.
- If you feel overwhelmed, anxious or uncomfortable, let the team know, particularly if the way you experience these states is not obvious to someone who doesn't know you well – for example, 'Could we stop for a moment as I'm feeling anxious and not able to take in what you're saying?'
- Think about how you best take in information. If you understand better through pictures or diagrams, let your team know.
- If you don't feel confident having a conversation in English, ask for an interpreter. Although many parents feel embarrassed to do this when their spoken English is perceived as good, under stress or when communication may not be clear from medical teams it's often useful to have another listening ear to help. It's your right to access interpreters, and their services are free.

(More information about conversations with the clinical team when circumstances are highly distressing or challenging can be found in Chapter 8.)

TYPES OF DECISIONS IN NEONATAL CARE AND 'SHARED DECISION MAKING'

Your medical and nursing team will be making a lot of decisions every day about the care of your baby based on their neonatal expertise. When you arrive on the unit this will have been explained to you, including what kind of decisions or procedures would be part of routine care, for example, regular examination of your baby, giving routine drugs, blood tests, etc. As these are considered to be low risk and provide the best care for your baby's needs, you won't be asked for your consent explicitly or to make a decision on each one.

As part of FiCare you are likely to have input into the timing of some of these aspects of care (such as being there for a feed), be involved in helping your baby (such as helping them manage pain when they take blood) and advocating for them if necessary (such as requesting tests or specialist visits to take place outside a quiet/rest time). It can be important to highlight decisions you'd like to know about in advance if possible, for example, your baby changing nursery or moving from an incubator to a cot, particularly if they hold special significance for you or might trigger anxiety and distress.

It's important to acknowledge that expressions such as 'routine care' can make it seem like what is happening is in some way not significant or shouldn't bother you; however, when your baby is in neonatal care, often nothing feels particularly 'routine'. Whilst these patterns of care will become more familiar to you over time, and typically feel less distressing as a result, you may need more support in the beginning. There might be certain aspects of routine care that you would like to be present for to support your baby, or you may find that asking a nurse to 'talk out loud' about what she's doing to you and to your baby can help with anxiety and uncertainty.

Nurses can help with worries by talking through what's happening for your baby

Remember, decisions about your baby's everyday care and routine that reflect your preferences and values as a parent (the kind of things you would make a decision about if you were at home) are something you can lead on and discuss with the neonatal team. This part of your role will develop as your baby gets better and needs less medical input.

There are other procedures, treatments and investigations where you are likely to be more involved in the decision making and giving consent. These might be early decisions in your baby's care, decisions relating to feeding, decisions about surgery and other common decisions such as participation in clinical research trials. You will also be involved in several decisions at *key points* in your baby's care (such as going home on oxygen).

Lastly, there are significant decisions you may be faced with, such as those relating to continuation of treatment or those that might have significant long-term implications for your baby. There may not be a clear 'right or wrong' for some of these decisions, and they will be guided by multiple factors for you as a parent and your neonatal team, with the best interests of your baby at the centre. In these circumstances there are many choices and areas to think about within an overarching decision, and it is usually a much longer and detailed process as a result. (We will consider these particular situations in Chapter 8, which will include a guide to the decision-making process and how to use the support and expertise within your unit to help you.) In general, neonatal units will invite you to be part of what is called 'shared decision making' (SDM), where you work together with the healthcare professionals to reach decisions about treatment or a course of action. This process acknowledges your own expertise and experience as your baby's parent and that of the team looking after them.

Urgent decisions necessary to save life or prevent serious deterioration will be taken by the neonatal team in the best interests of your baby. These decisions have to be made quickly to prevent harm. Although your team are likely to have discussed with you some of the decisions or situations your baby might face during their admission and when an emergency might occur, sometimes it's not possible to anticipate these events, and it can be terrifying if this happens in the course of your baby's care. Healthcare professionals will let you know what your baby needed and why as soon as it's safe and possible to do so. This may be a conversation you come back to several times, as part of a natural way of making sense of and processing something that can often be experienced as traumatic. (See Chapter 9, where we will think together about difficult events on the unit.)

COMMON FICARE QUESTIONS AND CONCERNS

'I don't feel like spending a lot of time with my baby'

Being on a neonatal unit and/or having gone through a difficult or traumatic time in pregnancy or birth can impact how you may feel about your baby. While we will think together about your relationship with your baby in more detail in Chapter 6, for now it's important to be gentle and compassionate to parts of you that might feel close to your baby, other parts that might be scared, and parts that could be unsure. As part of FiCare you will have plenty of opportunities to cultivate and grow the relationship with your baby, the role you play in their care whilst they are looked after in hospital, and to think about what matters to you as you grow as a family.

Ask yourself what else might be happening when you feel this way. For some parents this feeling is more linked to not wanting to come into the hospital and everything that this entails rather than not wanting to be with their baby per se. Parents often report feeling like they just want to take their baby away from it all, and that there is great sadness and frustration knowing that this isn't possible. For others it can feel too hard to see their baby so unwell, and it feels easier to retreat rather than go towards a situation that is so difficult. Again, all these reactions are understandable given the circumstances. Take time to unpack these feelings for yourself and consider sharing them with those around you.

'How can I be my baby's primary carer when they need so much medical expertise?'

This is a common question and concern, especially when babies are in intensive care. At this stage of your journey the medical team will need to do a lot to support your baby using their clinical knowledge, expertise and skill. This might mean that for long periods they are surrounding your baby and carrying out essential tests, interventions and care that help keep your baby comfortable and safe. At this point parental care is largely about your presence and support for your baby so that they know you are there, can be soothed by you and helped to manage procedures or events that might be painful or challenging.

Babies in neonatal care, especially when they are very premature or unwell, have some different needs to babies who are born healthy at term. You will learn with the help of your neonatal team how to help your baby in a way that fits with their developmental stage, even when they need a lot of medical care. You will also start with small tasks, which most nurses refer to as 'cares', and then, over time, the number of things you can do will grow – for most – along with your confidence.

'I don't know how to look after my baby'

Even very experienced parents can find themselves at a loss to know how to look after their baby when they need medical care. Much of the knowledge and skills you may have learnt in parenting classes or that have been handed down from friends and family may not feel relevant or a good fit. Not knowing how to look after your baby right now is not a failure or fault in any way. It will take time to learn how to be a parent in a different way, and looking after your baby in neonatal care means everybody learning a new set of skills.

Another common worry, particularly when your baby might be very small or unwell, is that you might hurt them in some way by touching them, do something wrong or 'get in the way'. Your nurse will show you the ways that you can touch and help your baby that give them what they need and explain why. Parent sessions on your unit will give you other opportunities to learn about looking after your baby from different professionals or veteran parents. Sometimes being able to talk with other parents who have similar concerns to you and who can share their skills and knowledge can be helpful and develop your confidence.

'What if I don't want to or can't take on caring for my baby at the moment?'

When there is a lot of emphasis on being involved in the care of your baby from the beginning, you may feel you don't want to or are unable to do so. Many parents fear being judged if they don't become heavily involved straightaway, and worry it may even reflect something bad about them as a person.

> Steve didn't feel able to start helping with 'cares' in the first week of being on the unit. He was worried about his children at home and his wife who was still recovering in hospital herself. He saw his main role as looking after his wife, making sure she wasn't in pain, and had regular contact with the children by video call. The unit staff often made him feel like he wasn't taking responsibility or an interest in his new baby. It wasn't until his wife was discharged and they were able to come to the unit together that he felt ready and able to focus on care for baby Jana.

What's important to remember is that there are many reasons you may not feel able to be involved with 'cares' for your baby straightaway. Some common reasons are:

- Feeling in 'threat' or 'survival' mode, making it difficult to do things that are outside immediate survival needs
- Feeling afraid you might hurt or harm your baby in some way if you get it 'wrong'
- Feeling intimidated or anxious by being watched by a nurse or doctor
- Feeling disconnected or far away from your baby
- Feeling worried that if you connect with your baby during a painful procedure they will associate you with pain and not comfort
- Feeling overwhelmed and unable to engage in tasks or activities.

You can help yourself by letting the team know what is happening for you. You don't need to give them a lot of detail, but knowing a bit of background can help them to support you more thoughtfully. They might talk with you about pacing your involvement when you are ready, using a graded approach. This means you start with something small that feels manageable and gradually build up to more when you're ready. You will notice we have talked about a graded approach to many things in this book. This is because it can be helpful to break down any task or process into smaller steps, rather than overwhelming yourself by expecting to get to the end stage or goal straightaway.

'What if I have more than one baby to look after?'

Having more than one baby on the neonatal unit can bring with it many additional stressors and challenges. Whilst every effort will be made to keep your babies together, there can be times when they may not be able to be in the same nursery or even the same hospital. Even with more than one parent, it's common to feel like the task of giving each baby what they need is an impossible one. If your babies are in the same unit and receiving different levels of care, it can be helpful to know that they will be keeping in mind the fact that they are multiples and will look to move them together as soon as it becomes safe to do so.

In terms of practicalities, if you are in a couple, it's helpful to decide how you want to split your presence when your babies are apart. This might be led by what's most important to you, or it might feel like a wholly pragmatic decision. If you decide to spend time with each baby separately for most of the day, consider how you can keep contact points throughout the day with each other. You may also want to schedule in time when you can be together with each baby.

If you are parenting on your own, you could nominate a friend or family member to be with your other baby. Each unit has different rules around who can be present and when. Similarly, units will have different policies around the use of mobile phones and videos, although it may be worth exploring whether you could have a video connection with your other baby/babies when you are on the unit so you can watch over them all, even if you can't be with them, and move between them according to need.

Ask whether it is possible for your babies to spend some time together. This usually becomes easier as they are more well, and some units have special cots that allow babies to receive comfort and regulation from each other. If babies are apart, finding ways to connect them with each other through their senses (such as providing a familiar smell) can be helpful.

Think about memory making and symbolic means of connection for your babies and for you. For example, you may wish to have photos of them or their footprints together in their cots, or a symbol such as a multipart flower or a coin with two parts that come together to make a whole. Some parents wear jewellery that helps them to focus on this sense of togetherness – Jane wore a set of interconnecting rings on a necklace round her neck. Some mothers find it helpful to focus on the feeling of their babies being together when they were inside them, and use that remembered 'felt sense' as a resource to connect to in their minds when they are struggling with disconnection and apartness. Others find fast-forwarding to an image in their minds of them being together in the future in a peaceful and calming place a helpful space to spend time in.

You may feel that one baby needs more of your care and attention when they are unwell or distressed. Although it can be an agonizing decision to feel like you are prioritizing one child over another, it may be helpful to think of this as being flexible and sensitive to meeting the needs of your baby as they arise. Parents continually change the way they allocate their time and resources between multiple children.

Finally, acknowledge that for a short time you are doing all you can to be with all your babies, but that at times it's just not possible. You are helping them to feel as cared for and loved as you can with all the constraints and challenges around you.

'My partner isn't often able to be on the unit – I feel like all the responsibility for learning how to look after my baby, talking to the team and making decisions that impact all of us is on me'

When a partner can't be on the unit regularly it can often cause tension, particularly around the shared experience, knowledge and skills needed to care for your baby. It can also be difficult for the neonatal team to know how best to include a parent they have little interaction with. Consider the following to help you plan as a family:

- Do you have a clear idea of what makes it hard to come onto the unit, for example, work hours pressures, needing to look after other children or feeling redundant or uncomfortable? Take some time to work these out together, and utilize any family support services available.
- Do you have a shared understanding of the value of the presence of both parents for your baby? Historically, fathers and non-birthing partners have been less included in their baby's care, particularly in the early days. Are assumptions being made about this or beliefs about roles? What might these be based on?
- Can the unit support you to help your partner see their role differently or work around their timings so they can be included in (1) what they would want to prioritize in terms of the relationship with your baby and (2) what they need to learn to help them to be more confident in caring for your baby? It's important to be aware that there are certain tasks they will *be required to learn to do* (such as what to do if the baby stops breathing) before discharge, and these need to be factored in with adequate availability.

- Can the unit help include your partner at key communication points? (See 'Being involved with or leading ward rounds' and 'Conversations about your baby's care'.)
- Talk about how you are feeling about your partner's role and time spent with you and your baby. Your partner may not realize the additional stress or feelings of abandonment or loneliness that can arise if you are spending long periods without them there, or the anxiety that can come with a sense of holding sole responsibility for your baby.

'I'm a single parent. Who will help me look after my baby when I get home? My parents have offered to help, but there's so much they don't know, and they think it's just like having a smaller term baby'

The knowledge and experience of your baby in neonatal care is not easily conveyed to family and friends. There may be a lack of appreciation of the differences not only in how your baby may *need* to be cared for, but also the impact of what you have been through on how you *wish* your baby to be cared for. If you are parenting without a partner, you may have already identified key people who can help with your baby. Talk to your neonatal unit about how many people can be authorized to come on to the unit, and explain that they will have a key role.

For those who have committed to helping in a regular capacity, it is helpful for them to be able to join you on the unit as much as possible, particularly towards discharge. The neonatal team can discuss with you how they can be involved and what they can learn. Sometimes it can be helpful for the team to know if there are any points of disagreement or tension that they can support you in clarifying.

> Moira was under pressure to have a large homecoming party for her baby, but was worried about him catching a cold, particularly as he was going home on oxygen. The team was able to give advice to the whole family about going home in a joint meeting, including some specific guidance about exposure to infection, looking after equipment safely and the needs of a premature baby.

'Will my baby think of me as a nurse and not a parent?'

How parents think about themselves and how they imagine their baby might experience them often weighs on their minds, particularly when they have long stays in hospital. Whilst it may feel to you that your role aligns more with a nurse, it's important to remember that your baby will simply be experiencing care, love and someone being there for them to contain their distress and help them feel better. You are someone your baby already knows by your voice and smell, and who can provide what they need through a safe and loving parental relationship, which includes looking after some of their medical needs.

Many neonatal parents describe how their identity shifts and changes through their neonatal journey – at any time you will be holding so many elements of your parental role, all of which form parts of your identity as a parent. Here are some of the roles that parents describe holding whilst their baby is in hospital:

Parental roles on the neonatal unit

YOUR ROLES AS A PARENT

Think about these roles and how they fit with your experience. Write what's most important about your experience so far here:

....

....

....

List other parenting roles that are important to you here:

1. ....
2. ....
3. ....

For some, calling themselves 'medical mum' or 'neonatal parent' is an important identity that helps them to feel solidarity with a group, share a sense of combined strength and also acknowledge what they have endured and gone through to have that title. Others don't wish this to be part of their identity moving forwards, and others sit somewhere in-between.

Wherever you feel you belong, to your baby you are always their parent.

SUMMARY

FiCare places you, as parents, as the most important people for your baby from the beginning. It supports you to provide their care and nurture as much as possible during their stay in hospital. At the same time the neonatal team act as your baby's 'medical guardians', working directly and with you to give your baby the best care, to meet their developmental needs and improve their long-term outcomes in the future. Whilst FiCare has many benefits, it can also bring all sorts of challenges. You have a lot to take on board and to decide what you're likely to be focusing on one moment to the next. Relationships with your neonatal team, friends and family are key to helping you stay emotionally and physically equipped to be in a place where you can help your baby and be their voice.

RESOURCES

There are many resources in all sorts of formats for supporting you on a FiCare neonatal unit. Here are some places to start that add to some of those you might have looked at from Chapter 1. Most units have their own bespoke resources for families, such as timetables of events, education and parent groups, as well as support you can access. Your unit will also be able to link you with what is available in your local area, which often includes charities that are dedicated to the needs of neonatal families.

Somewhere to find more information

FiCare (Family Integrated Care) provides a wealth of information on all aspects of FiCare, including the research behind the approach and the initiatives to implement it around the world: https://familyintegratedcare.com

FiCare apps, such as 'Integrated Family Delivered Care' (IFDC), are available on app stores and 'What matters to you' in digital form via vCreate.

EiSMART provides a framework and resources for things you can do to help your baby's development when they are born sick or premature: https://eismart.co.uk

Something to watch

'Daniela: FiCare is for every parent' is a short video from a veteran NICU mum, explaining how she built her confidence over time to know what questions to ask and to feel more part of the neonatal team. It's available on YouTube and also on the FiCare website: https://familyintegratedcare.com

Something to listen to

Episode 18, 'Family Integrated Care – What do parents say?' involves two mothers and researchers discussing FiCare and what mattered to them. It's available on YouTube, Spotify and Apple Podcasts.

Something to read

Caring for Your Baby in the Neonatal Unit by **Inga Warren and Cherry Bond** is an accessible guide to looking after your baby in neonatal care, including information about your invaluable role, your baby's development and how you can support your baby, with a straightforward explanation of your baby's medical care through each step of the journey.

CHAPTER 5

Becoming a parent when your baby is in neonatal care

The journey of a thousand miles begins with a single step.

CHINESE PROVERB

Whether you are a new parent or the parent of a baby in hospital for the first time, there's a lot that's different to what you might have hoped for or expected. It can be extremely hard to know how to parent or what it could look like, particularly when your baby is in intensive care. In Chapter 4 we thought about some of those early steps to become involved in your baby's care, many of which can help build aspects of your relationship with them and help you feel more like a parent over time. In this chapter we are going to look in more depth at your parenting journey, to help make sense of your life experiences and what they mean for you at this point in time.

We'll look at where your parenting journey began, the experiences and expectations of yourself and others, and the impact of what has happened in your more recent history (e.g., in your pregnancy or during birth). We'll also look at how this time in hospital differs from what you may have felt prepared for, and how to rebuild after these losses and challenges. Finally, we'll focus on the values and principles that guide you as a parent, and how you can put these into action straightaway.

YOUR PARENTING JOURNEY – WHERE IT BEGAN AND TAKING STOCK OF WHERE YOU'VE TRAVELLED SO FAR

Take a moment to ask yourself where the journey into parenthood started for you – was it when you thought about having a baby? Or perhaps later on, when you began to feel your baby move inside you? Perhaps you had always wanted to be a parent and had imagined it for many years? Everyone has their own story.

Wherever it begins, the process has long been recognized as a significant adjustment and an expansion or shift in role and identity across all cultures. This happens alongside physical (including the brain), psychological and emotional changes. Whilst the focus in the past has been mostly on mothers, there is now growing recognition that this journey into parenthood is also a significant process for fathers and partners as well as involving, to varying degrees, parents' wider family and community.

Whilst the media and baby magazines tend to focus more on the joyous aspects of becoming a parent, the reality is that this period, even when your baby is not in neonatal care, can be a time of very mixed emotions and ambivalence. Everyone comes to being a parent from a unique place.

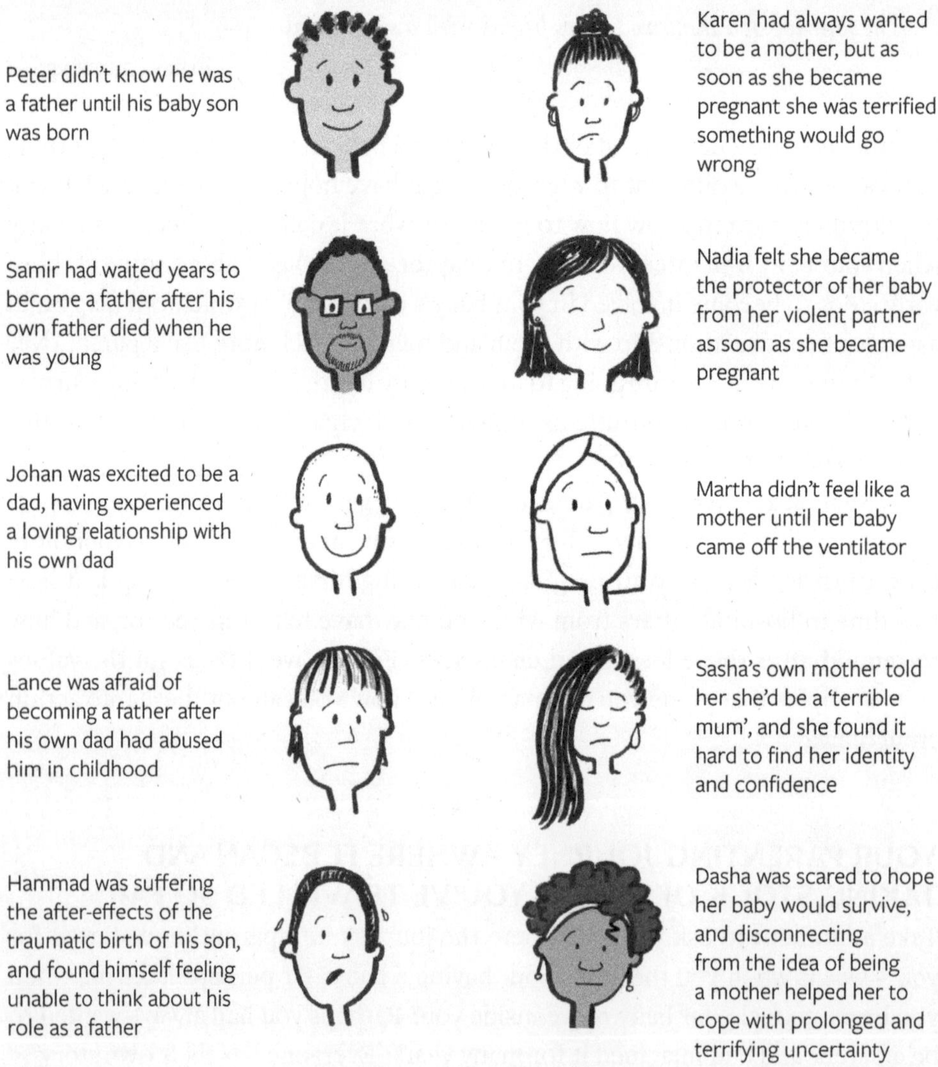

Different journeys into parenthood

YOUR JOURNEY INTO PARENTHOOD

As you read about these parents' different situations and journeys, take a moment to think about your own journey and story.

What's important to you about what you were hoping for or expecting? What's different and what's the same between you and your partner? Make some notes here about what matters most about your journey into parenthood:

....

....

....

....

....

....

....

....

....

....

ACKNOWLEDGING THE LOSSES OF PRE-BIRTH PARENTING EXPERIENCES IF YOUR BABY IS BORN EARLY

When your baby is born early or sick, there are a number of experiences, rites of passage and rituals that can be lost or significantly delayed. Each of these serve a *function* for parents-to-be. It's not just the loss of a specific experience but also the loss of what that represents. Here are some of the experiences you may have missed out on:

- Religious or secular ceremonies or rituals specific to this period of time
- Honouring traditions that may be unique to your family
- Classes – both parenting classes and those that prepare you for childbirth
- Hospital tours
- Later baby scans
- Baby showers or family events

- Choosing baby items such as a pram, car seat and key outfits
- Decorating the nursery or a special place in your home for your baby, including how you wish to reflect yourselves and their personalities and identity
- Having a 'nesting period' – a period of time typically peaking in the third trimester for mothers where parents prepare their environment for their baby (such as organizing), can have a burst of energy and a preference for familiar places and people.

TAKING STOCK OF SIGNIFICANT LOSSES AND THEIR MEANING FOR YOU

Think for a moment about some of the losses you have experienced as an individual and as a family. Make a list here of these:

....

....

....

....

....

....

What did these events, rituals or rites of passage mean to you and your family?

Let's meet Tammie, Catalin and Jane, who had important things they needed to do before their babies' arrivals that were full of meaning and had an important function:

Tammie had planned to have a long preparation period leading up to the birth of her first child. Being autistic she'd planned with her midwife to have time to get to know the hospital and meet some of the team who would be looking after her as well as make a comprehensive birth plan. When she went into premature labour she became extremely anxious as she arrived in the labour ward in the middle of the night, where everything and everyone was different.

Catalin had organized a special ceremony for her partner Jane that honoured their relationship as two mothers, and symbolized a new start for them both, having experienced a lot of hurt and rejection from one of their families. Being unable to go through with the event caused significant distress, and they felt their baby was born without the protection of the rituals and symbolism they had wanted.

For Tammie, losing preparation time before birth added a lot of additional stress and trauma to her delivery. She was clear what needed to happen and this had the potential to be well planned for, but there was no time with an urgent premature delivery. For Catalin and Jane, their pregnancy was a significant milestone in symbolizing a new phase of their lives. The ceremony they'd planned to mark this transition and prepare them both for what lay ahead had to be cancelled.

It's important, first, to give the feelings you have about these losses and changes space and acknowledgement. They can often be dismissed as minor or irrelevant, or even completely misunderstood. Comments such as 'You missed the scans but you got to meet them sooner instead!' can be an attempt by others to positively reframe a difficult experience, but they can also down play the grief and distress.

CREATIVE APPROACHES TO RITUALS, RITES OF PASSAGES AND KEY EVENTS IN THE NEONATAL CONTEXT

What can be helpful is to think about how you can bring some of the events and milestones you've missed into your neonatal journey. Although they won't look exactly the same, there may be elements of what they represented for you that can be captured creatively in the here and now. Let's have a look at how you might do that based on your list from "Taking stock of significant losses and their meaning for you'.

1. Identify which items on your list have a key function, meaning or role for you.
2. Work out the principles or main ideas behind that item.
3. Think of a way to incorporate this into your immediate environment or plan for the future.
4. Share and ask for ideas on the unit of how they could help.

Let's look at Catalin and Jane's example. They identified (1) the ceremony and (2) the items they wanted to prepare for their baby that reflected their identity and personality as priorities on their list. They were able to design a ceremony with a humanist chaplain in the hospital, with a small reception nearby that incorporated what they wanted. Now their baby was born, the staff thought with them about how to decorate the baby's incubator space to reflect their style as much as possible, and arranged a video link with the chapel so she could be included and present. On the unit Catalin and Jane repeated some of the readings in a more intimate mini-ceremony and left a small toy lion that symbolized their combined strength next to her incubator. When they had video updates, the messages written by the team from their daughter reflected themes of strength, resilience and new beginnings.

INFLUENCES ON YOUR EXPECTATIONS, FEELINGS AND THOUGHTS ABOUT BEING A PARENT

Our experiences in society, within our culture, religion, family and friends (as a child and adult) all play a part in forming expectations, hopes and fears during pregnancy and after birth. Even before you became pregnant you will have come across received wisdom, ideas and opinions about parenthood, pregnancy and birth. Whilst there is a lot to be said for advice and knowledge passed on, much of which can be helpful, there can also be particular messages that are less helpful or even harmful. Similarly, you will have an experience of being parented, and this can affect how you feel about your role and the children you parent.

You may already be a parent and have experiences to draw on that will have shaped your views and perspectives. When previous children have not been in neonatal care it can feel like you're embarking on a type of parenting journey for the first time, or you may feel able to bring your parenting knowledge and understanding flexibly into this new situation. If you've had a baby in neonatal care before, this can bring mixed feelings depending on what happened to you and your baby at that time.

When we start to try and understand our own journey and our emotional reactions, it's helpful to think about what's happening to us, and also what those experiences might *mean* to us. No two journeys into parenting a new child are exactly the same, and whilst one might feel better or worse, they may also just feel different.

✓ UNDERSTANDING WHAT SHAPES YOUR THOUGHTS, FEELINGS AND BELIEFS ABOUT BECOMING A PARENT

When thinking about how you feel at this moment in your parenting journey, consider your experiences in society, your culture, your religion and your family and friends in terms of how they have shaped your thoughts and feelings and beliefs:

- Pre and during pregnancy (including previous babies, if applicable)

- Experiences around birth
- Having a baby in neonatal care.

You might want to consider what messages they have given you (e.g., society can give a message that new parenthood is a wholly happy time or your family may have been an environment where distressing feelings or ambivalence about becoming a mother were unspeakable). As a child you may have experienced love and having your needs met, or perhaps you felt neglected or ignored. You may find that there are multiple messages or experiences in each area, reflecting the complexity of our lives.

Take a moment to think about your experiences and what messages you have been given in each of these areas. Short examples are included in the table to help start you thinking, **with some space to write about yourself underneath:**

	Pre and during pregnancy	**Experiences around birth**	**Having a baby in neonatal care**
Society	*The main message was feeling like I had to be happy and feel lucky I was having twins.*	*I was told I should 'hold out' for pain relief as it would reflect badly on me if I had it too soon. When it happened I was in such pain and thinking I was a failure because I needed an epidural.*	*I can't see my experience of neonatal care reflected anywhere I go – it feels like I have a secret!*
My experiences			
My culture	*The main message was I had to be strong and brave at all times. I have seen other members of my family really struggle with this – feeling ashamed and having to hide what they're going through.*	*My 'take home' was it's just what you have to go through – if it's hard, don't make a fuss – generations of women have done it without complaining.*	*I have to be strong otherwise it will affect the babies – it's hard to feel like I could be damaging them if I cry or feel overwhelmed.*

cont.

	Pre and during pregnancy	Experiences around birth	Having a baby in neonatal care
My experiences			
My religion and/or beliefs and values	*There is a definite sense that babies are a gift from God – this feels true and I am grateful, but it also left no space to say things weren't easy, like on the days when I felt so sick I wished I hadn't got pregnant.*	*I believe God will protect them and me – whatever happens is his will.*	*I must pray for their protection, and God won't give me more than I can handle.*
My experiences			
My family	*They are supportive and excited about the babies, but I have never felt like they want to hear what things are really like for me emotionally. I feel like I have to keep them happy by always being happy. As a young child I felt invisible. I learnt very quickly my feelings weren't important to them.*	*Everyone wanted to be at the birth – I know they meant well, but there was little space for my own opinion. When I told them I only wanted my husband with me, they were offended and I felt guilty and upset.*	*The message I got was they'll be fine if I pray hard enough. I'm almost not allowed to think about any other outcome or express my fears, so I keep them to myself at the moment, just as I did as a kid, but I might talk to the chaplaincy team next time they come by.*

My experiences			
My friends	*My friends have always been a huge support – they come from all backgrounds and accept me as I am. They could hear I was a bit nervous about having twins – and the message was that's okay, that it's normal to feel apprehensive about becoming a mother.*	*A few of them had given birth already – they told me how it was for real. I valued their honesty.*	*They told me I could call them any time, and I do. They are always on WhatsApp sending me messages, and often surprise me by coming to the hospital to accompany me on the way home.*
My experiences			

When you look at your responses for each of these areas, take a moment to pause and take stock. You might want to consider:

- Are there particular things that have come to light doing this exercise that are new, validating or helpful?

 ....

 ....

....

....

....

....

- Have you found yourself making any connections between the messages and experiences you have had in your life and what's coming up for you as you become a parent? If you have had a baby before, are there any differences this time? Are there things that you notice from your own experience of being parented as a child that arise for you?

....

....

....

....

....

....

- Notice how completing this exercise has made you feel about yourself. Do you notice any criticism, minimizing of difficult experiences or perhaps some compassion and kindness towards yourself? Are there things you are proud of or that give you a sense of achievement?

....

....

....

....

....

....

Let's have a look at some parents' stories and how these factors have influenced how they feel about themselves and their role as parents on the neonatal unit.

Raya felt that she cared less about what society thought than her family's strongly held views. She was told that it would be easy to get pregnant and expected to conceive quickly, but in fact it took many years to become pregnant with her son. During that time she felt like a failure and that she was letting down everyone around her. When she was pregnant she was given a lot of advice about what she should or should not do, and she felt like it was impossible to get it right or to please everyone. She began to feel low and anxious and withdrew from people. She felt like her pregnancy and her body was everyone's business, which was intrusive and made her lose confidence. When she went into labour early, she felt like it was her fault, despite the doctors being clear that it was unforeseeable. She did not feel able to inform her family for a month that her baby had been born, for fear of their reaction. The situation itself was frightening, but coupled with fear of judgement and shame, Raya felt overwhelmed.

Shazia was raised by her grandmother in a large and supportive family. Her family were Catholic and she was very involved in the church community, which helped her to feel valued and loved. When she became pregnant, she joined a mother's group at her community centre. This helped her become more confident in being a mother herself, which had been an early fear after her own mother had left the family when she was young. Shazia was excited but also anxious she would be able to cope and feel good enough as a parent. Her partner and his family also helped by welcoming her into their extended family and inviting her to spend time with the mothers and aunties. When she was told her daughter might be born prematurely, Shazia sought out the support and wisdom of her family, the church and local community. They supported her through prayer, and emotional and practical support, helping her to feel she was able to manage whatever lay ahead. This support continued through their admission to the neonatal unit, and Shazia's sense of being the mother she wanted to be grew over time.

Simon had grown up in a family where he was the youngest of four boys. Whilst he was talented at music and art, he was seen as 'weak' and 'useless' by his father for not being sporty and outgoing, like his brothers. Simon felt, over time, that anything he had to offer was not good enough, and that he wasn't strong or resilient. He pursued music as a career, finally meeting other men more like himself, and within this circle he met his wife, who became a source of encouragement. When they became pregnant Simon resolved to be a very different parent who could nurture and protect his family in the way he wished he had been as a child. When their baby was born by emergency C-section with a heart condition, Simon felt that he had already failed to make the 'perfect family'. He was devastated that he wasn't allowed to be with his family due to Covid-19 restrictions, and felt that he was abandoning his baby. Simon was unable to reconcile these events with his hopes for the future, convinced that he would be unable to 'fix' the relationship with his wife, and, most importantly, his son, after this start.

Reading these stories, we can see that we all arrive on the neonatal unit with different experiences that can colour events that are already difficult. For Raya, it was important to recognize that the fear of judgement and failure had come from many sources. She needed help and encouragement to find her own sense of worth and confidence as well as support to approach her family with the news of her baby's birth, and to develop healthy boundaries around their involvement and managing their reactions. For Shazia, the abandonment by her own mother understandably came more to the forefront when she found she was pregnant herself. However, the welcoming of her as an emerging mother in her church and local community as well as her extended family meant she felt able to develop her own path and confidence in her maternal role at the same time as acknowledging the grief she felt from when she was a child.

Simon's story tells us how some of the early events and losses that happen in neonatal care can activate fears and feelings that become overwhelming. The sense that early events with your baby 'set the course' for the future is a common fear that can bring with it anxiety and hopelessness. What's important is to acknowledge that there are many influences and factors that impact the development of a baby and the development of a family. For Simon, it was helpful to see that his insight into his own childhood had enabled him to know he wanted something very different for his family, and that his commitment was not altered or diluted by the circumstances he found himself in that were not his fault. By helping Simon to find ways to honour the values he wanted to live by as a parent whilst separated from his wife and baby, he was able, little by little, to find his role and feel more positive about the future.

We have thought together about how parents can come from many backgrounds and have many different experiences that they bring with them through the doors of the neonatal unit. But there are additional factors, those that relate to what happens on the unit itself, that are also important to think about. As much as it's vitally important to understand ourselves and where we are now in the context of where we've come from, it's also important not to underestimate the challenges that occur solely as a result of your baby being in neonatal care. These challenges are many, and they are not your fault. In the next section we will explore some of these in relation to becoming a parent, and we will also revisit this when we think about building a relationship with your baby in Chapter 6.

IMMEDIATE CHANGES TO YOUR PARENTING EXPERIENCE THAT HAPPEN AS A RESULT OF A NEONATAL ADMISSION

If you've had a baby before who has been well, the journey from coming into hospital, giving birth and returning home will be familiar. You will have a sense of those times where you felt like a parent, or perhaps first observe your partner taking that role. If you are a first-time parent you may have read books or attended classes that tell you about each stage and the many small moments that help you to feel like you're a parent right from the very beginning.

It can feel isolating and suddenly like you're not part of something when you're parenting in hospital. You may not have many friends or family who have been through anything similar. Those touchpoints of common experience that join us to others and give a sense of community and solidarity may be missing in your world outside the hospital. It can be helpful to acknowledge these differences and also the important similarities you share with other neonatal parents through a different set of touchpoints that connect you through this exercise.

MAPPING OUT DIFFERENCES BETWEEN NON-NEONATAL AND NEONATAL EXPERIENCES IN EARLY PARENTING MILESTONES

Some differences in non-neonatal and neonatal experiences parents often highlight as significant are outlined in this table. **There is also space for you to add experiences that you feel significantly differ and matter to you, and that might be shared and that might be the same for other parents in the unit.**

Non-neonatal experiences	Neonatal experiences
Birth of baby followed by immediate access/ access within hours to baby.	*Birth of baby where there's often only brief contact before long period/s of separation.*
Choice of clothes to dress baby, blankets, feeding preferences.	*No/few choices in early care or space to express parenting preferences.*
Easy access to pain relief, food and medication.	*Access to pain relief, food and medication can be restricted or challenging.*
Partner's/other children's/extended family's access to mother and baby (some variation post-Covid-19 across hospitals).	*Extended family and siblings often have restricted access.*
Discharge typically within 48 hours.	*Often facing long period of admission to hospital, variable facilities for parents and can be far from home and support systems.*

Non-neonatal experiences	Neonatal experiences
Immediate responsibility for baby including decision making and preferences given to parents.	*Immediate need for medical care from professionals and immediate decision making often made in the absence of parents or with limited input in baby's best interests.*
News of arrival shared rapidly with friends and family.	*Often difficult decisions about what news to share with whom and when.*
Cards, presents and congratulations given from friends and family.	*Friends and family often uncertain of what to say or how to respond.*

My own previous experiences outside of neonatal care and/or those I had hoped for	My neonatal experiences

As you look back at this list, notice what this brings up for you emotionally, without judgement. It's important to compassionately acknowledge the losses, disappointments and changes that you have been through as a result of your baby being admitted to neonatal care.

As you acknowledge these, you may feel a range of emotions. Take a moment to make a note of these here:

....

....

....

....

....

....

As you take stock of these emotions and the journey you have been on into parenthood, you will also find yourself growing into and adopting the different roles we talked about at the end of Chapter 4. Take a moment to look back at this section, and think about what each of those roles means to you in light of your parenting journey so far. You may notice that some of them feel particularly important, and these might be roles you want to focus on in these early days. For example, Simon felt that the role of protector and guardian was his first priority. As his parenting journey continued, he was able to think about his role as a nurturer and give his son the love and care he had craved throughout his own childhood.

REVISITING PARENTING ROLES ON THE NEONATAL UNIT: 'WHICH MATTER TO ME MOST RIGHT NOW?'

The parenting roles we thought about in Chapter 4 included: guardian, protector, encourager/cheerleader, holder of hope, nurturer, comforter, observer, advocate and ally and delight-taker. You may have added some of your own too.

Think about what roles matter most to you right now and why, and write them in the table. *This will help you to focus on what you can do, even when there can be a lot of things you feel you can't yet do.*

If you have a partner, you might want to do this exercise together and think about the answers for both of you. What is similar and what is different? How can you develop an understanding of each other's parenting journey to help you grow together?

Role	Why it matters to me
For example, Advocate	*For example, I grew up learning to speak up if something wasn't right or needed to change. I feel this is something I can do straightaway for my son.*

IDENTIFYING WHAT YOUR VALUES ARE AS A PARENT AND PUTTING THEM INTO ACTION

We can think of our values as being a guiding set of principles that direct what we do. Values influence how we operate in all our multiple roles as adults – son/daughter, sibling, partner, professional, etc. – but are particularly important when it comes to parenthood as they profoundly affect the decisions we make, what we prioritize and our relationships. In this final section on your parenting journey let's find out more about your values and how you can put them into practice on the neonatal unit.

To identify values, think about the kind of relationship you would like with your baby, and what you want for them, and then what values that involves. For example, having a relationship where your baby can openly express how they feel from the very beginning might reflect values of love and acceptance. If you prioritize them feeling secure and protected, this might reflect values of caring and safety.

If you are parenting with a partner, it can be helpful to discuss with them what their values are, where they may have originated from, and how you might bring them together with your own, now you're a family. If there are significant differences, it's worth spending some time working out how you might compromise in some areas, as well as being clear what values feel non-negotiable for you. Like we saw with Simon, think about prioritizing your values according to what matters most to you right now. This can give you a focus for this first part of your neonatal stay in all your different parenting roles.

Let's meet Jason and Connie, who hadn't thought about their parenting values ahead of their baby Jess's birth. They both came from very different families and backgrounds, and when they discussed parenting values, they discovered they had very different priorities.

Connie's difficult childhood meant that loving behaviour, connection and safety came top of her list. She didn't want Jess to feel alone, and it was very important to her that she was there at key points in the day (such as first thing in the morning and last thing at night). Jason felt that independence and self-care (for himself and for Connie) were most important. He felt Connie's insistence of being with Jess for very long hours meant they had no time together, and that Jess needed to learn to be by herself as well as with them.

When they talked about their differences, Jason was able to understand that Connie's position of Jess not feeling alone was not one she was willing to compromise on, particularly whilst she was in hospital. Connie also understood that Jason was fearful that their relationship, and therefore their 'united front' as parents, would suffer if they had no time alone, particularly as it had been under strain during a stressful pregnancy.

They agreed that they would spend some time together away from the unit in the middle of the day, if Jess was asleep and settled. They developed a routine for the evening that involved them both, and between them they noticed that Jess was able to settle back into sleep from a lighter sleep state without always needing Connie to intervene. Equally, Jason saw that when Jess was distressed, she was able to calm more quickly when they both helped her to move into a regulated and calm state. They both found a way to honour their values and learnt more about each other and what mattered as joint parents of their little girl.

It's important to also remember that different ways of doing things don't usually mean they're wrong. Part of adjusting to each other's parenting role is being able to accept your baby can be parented in different ways, with different expressions of love and care.

SUMMARY

Becoming a parent for the first time, or navigating this role with a hospitalized baby, is challenging in many ways. In this chapter we have thought together about your journey into parenthood, and the complexities and richness this can bring. We have also looked at the differences to the parenting experience that take place as part of the neonatal experience, including the many changes and losses, and how difficult it can be to make those early connections in such a high-risk and technological environment. You've started to make those brave first steps into your parenting role as you also understand your own background and messages you've received in your life about pregnancy, birth and becoming a parent whilst your baby is in neonatal care. Take a moment to take stock in these early steps and the courage it takes every day.

RESOURCES

Somewhere to find more information

Parenting for Humans: How to Parent the Child You Have, as the Person You Are by **Emma Svanberg** explores what we bring to our parenting journey, how to parent the child we have, and how to gain confidence in our role as a parent.

Something to watch

'Neonatal care: Navigating the journey for parents', a video from the **Just One Thing series**, with **Dr Bettina Hohnen**, is available as a podcast and to watch on YouTube. This outlines some key concepts when navigating being a parent on the neonatal unit and acting in accordance with your values: www.youtube.com/watch?v=udg-fHNcwAY

Something to listen to

'Grief + Growth through mothering', from **Seasons of Matrescence – The Podcast** with **Julianne Boutaleb and Nikki McCahon**, is a powerful podcast exploring the process and complexity around becoming a mother, touching on themes of identity, relationships and the constant process of 'becoming'. It is available on Apple Podcasts as well as, for example, Podtail.

Something to read

Dear NICU Mama, 'Letters of hope written by NICU moms for NICU moms': These letters cover the experience of being a parent in neonatal care and the range of challenges, joys and experiences from mothers with a wide range of backgrounds and circumstances: www.dearnicumama.com/letters

CHAPTER 6

Building a relationship with your baby

Nurturing itself needs to be nurtured.

SARAH BLAFFER HRDY

Feeling connected to your baby and building a relationship with them can be really hard when they're in neonatal care. There are often many worries and concerns about bonding that can be hard to talk or think about because they carry anxiety, guilt and shame. It's important to remember that the barriers to feeling a bond with your baby when they are in neonatal care are not your fault.

In this chapter we'll look together at the factors that can impact your connection to your baby in this high-threat, high-stakes, high-tech environment. We'll also explore how these factors and others from within your own life, including your own experiences as a child, play a role in how you might bond with your own baby. Once you have a picture of how these elements link together for you, we will think about how you can make the first steps towards building the relationship, holding you and your baby compassionately in this journey together.

'WHAT IS "BONDING" AND IS WHAT I'M FEELING "NORMAL"?'

The process of bonding is the forming of a strong attachment and emotional connection between you and your baby where you have a desire to care for them and for it to feel rewarding when you're together. Many parents, even when they know their baby will be in hospital, come with high expectations of feeling instant and intense love, immediate connection and an immediate desire or ability to care for their baby. It can be unsettling and devastating for the parents whose reality feels so different to those expectations when they don't feel an immediate bond, even though this experience is common.

Although other parents feel connected to their baby straightaway, this can lead to being terrified about what might happen to them. There can be fears about their survival that can be overwhelming, or worries about the impact of the neonatal experience on their baby's emotional and neurological development. In some ways it can feel as if it's impossible to know what to feel or allow yourself to feel in these circumstances, or what might be 'best'.

> However you come to form the relationship with your baby, it's important to remember that rather than being seen as a 'one-off' event, bonding and connecting to your child is a lifelong process.

Let's look first at the different kinds of experiences parents can have around connection with their baby. Jessica, David and Sharon all have babies in the high dependency unit (HDU), and have been on the unit for a few weeks:

> Jessica sits quietly in the chair by her baby, occasionally looking into the incubator and then looking away. Three weeks into her neonatal journey she finds herself struggling to come into the nursery, arriving later and later and leaving earlier than she had planned. The team have told her all about holding her baby and being involved in his care, but what she feels ashamed to tell them is she doesn't really want to be around him. She doesn't feel a 'rush of love' when she holds him, and finds their comments about her being a mummy make her anxious and angry.

> Sharon is finding it hard to be in the hospital with her baby after a traumatic birth. Even though she knows it's not her baby's fault, every time she sees her it triggers traumatic memories that are overwhelming and difficult to cope with. She is also terrified that her baby might die, making her afraid to feel anything for her.

> David looks at his daughter but cannot see any response to his presence. He feels like it makes no difference whether he's there or not, and is resentful for the changes her medical condition have brought to the family. He sees little point in investing in her, and feels like she might even be better off being looked after by someone else. Since her diagnosis of a genetic disorder, he hasn't wanted to talk about the future or make plans. He feels alone with these experiences as he feels they are unacceptable to tell anyone else, and as a consequence he becomes more and more withdrawn from his baby and his family.

All three parents are experiencing some complex emotions when it comes to forming a connection with their baby. For Jessica, the pressure and expectations of being a mum and fulfilling these is overwhelming, especially whilst she feels watched by others. She feels numb at this moment in time, and this sense of numbness extends to her baby. Feeling nothing is hard to explain, and so she stays away, resentful of attempts to engage with her baby's cares and spend time on the unit.

Sharon is also feeling disconnected from her baby, but this comes along with terror that something will happen to her baby. Without perhaps being consciously aware of it, she is holding back from an emotional connection with her baby as she believes the pain would be too great if she were to die. Her baby also reminds her of several traumatic moments during the birth that cause flashbacks. She feels torn by her intense feelings that confuse her and those around her.

For David, the lack of response from his baby means he doesn't feel being with her is rewarding or meaningful, which would help him feel motivated to engage with her. He's also grieving, confused and angry at her recent diagnosis, where he feels he's had no positive conversation about her with anyone. His loneliness and withdrawal mean he's also losing key points of social connection in his other relationships, and he begins to view himself as selfish, hopeless and unable to love.

EXPLORING HOW YOU FEEL ABOUT YOUR BABY

As you read these stories, take a moment to think about how you feel about your baby.

What kind of thoughts or feelings come up for you? As you notice them, try to capture what goes through your mind as well as what you might feel in your body without judging it. Just be curious about what's there right now, and make a note of it here:

....

....

....

....

....

....

To help unpick these feelings and to understand them it can be helpful to recognize the kinds of experiences and barriers to an emotional connection with your baby that exist in the neonatal context in addition to those that we have thought about in 'Immediate changes to your parenting experience that happen as a result of a neonatal admission' (Chapter 5), which are about your parenting experiences and context.

EXPERIENCES AND BARRIERS THAT CAN IMPACT THE FEELING OF EMOTIONAL CONNECTION/ BONDING TO YOUR BABY IN NEONATAL CARE

Even when a baby is not in neonatal care, around 40 per cent of first-time mothers and 25 per cent of women with two or more babies actually describe feeling indifferent when their baby is born.[1] In some cultures, a feeling of indifference is the norm whilst a mother recovers from birth. It's important to remind yourself that this is so common, even when your baby does not require neonatal care.

It's important to recognize that some of those early opportunities for processes that facilitate bonding and connection are absent or reduced *through no fault of your own*. Some of these are a product of the differences in how your baby looks and behaves or how likely you feel they are to get better; some are related to previous or recent loss; some a product of the physical environment; and others are related to how we respond under threat or experience low mood.

If your baby is born early or is sick, there is often a question about their survival or longer-term outcomes. Thinking about this in evolutionary terms, delayed bonding can be viewed as an evolved response of holding off investment until survival is more assured. This delay may not be something that is done consciously, but it's often the case that parents will describe a point where they feel it is possible to invest and 'take the risk'. If you have experienced previous losses during pregnancy or on a neonatal unit, you may feel this particularly acutely. There is often quite a lot of variation in the time where it feels 'safe' to invest and when the threat system becomes less activated, allowing feelings of soothing safety and connection.

In the case of twins or triplets, where one or more babies may have died and you have a surviving baby, there is additional complexity. You may feel a range of emotions, from extreme fear of another loss to ambivalence about your surviving baby. The death of their twin or multiple may leave you afraid of what is to come, of investing in them or struggling with the impact of constant reminders of your other babies. Your sense of threat and danger may also be triggered by having to come on to the neonatal unit where you have experienced a death of a baby in another family, making the foundations of closeness and connection harder to establish (see Chapter 9, 'When a baby on the unit dies', for more information).

In addition to this high-risk situation around survival, our readiness for bonding can change if we are in a situation where we don't have, or don't feel like we have, the resources to care for our baby – for example, feeling very unwell, having an absent or unsupportive family or a lot of worries about how we might provide

1 See the article by Robson and Kumar (1980).

for our baby. Growing support around you, as discussed in earlier chapters, can help you feel more resourced to be able to feel a connection with your baby.

If you are feeling depressed or very low, this is another situation where these feelings of connection can be dampened, and what's important is to view these compassionately, without making assumptions – for example, 'I'm a bad mother because I don't feel anything for my baby'. It's helpful to place some hope into the darkest and most desperate thoughts that you may be having, even if it's one word... 'I don't feel anything for my baby *yet*'.

When babies are born prematurely, they don't look the same as we often imagine babies to look. Very preterm babies have translucent skin, little fat or muscle tone, are often covered in soft hair and may not be able to open their eyes to start with. Even when they do open their eyes it is unlikely to be for long periods. If your baby is born with a visible difference or a medical condition that impacts how they look or behave, this can also mean they don't appear in reality how you may have imagined them in your mind.

How your baby looks can impact how close you feel to your baby as babies have evolved to have particular features and behaviours that encourage caregiving and stimulate hormonal changes, such as looking cute (having large eyes and a smaller nose and mouth). Several of these features may be less obvious or absent when your baby is very premature or unwell.

Many parents also describe how they didn't feel that their baby looked like a *real baby* in the early days, and how it can be hard to think of them as a person. This is understandable as it can be difficult to even see their whole face without equipment, or to work out who they might look like in the family. It's quite natural to wonder if your baby looks like you, and when this is obscured or uncertain there can be a loss of continuity and connection from the baby you have grown inside your body or watched develop in close proximity and the one you have.

Babies who are premature or unwell may also not respond to us in a way we expect based on a well term infant. Even when they have periods of being awake they may look away or become unsettled as they struggle to achieve or maintain a regulated state. For some parents, even with the knowledge that their baby is responding differently for a reason, it can feel difficult when these responses occur. For example, your baby looking away from you may feel like a rejection or that they don't like you. With a baby that is finding it hard to settle, move into a more regulated state or sleep, some parents feel irritated or frustrated by their baby. These emotions and things they may bring up for parents are sometimes hard to make sense of or to talk about.

Physical closeness is another factor that plays a role in the formation of early bonds, and our brains are wired to reinforce this and other nurturing behaviours.

The biological underpinnings of physical closeness

Physical closeness is one of the elements that stimulates the production of the neuroendocrine hormone oxytocin (which, for the majority of people, gives feelings of calmness and soothing between the baby and parent) and the monoamine dopamine (which gives a pleasurable feeling of reward and is linked to the motivation to attach). In addition, when babies are able to respond to parents and parents to them (sometimes called 'reciprocity'), this also produces feelings of reward and a sense of wanting more in the parents' brains, setting up a positive feedback loop with the baby.

Babies who are medically unstable may not be able to spend any or very limited time in skin-to-skin contact with their caregivers. They are also separated by incubators, medical equipment and other physical barriers. Some of the early things you may have done together such as breastfeeding, which often bring feelings of closeness, may be a long way off in the future, or challenging and anxiety provoking. Even when you are encouraged to put your hands through the holes in an incubator, this is no replacement for total proximity to your baby's body, especially their face.

Many parents describe a distinct change in how connected they feel to their baby when these physical barriers are reduced, for example, once they are in an open cot or breathing support is no longer needed. Limited opportunities for this contact and interaction, coupled with a high-threat environment, might leave you feeling physically disconnected from your baby, reducing a sense of emotional connection. It's common for parents to report it feels like their baby isn't theirs in the early days, and that the baby belongs more to the neonatal team.

WHAT IMPACTS YOUR SENSE OF CLOSENESS AND CONNECTION TO YOUR BABY?

In addition to these experiences listed above there will be other factors that can have an impact on your sense of closeness and connection. Take a moment to list any others that you feel are relevant for you here:

....

....

....

....

....

For babies, separation from their caregivers often causes them to experience a stress response as they don't have access to the regulating presence of you, as their parent. They have a lot to navigate such as painful procedures and a sensory environment that is difficult to manage for their immature nervous systems. Being close to them and building the ability to 'tune in' to their needs and to understand how they are communicating with you will benefit their development and emotional wellbeing in the short and longer term.

THE IMPACT OF YOUR OWN PARENTING EXPERIENCES ON YOUR CONNECTION WITH YOUR BABY

All of us have our own experiences of being parented, and we thought about how this can impact us when we become a parent ourselves in Chapter 5. Another area to consider is our own experiences of the 'building blocks' of attachment with our caregivers. For example, did you have parents who were sensitive and responsive to your needs and who provided you with a relationship that was safe and loving as a baby and a child? Those who have experienced a secure and loving relationship with their own parents have a 'blueprint' of what this can look and feel like, which can be helpful when making a connection with their own baby.

For those who haven't experienced this as a child there can be (but not always) difficulties in creating and sustaining the kind of relationship they would like to have with their own children. Some examples include:

- If you didn't have a healthy emotional connection with your parents when you were a child, you may struggle to make this connection now with your baby.
- If you experienced erratic or unresponsive parenting, you may feel quickly dysregulated or overwhelmed by your baby's distress, or feel like things are out of your control.
- You may find your baby's distress can bring up your own feelings of distress from childhood where your needs may not have been noticed or attended to.

Take a moment to reflect on your emotional experience and attachment patterns in your own childhood. Notice what is most emotionally present for you, or any reactions that arise in your body. It will be important to pay attention to any responses that you notice as you begin to build your connection with your baby, and you may wish to keep a note of these as you work through some of the exercises and activities in this chapter.

In the next section we will look at how you can start to find ways to connect with your baby whilst holding gently your own understanding of your experiences and their impact. All the time you are seeking to connect with your baby, even if it feels hard or scary, they are also building a connection and an attachment to you. Care that you give that is attentive, sensitive and responsive helps them to feel safe, secure and loved when they are around you, which is an important foundation for their wellbeing.

CORE PRINCIPLES OF STARTING TO BUILD A CONNECTION WITH YOUR BABY

We have thought about the many experiences and processes that may have made first steps in feeling connected to your baby more difficult. Moments of connection build to form a bond, and we know that this is an ongoing process. The approach and exercises in this section are all offered in the spirit of some core principles for starting to build a connection with your baby:

- Start where you're at. Every relationship is a journey, and even though we might not be where we'd wish to be, we need to start gently from where we are. If you need to compassionately remind yourself of this, take a moment to do that now, before you read further.
- Build and nurture using 'baby steps'. Whilst we might wish things to move faster or feel the need to 'do something' to speed our feelings up, we can think about the bond with our baby like growing a rich and beautiful garden. We can cultivate that garden, watering over here, pruning over there. We can tend to each element up close, and there will be a moment when we step back and see the whole garden as one.
- Ask for additional help if you need it, and make use of expertise on the unit. For some families the process of bonding will happen over time, without additional help. Others will benefit from a range of professionals who can help specifically in this area – from neonatal nurses and nursery nurses to allied health and psychological professionals. Staff are trained in this area specifically because it's recognized it can be hard. They are there to support your process, not judge or criticize it.

BEGIN TO RECOGNIZE AND RECORD THE VARIETY OF WAYS YOU MIGHT FEEL CONNECTED TO YOUR BABY IN NEONATAL CARE

RECORDING 'MICRO MOMENTS' WITH YOUR BABY

We can often miss the small ways that tell us a connection is beginning. How do you feel when you leave your baby (e.g., feeling a physical change or that something is missing)? Do you think about them when you're not with them (such as wondering what they might be doing or who is looking after them)? Do you have any moments, even if they last only a few seconds, when you experience a feeling of love or pleasure?

Make a note of these moments when they happen and how they feel. Extending our gardening metaphor, keep a record of the 'buds' that start to emerge. They may not be big moments, the grand flowers or blooms, but they are still important and will accumulate over time.

Here's an example from Phoebe's 'micro moments' list:

- I felt an ache in my body when I stepped away to go home for the night.
- I held her hand and noticed her fingers curl around mine – that moment felt like a real connection.
- The nurse said she was calmer when she heard my voice this morning – I noticed that made me feel something – was it pride? Also like I mattered to her, I made a difference.
- When the monitors stopped beeping I felt I could look at her, really look at her, without fear.
- When I gave her a feed I felt like I could nourish and provide for her.

It can be helpful to look back at this record as you are able to do more with your baby over time and take stock. You may find that they emerge from specific ways you have been encouraged to become involved in your baby's care (see Chapter 4).

EXPANDING A 'MICRO MOMENTS' LIST TO ENCOMPASS MORE ABOUT YOUR BABY AND YOUR CONNECTION WITH THEM

There is an opportunity to extend the use of diaries or positive micro moments logs to help consolidate your moments of connection and to develop a map of your baby over time as they change and may feel more like a little person.

Other areas you could consider keeping a record of include:

- Moments when they feel very much like a baby and/or feel like *your* baby.

  ....

  ....

  ....

- Moments when you notice them responding to you specifically – what do they do and how do you know?

  ....

  ....

  ....

- Activities or moments where you feel more of a connection (and ones you might like to try).

  ....

  ....

  ....

- What kind of characteristics they have now or are developing – glimmers of their unique personality or physical appearance, for example.

  ....

  ....

  ....

- What soothes them and helps them to feel safe and secure.

  ....

  ....

  ....

- How do they communicate with you? What are their cues and what do they mean? Have they changed over time?

....

....

....

What other things would you find it helpful to keep track of with this connecting focus?

....

....

....

What things help you to feel like your baby is a unique person? Make a note of them here:

....

....

....

....

....

....

....

....

FOCUS ON YOUR BABY'S STORY SO FAR AND WHO THEY ARE AS A PERSON

There are many ways in which your baby already has a story to tell. A starting point is their name – consider why you chose this name and what it means. You may have chosen a first or second name that represents an important meaning or person in their neonatal journey. Think about what your baby has shown you in terms of their personality so far.

Laura felt like her baby was feisty and 'always proving the team wrong' in terms of progress. She felt like her baby's determination and fighting spirit was what helped her exceed expectations of her progress, and it became a core feature of her stay (as well as the root of many nicknames!). It also helped her to consolidate this sense of her baby's personhood by being able to talk about it with the team, and for nurses to share their observations, gradually building an enriched story about her baby that wasn't wholly focused on medical facts and progress.

MOVE INTO AN EMOTIONAL PLACE WHERE YOU FEEL ABLE TO BE CLOSE TO YOUR BABY

The environment and circumstances of neonatal care can cause our minds and bodies to be in a state of high threat for prolonged periods. This can change how we are able to respond to our baby – both in how connected we may feel to them emotionally and in how able we are to build those connections through being attuned, curious and sensitive to them. It can help to mindfully see if we can move into a more soothed and content state that provides the fertile ground for those early relationship feelings and bonds to happen, rather than feel rushed into an activity or encounter when we are still very much in threat mode. It can also help when bringing your baby to feed or beginning to express milk. It might only need a few moments each time.

MOVING INTO A SOOTHED STATE AS YOU COME TO BE WITH YOUR BABY

This is a guided exercise to help you move into a soothed state as you come to be with your baby. You may wish to listen to this exercise or read it through yourself.

Take a moment to acknowledge everything that may be going on around you, and then bring your focus to your breathing. You may want to close your eyes, and look at your baby or a part of your baby that feels okay or good. Just notice your breath coming in through your nose, and released slowly out through your mouth.

Slowly try and make the out-breath a little longer each time. As you breathe in you may want to imagine that air has an energy or a wish for you – one of protection, calm or safety or any other feeling that you need right now as you get ready to be with your baby.

Notice your body, scan from the top of your head slowly all the way down to your feet. Notice if there are any feelings of tension or distress and then imagine directing the air coming into your body to those areas, giving them what they need.

You might want to focus on your hands that will touch your baby or your chest as you prepare for them to rest there during skin to skin. Imagine what you would like your baby to experience as you come together. You might want to spend a moment focusing on this space between you, imagining it is protected from or just away from everything else around you. Maybe you can change where you imagine you are, for just a few moments, and take you both to somewhere real or imagined that you would like to be together.

Notice as you create this space for you both how it feels, the flow of energy through your body and your mind as you breathe in what you need. Give yourself permission to stay in this mental and physical space as you go into your connecting time.

If you find this is difficult to do, be gentle on yourself. These exercises, like many in the book, take time and practice. Notice if being in a more soothed state changes how it feels to hold your baby, or spend time watching and being curious about them.

BABY BODY SCAN

This exercise is another way to connect with your baby even if you can't hold them or there are reduced opportunities for touch. You may want to start to use touch in this exercise when they are ready. Make sure that your hands are warm and that you talk to them gently as you approach their body slowly and calmly. Begin with the 'Moving into a soothed state as you come to be with your baby' exercise if you feel that you are in an anxious or threat-based state.

When you are ready, find a place to stand or sit where you feel you have a good view of your baby – you might need to move around a bit if they are in a closed incubator.

Start at the top of their head. Notice if they have any hair or what their skin is like.

Move down towards their eyes. Notice if they are closed or occasionally open. If their eyes are open, spend a moment looking directly into their eyes. Notice what it feels like to see their eyes if this is something new for you.

Gradually notice their face – the parts you can see directly and those that might be less visible for now. You might want to connect with your own face as you do this – is there anything you can see that's similar? Are their parts of their face that you love particularly? If your baby has less medical equipment you might be able to notice their expressions or reactions in this area.

As you move down their body, notice the shape of their torso, their arms and their hands. Spend a moment pausing on their fingers, looking at each one in turn. As you do this, be mindful of your own breathing, taking a moment to keep it steady and calm. If any worries come up as you go, about your baby or what the exercise brings up, just acknowledge them and let them go for now, bringing your attention back to your baby.

As you move down towards their legs, spend a moment noticing how they are positioned, how they might move or be comfortable, nested and still. Notice their feet, the shape of them, even though they may be very small. As you make your way down through their body you might have a wish for a particular part of their body that you can think or share with them, which might be a part that needs to grow in strength or size to help them or simply a wish that they will get better every day or feel more comfortable.

If you are able to touch, you could imagine that wish and energy flowing through your hands into them, from your body into theirs.

At the end, use a containing hold of the whole of your baby with your hands. Before you slowly remove your hands, let them know that you are ending the exercise for now.

You might notice in both these exercises that you begin through mental connection and touch to regulate *each other's* states rather than it feeling just one way, particularly as your baby becomes more well and stable.

> Matt noticed that as he spent purposeful and focused time with his baby, his body relaxed a little more each time when they were together. By the time he was in the special care nursery he made time to prioritize skin to skin with her every time they were together, and also found it helpful to reconnect with that state when they were apart, to help him feel calmer.

Make a note of these changes when they happen as another set of 'buds' that emerge over time.

SKIN-TO-SKIN CUDDLES OR 'KANGAROO CARE' WITH YOUR BABY

Skin-to-skin contact (also interchangeably referred to as 'kangaroo care') is important for growing feelings of closeness and connection. Its many benefits for you and your baby have led to it being considered a key intervention on the neonatal unit. For parents, skin to skin has been shown to have a positive impact on bonding as well as on mood, anxiety levels, confidence and milk production. Finally holding their baby against their body can be the first time many parents feel like their baby is theirs or more real.

For babies, skin-to-skin cuddles improve many significant health and development outcomes. During skin to skin parents can soothe and help their baby maintain a regulated state where they experience less stress. This, in turn, can help parents' own regulation, levels of stress and anxiety. Babies show positive changes in their autonomic reactivity (how their body reacts flexibly to changes in the environment or emotional contexts) during skin to skin, and these positive changes also play a part in how their nervous system works to regulate them later in life and form an attachment to the parent, as a safe, loving and soothing person.

Having kangaroo care is something that has become possible earlier and earlier in babies' journeys, thanks to its importance being recognized at all stages of care. You may have been able to do it straight after your baby was born, before they came to the unit. The ability to have regular skin-to-skin contact can depend on what staff are around to help you and how stable your baby is at the time. Although these factors are not in your control, it can be frustrating and upsetting when it's not possible.

Some things to consider when you are able to hold your baby include:

- You may feel scared you might hurt your baby in some way. This is a common fear. Ask your nurse to talk through how they transfer your baby to your chest, and how they manage the wires and equipment. Also ask them what can happen during that transfer so you feel prepared for any changes, for example, a temporary change to stats on the monitors, as well as what will happen if they need to transfer your baby more quickly back to the incubator.

- Take a few moments to prepare yourself for holding your baby – not only in terms of practical elements (such as using the toilet and having a drink within reach) so that you can experience uninterrupted time, but also emotionally. Holding your baby can bring some wonderful feelings of calm and closeness, but it can also bring other feelings such as sadness (e.g., that they are in hospital or have been born so small) or anxiety (e.g., that an alarm may sound or that they won't settle on you). If you are noticing your heart racing or feeling anxious, before you start skin to skin take some moments to do your 'Soothing breathing rhythm' exercise.

- Take a moment to connect with your intention towards your baby – for example, to help them feel loved and cared for. Remember, your love and nurture will benefit them throughout their lives, and is a fundamental need for every baby.

- Talk gently to your baby in a soft voice, looking carefully for cues from them as you speak. Holding them close can be a very intimate moment when it can feel easier to share things with them than speaking through an incubator. Focus on how it feels to have their body connected back again with yours, and all the sensory elements such as the feel of their breathing or their smell. If they are lying on your chest, you can use a small mirror so you can see their face more easily against you. You may also have an opportunity to touch and explore parts of their body more closely – take your time to do this and know them in this special way, playing close attention to how much they can manage at one time.

- If skin to skin has helped you to feel close and calm, it can be helpful to take a mental 'snapshot' in your mind of this moment and all its elements to come back to later. It can be particularly helpful to connect with this moment if you are away from your baby or feeling anxious or disconnected.

- You might also find it helpful to speak to yourself with compassion, care and understanding as you hold your baby for the first few times. Let yourself know that it's okay to feel a bit overwhelmed or frightened, and that you are doing something courageous to help you both. This can be particularly important if your baby struggles to adjust to being on you for the first few times. Remember that it is an adjustment to being held by you, and this doesn't mean it will always be tricky.

FEEDING YOUR BABY

Feeding your baby can be another way to feel close and connected to them. It can mean many things on a neonatal unit, from giving your baby milk through a tube to breast and bottle feeding. In the early days your baby may be fed directly into their bloodstream with liquid that provides some or all their nutritional needs. At this moment in time, it can be reassuring to know they're receiving what they need, even if this doesn't involve feeding as something you do actively together in the same way. It can be helpful to feel you have an important role in nourishing and helping your baby to grow.

It's also the case that feeding can bring with it a lot of strong and mixed feelings, such as joy and fulfilment, frustration, sadness and grief (perhaps missing out on feeding your baby as you'd have wished). If your baby is in NICU, they can have a long road ahead of them to come to a point where they can manage the skills needed to feed by mouth. It can be very difficult to express milk for a long time whilst waiting for the moment you may have imagined to arrive. You might find that expressing milk helps you to feel close, particularly if you're next to your baby, although this isn't the case for everyone.

Some things to consider when you are feeding your baby are:

- Remember that the time you spend getting to know your baby and how they communicate, the many opportunities for closeness and helping them develop a sense of safety and being soothed will all be of benefit as they move towards feeding with you. Be gentle with yourself as you are with them, as you're discovering and learning.

- Notice what goes through your mind when they're feeding. How do these thoughts affect how you feel about feeding and your baby? If you notice a lot of difficult thoughts relating to yourself or your baby (e.g., 'My baby doesn't like me'), this can change the way you feel and interpret what's happening. It can be helpful to remember that babies in neonatal care often struggle with aspects of feeding, and may need plenty of time and patience to coordinate the many elements involved.

- Talk to your team about ways they can help you feel close to your baby however they're feeding, such as holding them skin to skin near the breast during a tube feed.

- The feeding journey can be long, frustrating, disappointing or rewarding. Compassionately remind yourself that you're doing the best you can to feed your baby at whatever stage they're at, and there are many people on the unit to help you work towards what's right for you.

GIVING A VOICE TO YOUR BABY AND STARTING TO WONDER ABOUT WHAT THEIR WORLD IS LIKE FOR THEM

Being curious about the world through your baby's eyes is a helpful way for you to know and understand each other better, for you to communicate with each other, and for you to meet your baby's needs. You can start doing this by wondering (either to yourself or when speaking to them out loud) about what's happening – for example, 'You're starting to hiccup, I wonder if you've had enough for now?', 'You've woken up all surprised this morning!' This ability to think about their mind and their experience is an important foundation of being sensitive and attuned to their needs, and is part of the journey in how you build communication between you both.

CREATING TIME WITH YOUR BABY ALONE AND ALSO AS A FAMILY

Although many activities and moments are very much between your baby and yourself, you can also begin to consider the time you might spend together as a couple or a family. Part of your baby's identity is formed in relation to those around them, and you might notice that their connection with their siblings or a grandparent is different or reveals new things about them. Many parents also describe family time as feeling more 'normal' as the responsibility and enjoyment is shared between people, as well as your baby feeling more real for others. Grandparents, for example, who can take a photo of you with your baby and are able to engage in holding or doing an activity with your baby or seeing you both safe together often feel more encouraged and empowered in their supporting role as well as their own grandparenting role. This 'coming together' with supportive others can also help build a sense of community and social support, which can, in turn, facilitate bonding and connection.

WHEN TO ASK FOR MORE HELP

We have thought together about the many ways you can start to get to know and form a bond with your baby yourself, and how some experiences before a neonatal stay and after admission can make this more challenging. Although you may have found some of the exercises in this book beneficial, there are times when you might feel you need more help with this relationship. You might need extra help for a range of reasons, and this is not a reflection of failure. Rather, you could see asking for help as a part of your parental role, seeking additional input where you recognize it's necessary – for your baby and for yourself.

Some examples of situations where you might seek extra help include (but are not limited to) where the following are having a significant impact:

- Struggling with feeling connected to or interested in your baby, and these feelings aren't resolving or changing as you might expect
- Finding it hard to feel like your baby is yours or feeling estranged from your baby
- Feeling continually fearful about something happening to your baby
- Feeling continually angry or frustrated with your baby
- Experiencing strong feelings of being inadequate or worthless as a parent to your baby
- Feeling that your baby is impossible to understand or 'tune in to'
- Struggling to process the loss of another baby (in the same or different pregnancy), which is having a significant impact on relating to your surviving baby/babies.

Whilst a whole range of professionals can help with bonding difficulties, psychological professionals and occupational therapists are the two main specialists who will be able to help, often working together and with the broader neonatal team. You may have access to these professionals on your unit, or you may access them in the community.

On the neonatal unit there are several collaborative tools and approaches that these professionals may use to enhance their work with you, such as the Newborn Behavioural Observations (NBO) system. A specialist on your unit can provide you with detailed information about what they involve and how they can benefit you and your baby, as well as the typical time in your stay that they can be used most effectively.

You may also benefit from a range of psychological therapies that can help you explore more about your life and current circumstances that may be having an impact on your experience as a parent and your capacity to form a relationship with your baby. Psychological professionals think with you about how to move forward based on this shared understanding, which is often referred to as a 'psychological formulation'.

Once you leave hospital, some areas have parent-infant relationship teams that have multidisciplinary (more than one profession) expertise in helping you and your baby to relate to one another,[2] or you may access a range of interventions

2 Details can be found on the Parent-Infant Foundation website: https://parentinfantfoundation.org.uk/our-work/map-of-teams-and-services

through a Perinatal Mental Health Team (PMHT) or a Maternity Mental Health Service (MMHS). You can ask your neonatal outreach team, neonatal psychological professionals or your health visitor or GP about what might be available to you in the community, including what's on offer via the charitable sector and online. Some units also have follow-up parent groups, where this topic is often included in parent sessions.

SUMMARY

In this chapter we have talked about making a relationship with your baby as well as developing your sense of who they are as a unique individual. You are both finding ways over time to communicate, interact and get to know each other. The journey is a lifelong one as your own role and your relationship adapt and change as circumstances change around you. If you find you need some extra help, there are professionals who specialize in these areas to support you on this journey and who will help you to make sense of what you're experiencing. Also remember that wherever you are in the process, or however you feel about it, there's a way forward, starting from where you're at right now.

RESOURCES

Somewhere to find more information

The European Foundation for the Care of Newborn Infants (EFCNI) has a huge range of information on budling a relationships with your baby and can be found on Instagram. They also have a publication that gives more detail on the importance of the relationship between you and your baby, including your role in developmental care and looking after their needs. It also has a section on further resources and interventions: https://old.efcni.org/wp-content/uploads/2023/04/EFCNI_BondingCare_EN_web.pdf

Something to watch

'The 5 step dialogue: A mindful connection' with **Cherry Bond**. Join Cherry as she talks through five steps to mindful connection to your baby in neonatal care. Whilst this video is aimed at neonatal staff to help parents, it is also useful to watch as a parent yourself, from an expert in the field: www.youtube.com/watch?v=O7dDyOKHZ3s

'Bonding with the baby while in hospital for neonatal surgery' from **healthtalk.org**. This series of videos reflects a range of parent experiences around bonding and what was helpful: https://healthtalk.org/experiences/parents-experiences-neonatal-surgery/bonding-baby-while-hospital-neonatal-surgery

Something to listen to

'Bonding with your NICU baby roundtable', Series 5, Episode 11 of Dear NICU Mama podcast. Listen to mothers who have had a baby on NICU talk candidly about their own experiences of building a relationship with their baby whilst on the neonatal unit, and their reflections later on looking back. Available on iTunes, Spotify, Google and on the Dear NICU Mama website: www.dearnicumama.com/podcast/bonding-with-your-nicu-baby

Something to read

'Understanding your preterm or sick baby in hospital', a postnatal (0–6 months) course module. This is a free online interactive module that can help you develop further understanding of your baby and build a close and loving relationship with them, written by clinical psychologists with neonatal expertise: https://inourplace.heiapply.com/online-learning/course/98

Mother Nature: A History of Mothers, Infants, and Natural Selection, by **Sarah Blaffer Hrdy** (1999).

Robson, K.M. and Kumar, R. (1980) **'Delayed onset of maternal affection after childbirth.'** *The British Journal of Psychiatry* 136, 4, 347–353. doi: 10.1192/bjp.136.4.347.

CHAPTER 7

Helping other children while your baby is in hospital

Baby in incubator, by Sam, aged 6

As a parent, there's a strong desire to protect your children from harm and hurt. Seeing them distressed or struggling is painful and difficult. When you have other children to care for as well as your new baby it can be overwhelming and exhausting as you try to meet all their needs in different locations with many competing demands. Some parents describe this time as trying to bridge between two worlds – daily life on the neonatal unit and juggling 'normal life' as it goes on outside – the school day, homework, exams, friendship troubles, etc.

It's important to acknowledge that you are doing the best you can in extremely difficult circumstances, and that it is at the same time distressing to perhaps feel like you aren't being the parent you wish to be for everyone. Whilst there are things about your situation you cannot change, this chapter aims to provide some practical suggestions to help you help your children at different ages, with advice on how to nurture compassion towards yourself and your parenting role under a period of enormous pressure. This guidance is also relevant to other children in your family who may be affected by the neonatal experience.

EXPLAINING TO YOUR CHILDREN WHAT'S HAPPENING

There is a lot of understandable worry about how to help older siblings understand what is happening when their baby is admitted to the neonatal unit. There can be fears about upsetting them or frightening them or that they will be too young to understand and perhaps that it's better not to say anything.

Being honest about what is happening with children is important. What's key is tailoring how you speak with them so it is appropriate for their age and who they are as a person, which you will know better than anyone. Remember, you are an expert in your own children. You don't have to include all the details or talk about things you aren't yet sure of yourself (such as when your baby might come home). Often something very simple and short will suffice, such as: 'Our baby came early and is in hospital to help them breathe and get used to being outside mummy's tummy. Mummy and daddy will go to the hospital every day to look after our baby, and then we will come home again to look after you.'

Children notice more than we often give them credit for. They might already have picked up more than you realize from conversations they have overheard with adults, letters or appointments you have attended in hospital, or the 'emotional temperature' of the household. It is important to be honest, because they will often use partial information to make sense of what is happening, and it may lead them to come to a different conclusion that is even more distressing – for example, that their mother has died if they have not come home from the hospital, or that they are not seeing much of their parents because they are more in love with the new baby than them.

Whilst exact phrases and words will vary between families, the following principles can be helpful when talking to children:

- Choose the right time to talk when possible – when they are not too tired, hungry or distracted. For older children and teens, offer them a choice about when they would like to talk about what's happening and the location.
- Use honest and straightforward language appropriate to their language level and age.
- Use pictures, toys and props for younger children to help make what you're talking about more concrete and easier to understand.
- Check back they have understood what you've said, acknowledging that understanding can take time and it will not be a 'one-off' conversation.

- Let them know that you love them and are there for them.

Although these same principles apply whatever the situation, there are some additional considerations if you are facing specific situations such as longer-term disability or end of life, and you can find more about how to support your other children with this in 'Supporting your other children' in Chapters 10 and 11.

EXPLAINING AND EXPLORING THROUGH PLAY

Very young children explore and learn through play. Finding ways to help them understand and express themselves whilst playing will give you a window into their emotional world, and it also gives you a chance to correct any misunderstandings or help them with their fears. You can easily adapt what you have at home for this play, and there are also toy companies such as PLAYMOBIL® and Mattel (Barbie) that have some toys that look very similar to the equipment and surroundings they will find in the neonatal unit. You can also purchase dolls that have medical equipment or devices such as stomas or feeding tubes, which can help normalize what your child will see and experience.

Becoming familiar with the neonatal environment through play

Invite your children to use toy figures, dolls or soft toys to represent all the important people in their life. Notice if they include the baby. Do they know where the baby is? Do they think the baby has been born yet? You can decide how to explain what is happening with the toys – you may wish to show them where their baby is and what is happening or tell them what happened when their baby was born in the hospital step by step. The key ingredient to play is curiosity – be curious to understand through their eyes first. Then you can gently help them to understand what is going on and introduce new information – for example, if they are worried their baby is all alone in the hospital, you can show them how they are being taken care of.

Be guided by your child as to what they need from the play. This may change over time. There may be occasions when it is more focused on information and others when the focus is on exploring feelings.

USING PLAY TO HELP YOUNG CHILDREN EXPRESS WHAT THEY NEED FROM OTHERS

Claire noticed that her daughter Zena was upset and not herself when she came home from the hospital, but attempts to ask her what was wrong met with further upset or anger. One day Zena did not want to greet her and stayed upstairs. Claire began to dread coming home to see Zena; she felt rejected by her and also frustrated that the time she had with her was so fraught. She then felt guilty that she was having these feelings and that she couldn't do anything right as a mother.

When Zena was playing with her dolls, Claire joined her. She took one doll to be mummy and invited Zena to find one to be a little girl. They played for a while in a pretend park, and then Claire changed the play to home time. Through this play Claire discovered that Zena felt angry that her mother spent so much time at the hospital and that Zena was upset that their new baby was always the topic of conversation, even when she was home. The special, fun times had gone, and she was also sad that they didn't play much anymore.

Claire swapped the dolls around and pretended to come home again. With some encouragement Zena was able to show her mother what she needed by showing her what she'd like to happen instead, and they made a plan for home time together. They didn't talk so much about her brother unless she wanted to, and they made time for play every day, which Zena chose. Claire also found creative ways to let Zena know she was thinking about her when she wasn't with her.

(See the exercise 'Creating symbolic ways to feel connected and keep each other in mind'.)

USING THE POWER OF STORIES

We all have stories about experiences in our lives, and stories help children in many ways. They can give information, help them recognize emotions and experiences of others and how they are similar to their own, and they often help children make sense of what is happening to them. There are several beautiful books written for children who have a sibling on the neonatal unit that cover a number of scenarios and topics. There are also books that address particular themes that may be relevant, such as missing each other, connecting with each other when apart and feelings (see, for example, the story book *Wherever You Are, My Love Will Find You* by Nancy Tillman).

It is particularly powerful, however, to create a story for your child that you can tell them at bedtime or record for them to listen to if you're not able to be there. By creating your own story, you can incorporate everything about your child and your family that is important to them, and include messages that guide what they understand and remember about the situation.

Illustrations created for Ben's story

Here is Anne's story for her child, Ben:

> Once upon a time there was a little boy called Ben who had two mummies who loved him very much. One day Ben's little sister Kim was born and was poorly, so his mummies had to spend a lot of time in hospital. Oh how they missed Ben! They missed playing with LEGO®, cuddling watching *CBeebies*, eating pasta and bubble baths. They missed Ben's laughs and hugs and wished they could bring him to the hospital every day. Ben missed them too; he sometimes felt sad and missed his special cuddles. Everyone was finding it hard to wait to be together again. Mummy Anne found a special power that helped her to be close to Ben. She put her hand on her heart, closed her eyes, and imagined he was sat right there with her. When Ben missed her, he did the same, and could feel his hand and then his heart filling up with a bright yellow sunshine, a sunshine of his mummy's love filling up his body. Kim was going to be home soon, and then the bright yellow sunshine could be all around them, shining in their safe and special family.

You may also wish to create a story for your baby that tells them about their journey and all the people who have helped them along the way. This can be helpful when they are older and may wish to know more about what being in hospital was like, and can also help you as a parent (you can use some of the content you have created through diaries or milestone recording – see Chapter 1, 'Celebrating and marking small steps and milestones, and memory making').

CREATIVE WAYS TO EXPLORE FEELINGS

Finding the words to describe what's going on inside is not always easy for younger children. Creative ways to do this means you can develop an understanding of how your child is feeling, and then begin to help them in a more targeted way. Children may also show their feelings through behaviour, and remembering all behaviour is communication can be helpful to keep in mind.

Understanding what it feels like and finding ways to help

We don't always need to know or use the same words to describe feelings, and children may not necessarily use the same words to describe emotions as adults.

> Taylor said he had a horrible feeling in his tummy when the phone rang at home (the hospital had called many times in the last week when their baby was unwell, sometimes late at night). He couldn't identify this feeling as anxiety, although his

mum suspected it. She started by asking him some questions, being curious about his experience.

QUESTIONS TO BUILD A SHARED UNDERSTANDING OF EMOTIONS WITH YOUR CHILD

Sometimes the way we ask questions can help children express and articulate what they feel in ways that make sense to them. These questions help you and your child to build a shared understanding of their experience. Summarize back what they've told you or drawn for you so they can experience being heard, seen and understood, e.g., 'I can see that this feeling coming up is really big, it feels really dark and spikey, like a hedgehog'.

If there are other questions or phrases that have worked well with your child/children, add them here for reference:

....

....

....

....

....

....

- How big is this feeling? (Huge – takes up all my body/bigger than me, or smaller?)
- Does it have a colour? (Explore why it has that colour, it is red because it feels hot, for example.)
- Does it have a shape? (Is it spikey or heavy or cold?)
- Where do you feel it in your body?
- Does it have a name? (It can be a made-up name or the name of a person or animal.)

Questions to help you find a way to manage feelings together

Creatively using questions can help you find solutions together. Once you've understood how they're feeling you can start with some general questions linked to what they tell you. You may want to make their answers into a plan that they can feel part of. Check in every few days to see how it's working and if you need to make any changes.

Jot down some questions you may also use with your child here, and any other notes that might help you make a plan together:

Here are some examples of questions you could use when being curious about feelings and experiences with your child:

- What makes/when does the feeling grow bigger/darker/heavier?
- What makes/when does the feeling become smaller?
- Is there something we need to do with this feeling together?
- What can prevent it from getting bigger?
- How can we help it to become smaller?

Understanding when everything feels overwhelming

It is helpful for children to know that worries and other feelings can build up over time, and sometimes, when there are too many all at once, they can bubble over the top and feel overwhelming. For children this may manifest as a change in their behaviour, such as being very 'clingy', a return to younger behaviour, such as wanting a dummy, or being more angry and 'acting out'. To help children understand this you can draw a jug and ask your children to colour it in or stick on pictures of things from catalogues or newspapers that represent their thoughts and feelings. Help your child to notice when their jug is becoming too full by asking some simple questions:

QUESTIONS TO ASK WHEN THINGS MIGHT FEEL OVERWHELMING FOR YOUR CHILD

- What would you notice first if your jug was becoming too full?

- What would mummy or grandad (for example) notice?

....

....

....

- What could you do to help straightaway if you noticed one of your signs that your jug was becoming too full (e.g., heart racing, crying a lot, feeling angry all the time)?

....

....

....

Helping children to understand what is happening internally gives them more of a sense of control and knowledge that they can do something to help themselves as well as reach out for help from caring adults around them.

Using visual or number scales

Use a visual or number scale for older children and for those who find it easier to work with numbers and prefer less talking. For example:

- Thermometer
- Ladder
- Traffic lights
- Facial expressions
- Different animals (from a lion to a mouse).

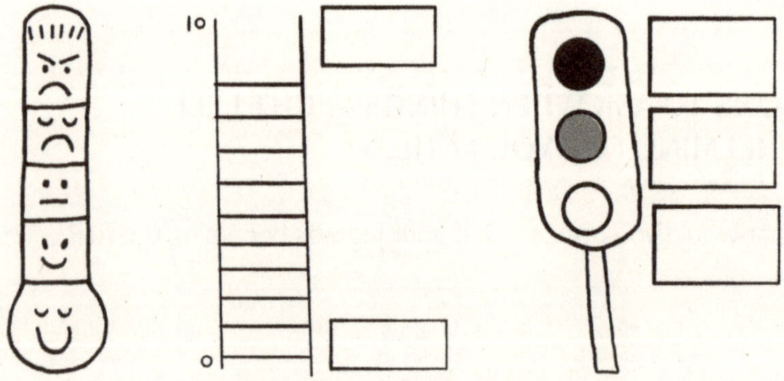

Example of some visual and number scales

USING EMOTION SCALES TO HELP FIND SOLUTIONS

Once you have some understanding of your child's emotional experiences, use one of the number scales to map out what each stage of the scale would look like for them. Starting at 10/10, explore what this would feel like for them and how others would know. Do the same for each point on the scale. You then have a shared 'shorthand' for assessing where they're at.

Given there are many times when it's not possible to take away the feeling completely, scaling helps them to realize feelings aren't 'all or nothing' and that small changes can be helpful.

See how Anish and his dad used his worry scale to help think of some practical steps to help in the following example.

> Anish gave a rating of 8/10 for worry most of the time. His dad asked what could make it 7/10 for tomorrow. They worked out that having a phone call to let him know what was happening if they were going to be late from the hospital would help.

Note: This only moved the anxiety down one notch, but often it's finding small ways to reduce worry, being interested in what your child suggests (it can often be very different to what we anticipate), that helps them to learn there are things they can do or that others can do that change how they feel – and that can be empowering at a time when there may be a lot that feels out of their control.

Children can benefit from something concrete to use when they are struggling emotionally. As you work out together what they find helpful when they are upset/angry/lonely (or their own description), you can place these objects into a special feelings kit bag designated for the purpose.

MAKING A FEELINGS KIT BAG

Explain to your child that this bag can stay with them, and help them to remember what each item is for. It can also be helpful to have a guide card for teachers and other caregivers so they can help them to use the contents most effectively. Here are some examples:

- Squeezy ball for when I'm stressed.
- Photo of me and my mum and dad for when I'm sad.

- Small teddy to cuddle with mummy's perfume on if I'm missing her.
- A book of puzzles to help me re-focus and feel calmer.
- My favourite snack that feels familiar and comforting.
- A souvenir from my holiday to remind me of fun and happy times.
- Bubbles to help with my soothing/calm breathing.

A 'Feelings kit bag' for children

USING IMAGERY AND BREATHING TO FEEL CALMER AND SAFE

Children often have wonderful imaginations and the ability to visualize, and we can harness these abilities so they can benefit from adapted imagery exercises and soothing/calm breathing.

CREATING AN IMAGE OF A SAFE/HAPPY/ CALM PLACE WITH YOUR CHILD

Invite your child to imagine a place that helps them to feel safe, happy or calm. Ask them if they can travel there in their mind and describe it to you, including what they can hear, see, touch, smell or even taste. They can decide if they want other people to be there, or certain animals or pets. You can encourage your child to include real or imagined places, people and animals in their created place. The aim is for them to include whatever they need so that it helps them to experience a helpful change in their emotional state.

Encourage them to 'take a photo in their mind' once they have been through the exercise, or they may wish to draw it or find an object that represents it. They can put this object or drawing in their feelings kit bag, or put it up on a wall at home.

SOOTHING/CALM BREATHING FOR CHILDREN

Keep explanations simple when introducing soothing/calm breathing to children. You might explain it as 'a way of breathing that helps our body put on the brakes and feel calmer. We breathe in through our nose and out through our mouth like this...' (and show them). Children can imagine blowing a feather away from their body when they breathe out through their mouth, or if they struggle to imagine something, they can blow actual bubbles as a way of keeping their out-breath long and steady.

Enhancing this exercise with colours can be a useful addition. Invite your child to imagine breathing in a colour that represents all the helpful, good feelings they want to have more of, imagining them travelling all the way through their body to exactly where they are needed, and breathing out some of the tricky feelings through their mouth, watching them vanish and dissolve into the distance. This could be breathing in a warm yellow colour, and breathing out a grey colour – check in with them what fits best with their internal experience.

CREATING SYMBOLIC WAYS TO FEEL CONNECTED AND KEEP EACH OTHER IN MIND

When you and your children are separated, it's helpful to find ways to let each other know you still have them in mind and are thinking about them. Younger children find more concrete ways to show or represent this helpful. Older children may also value objects or physical gestures, as well as making use of electronic communication and technology.

One of the most powerful ways to connect you with younger children is to use connecting hearts on your hands or arms, which is simple and free. Draw a small heart on your hand or arm and invite your child to draw a small heart on theirs. Explain that you are going to charge this heart full of love (and anything else they need such as feeling close to you or safe). Touch the hearts together, and charge the heart with what your child needs. Remind them that if they ever need to feel you/feel loved or safe, then they can put their hand to their heart or their face and they will be able to feel it. It can also help you as a parent to have a visual connection to your child.

Note: Due to hand hygiene in the neonatal unit you may wish to place your heart on a different part of your body such as your arm, so that it doesn't wash off!

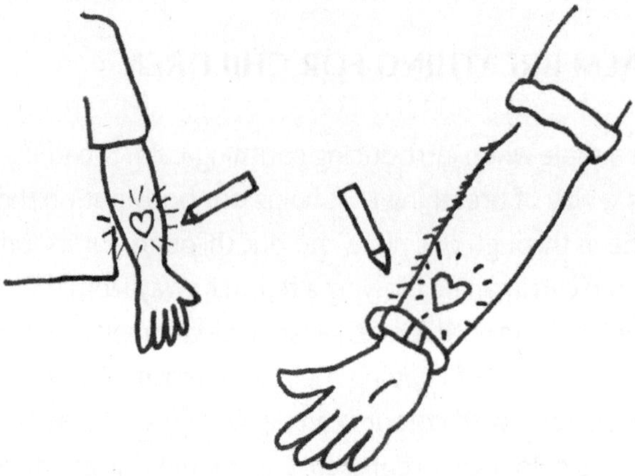

Connecting to each other through shared symbols

Using a locket, small teddies or objects to exchange can also be helpful as an alternative or in addition. Having a photo of you with them or something that represents your special bond can be helpful. A locket that keeps your photos together that your child can hold or open when needed, or two identical small soft toys (perhaps adding your perfume or cologne to theirs), can also be comforting. There may also be objects that have a special significance for you, such as stones or shells that you can keep with you and hold to remember and connect with each other.

When the focus of adults is mostly on the new baby, experiencing being held in mind is a powerful experience. This also comes through small but frequent gestures and points of connection, such as:

- Surprise cards – pop a card into your child's lunchbox or school bag if you are at home, or send them postcards if you are experiencing time apart
- Cooking their favourite meals or buying their favourite food
- Remembering to ask about key things that are happening in their day, friends and interests
- Putting some time aside every week that is just for you and your child/children alone – one-to-one time that they know is uninterrupted can be powerful and containing, even if it's short.

You can create a unique friendship bracelet to create a wearable representation of your child's sources of support and comfort. This helps create a unique reminder of support that your child can wear and keep with them at all times as a visual reminder. Here are the steps to making a friendship bracelet.

Step one: Help them to map out their sources of support, comfort and any other people, places or things that are important to them on a piece of paper.

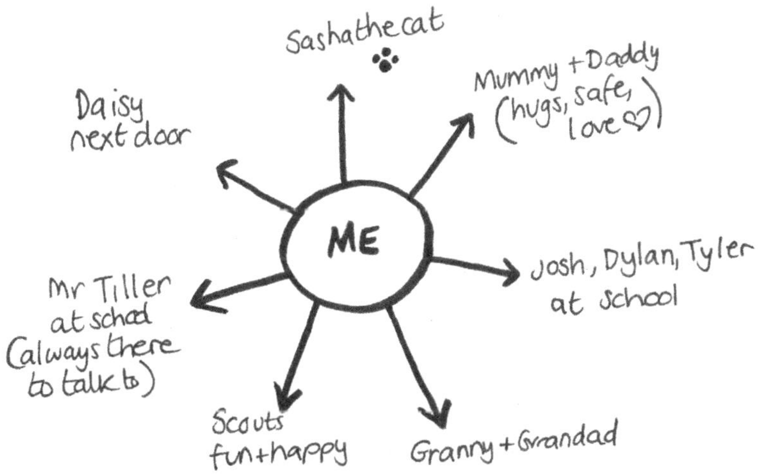

Step one

Step two: Ask them to choose a colour of yarn that represents each of these items/ people/places.

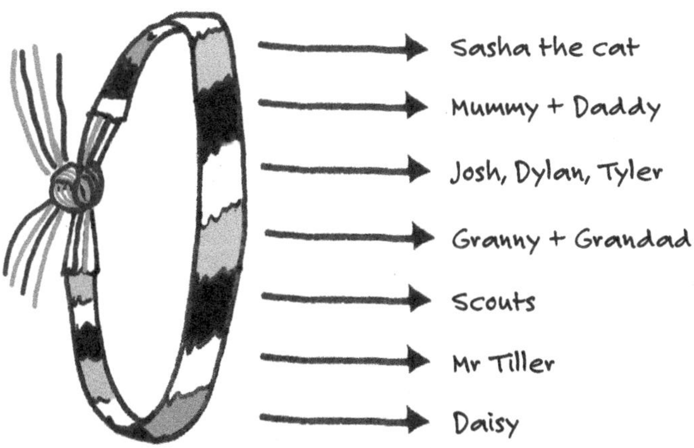

Step two

Step three: Weave the threads into a friendship bracelet. You can find information on how to make a friendship bracelet online without any special equipment.[1]

Alternative ideas are using the threads to make a dream catcher if your child is distressed at nighttime.

KEEPING THE 'KEY INGREDIENTS' FOR YOUR CHILD – ROUTINE, ANCHORS AND FAMILIAR ADULTS

Routine and predictability (without undue rigidity) helps children to feel safe and secure. It is likely that a lot has changed in your family fairly quickly, and this can be unsettling. If possible, try to keep as much as you can in your routine as a family. Even though you may feel you want your other children with you more, going to nursery or school will help them by providing structure and familiarity. It will also give them time to be in 'normal life', where they can focus on other things and play.

It is important to let your child's school or childcare provider know what is happening so they can understand if your child seems different to their usual self and know how to help. Teachers are experienced in supporting children through adjustment and change. Open communication will allow you to provide a consistency of approach (such as the language you use to describe what is happening) between home and school.

When you are spending a lot of time at the hospital, it can be easy to lose track of the day passing by outside. When they are small, children think about their days as a set of tasks or stages rather than in the sense of time: breakfast time, school run time, break time, bath time, story and bedtime, etc. Some of these moments in the day are particularly important for children (such as bedtime), and provide an anchor in the day. If the situation in the hospital allows, try to be with your child at some key times for them – for example, be home to do bath time or let them know they will see you at breakfast and take them to school before heading to the hospital. If who is going to be home for what is likely to be different day by day, a weekly chart so they know what to expect, stuck on the fridge or front door, is helpful.

Children benefit from the continued care from familiar adults. Whilst you may be inundated with offers of help, think about who is known best to your child. If you do find you need to call on people they don't know well, if possible give them a period of settling with that adult so that they feel comfortable and secure. If your

1 An easy to follow example can be found at: www.youtube.com/watch?v=IAQhiYI48y4

child can see you happily interacting with that adult, they will learn that they are a safe and fun person to be with.

NEEDS OF OLDER CHILDREN AND TEENS

Whilst some of the ideas in this chapter will be applicable to older children and teens, there are some specific considerations for this age group when thinking about how to support them through the neonatal journey:

- The fact that they are older and more independent doesn't mean they need you any less emotionally, so making space and time for them is important. This can include small or shorter moments of connection as well as longer conversations. You may want to schedule in a weekly coffee or ice cream trip or a walk where being together is guaranteed. If they want to talk about worries or concerns it can be helpful to know there is a protected space and time for this. However it's also important for them to know they can spend this time as they wish, and that may also be for fun, connecting and regulating things too.

- Important conversations also often take place in the car, during activities or 'off the cuff'. Many older children and teens find it easier to talk whilst doing something.

- If they don't feel able to ask you questions face to face, give them other ways (such as texting you or dropping questions into a jar). They may not wish to ask you some questions through fear it may upset you (such as fears about whether their sibling might die), in which case you may be able to arrange a time for them to meet a support worker on the unit by themselves.

- If you feel like they need their own regular support, ask your unit about psychological professionals who can offer this service on the neonatal unit or about support in the community.

- Older children and teens will be more able to understand the details and nuances of what is happening but may still need some help to grasp the implications or facts – some of which they may have overheard or got 'snippets' of along the way. If you are facing a longer neonatal stay you might want to give them a weekly update so they know when to expect new information. Honesty and openness remain key, including telling them when you don't know the answer.

- They will have their own emotional response to events that may be similar or different to your own. Be prepared to listen to what they tell you openly, and let them know that all emotional responses are valid and important.

- Think with them about whether they would like to let their school and friends know about what's happening, giving plenty of choices and autonomy in making decisions.

HELPING CHILDREN WITH ADDITIONAL NEEDS

If you have other children with additional needs, the impact of a neonatal admission brings many other considerations. Changes to routine can cause significant distress, absences can be harder to explain, and you may have concerns about the competencies of adults stepping in to help to look after them, even with the very best intentions. Here are some things to consider that may be helpful:

- Contact your child's network as soon as possible to let them know about the significant change in your family. It will be important to be explicit about what a neonatal admission means for your child as it is unfamiliar for many – that you will be spending long periods of time away from home, that you may not be able to predict when you will be around as easily, for example.

- Use tools and resources that have helped them to manage in the past (such as social stories), and as much as possible keep the same familiar adults in regular contact.

- If there are specific needs from a visit to see their baby, let the neonatal team know – such as providing headphones to manage the sounds on the unit, thinking about the time of the visit so there are fewer procedures happening in the room or people at the time, sending photos ahead of the visit so you can do some preparatory work on what to expect, having some time for your child to speak to their baby's nurse on their own to ask questions.

- There are likely to be times when you need to spend time with your child at home and cannot come to see your baby so regularly. Compassionately remind yourself that whilst you cannot be with both your children at the same time, for now your love remains with them both and knows no boundary or distance.

INVOLVING YOUR CHILDREN IN THE CARE OF THEIR BABY AND PREPARING FOR IN-PERSON VISITS

Units have a range of policies about siblings coming on to the unit, so it is important to check what these are in your hospital. Children can feel a range of emotions when anticipating a visit to their baby, and it's important to encourage openness about this and to help them prepare.

Here are some things to consider when preparing your child for a visit:

- Talk your child through what will happen, stage by stage. Use photos and videos if possible, to show them what the unit looks like and what their baby looks like. Many units now have virtual tours and photos on the hospital website or social media. Be honest and calm about the equipment around their baby – for example, 'This is a tube to help them to breathe, the beeping helps us know they have enough oxygen, etc.' There is also an app called Nell and the Neonatal Unit (see 'Resources' at the end of this chapter) that can help your child prepare through interactive games and activities.

- The neonatal unit is an environment that can be taxing on the senses, so prepare your child for what they are likely to see, hear, smell, touch and even taste (sanitized fingers in the mouth, for example!).

- You can explain who the different people are that they are going to meet, and see if they can spot different things about them, such as 'Doctors always wear blue, nurses are always in green', 'They wear clothes called "scrubs" that sometimes look like grown-up pyjamas!'

- Explain how their baby may look different or be a lot smaller than other babies they have seen, and that it won't always be possible to pick them up or to play with them.

- Show them where they will wash their hands and put their things.

- Don't expect them to want to stay very long – it doesn't mean they don't care or love their baby, but even the most welcoming neonatal units have little to hold the attention of small children. They might be disappointed that their baby doesn't 'do more', and it's okay to reassure them that their baby will change as they get bigger and get better.

- Tell them how they can become a 'baby protector super hero' by washing and gelling their hands, speaking with a soft indoor voice, keeping hands away from buttons and wires (even though they look interesting), and come with plenty of love and affection and a bit of patience too!

- Take smaller children for a good run around or play in the park before and after the visit – space on units is limited.

- Bring plenty of snacks and drinks and schedule regular toilet breaks.

What can they do when they are on the unit?

- Talk to your baby's nurse and ask them for ideas to plan for your child's visit. Nurses often have many ways to make siblings feel special.
- Be aware that your child may not want to see their baby or touch them. Do not force them if they aren't ready. If they are not ready to go into the nursery, let them know it's okay to peep through the door and that they can take meeting their brother or sister at their own pace.
- If they have been interested in the equipment round their baby when you have prepared them for a visit, see if they can spot the different things they saw in the pictures.
- Take small quiet toys or electronic devices they can play with safely in the nursery.

GIVING YOUR CHILD AN IMPORTANT ROLE WITH THEIR BABY

Having a list of things your child can help with, even if the things are small, helps them to feel important, involved and have an active role in the family. You can do this by making them a list of 'duties' that they can do for their baby and then tick them off. Ask the unit if they can laminate this for you so it is wipe-clean and also reusable.

Nurse Sacha's duties for baby Finn

Give him a gentle kiss and a cuddle with my hands.

Check with some help that his nappy is clean.

Make sure his teddies are tidy and neat.

Read him a story (my choice).

If their baby is going to be in the unit for a longer time, they may wish to add to their neonatal unit-related items by having mini scrubs or a special badge. Take the lead from your child about how invested or interested they are in this role.

Make sure any pictures they have drawn are up near the baby so they can see them – as well as anything else they have sent the baby.

Have something from the baby for them on occasion – a message, a sweet treat or a little teddy.

Be mindful of what they may see or hear when they are on the ward – neonatal environments are not always predictable, even with the most careful planning.

INVOLVING YOUR CHILDREN IN THE CARE OF THEIR BABY AND PREPARING FOR VIRTUAL VISITS

If it is not possible to visit in person, finding ways to help your child connect with the baby can be challenging. The baby may already seem a very abstract idea to them, and their interest may wax and wane.

Here are some ideas to try with your child, remembering that if they are not ready to start making a connection with the baby, you can try another time when you feel they might be:

- Write a card for the baby, draw them a picture or send a message (although it is important that something can come back from the baby in return).
- Send the baby a song or story by video message or audio.
- Plan for the baby – design their room or what things they'd like to show them at home first or teach them how to do.
- Watch videos of the baby with you so you can show them that they have the same hair colour or use the same blanket as when they were small.
- Choose their outfits for the day (when appropriate) or other small choices such as the lullaby they will have at bedtime.
- Encourage them to tell the baby all about their life, their day at school – things that matter to them.

BEING COMPASSIONATE TO YOURSELF PARENTING DURING A REALLY HARD TIME

It is effortful and difficult to afford the energy into parenting at a time when your own resources are limited. Alongside the need for routine comes the need for predictability and containment in other ways – from you as a parent and also the other adults who care for your child. There is a balance to be struck between letting some things go and also being containing and consistent for children who need the boundaries and predictability at a time of tumultuous change and adjustment. Having some shared principles amongst everyone who looks after your children will help them feel secure.

This may be a time when you are facing not being able to be the 'best' parent you can be at all times. You may be struggling to contain your emotions when your other children squabble or need something from you. Their needs may feel inconsequential or impossible to relate to when you are sitting with fears that your baby may not survive. It might feel that you have no love left to give anyone else. Sometimes situations are greater than we feel able to bear at the time – this isn't your fault. Remember that expecting yourself to be at your best in the middle of a crisis is a huge expectation. Most likely we would not expect this of our friends or other family members, yet, as a parent, it can be hard to acknowledge to start with.

If you feel you are struggling to cope, talking about it with someone who can help – such as a friend or a professional in the hospital – is important. They aren't there to judge you or tell you what you could be doing better, but they can offer a space to think and plan when overwhelmed. This may mean a few days away from the hospital or home to slow down the demands and to reset.

Also notice how you respond to yourself when thinking about your parenting. If you are noticing a highly critical voice when you are struggling, you might want to consider the following exercise. This will gently guide you towards a compassionate response to how hard it is to parent all your children, at this moment in time.

BRINGING COMPASSION TO YOURSELF AS A PARENT WHEN IT'S HARD

Remember in this moment that you are doing all you can to parent all your children amidst your struggles and difficult feelings. Take a few moments to bring to mind the things you are finding most difficult. Allow yourself to be honest about what you are struggling with and how it is feeling. Notice as you bring your attention to these things how your mind and body respond to them. Are there critical thoughts there, judgements or viewpoints from others? What do you notice happening to your body as you think about what you are finding hard?

As you notice these, imagine what it would be like to bring a compassionate presence to all your turmoil and struggle. You might be able to find this within yourself, or imagine being with a perfectly compassionate being who understands you and what you're going through. (See 'Creating a compassionate companion to help at times of distress and difficulty' in Chapter 2.) Imagine what they would say and what they would do that would bring a sense of comfort and ease to your suffering. Imagine them drawing entirely alongside you as you struggle with your parenting task at this moment in time.

As you draw alongside what's hard, think about:

- Bringing empathy to your distress. Acknowledge what you are thinking or feeling and how it is affecting you – how hard it is to feel split between two places and more than one child, for example. Remember that this would be hard for anyone – no one expects to have to do this as a parent. Finding it hard is understandable and neither a fault nor a weakness.

- Focusing compassionately on the whole picture. Notice what your mind is being pulled to focus on. You may be focusing solely on all the things you feel you've failed at or have missed out on. Think about what is also helpful to pay attention to, such as all the times you have felt like you have been a good parent or done something wonderful for your children.

- Nurturing compassionate thinking. You might also notice you are currently quite self-critical or taking on a huge responsibility for events as a parent. When under situations of threat, the way we think changes and can become very absolute, unkind towards ourselves or catastrophic in terms of what might happen. *Consider what a wise, non-judgemental and caring response would be to your situation right now.* For example, 'You are in a very difficult situation that is not your fault. You are doing the best you can in these circumstances for all your children, even though it can be hard to accept that about yourself. This situation feels like it will last forever, but it won't be forever.'

TAKING COMPASSIONATE ACTION

It is important to think about what action you can take to reduce your distress. This is not just about being 'nice' but also thinking about how you can act in a way that is wise, courageous and supportive towards yourself right now, in your parenting role. Being open to experiencing care and support from others, and also directing this support towards yourself in tangible ways, can help when you're overwhelmed or struggling. This may involve seeking support for help with children at home, or company to help you whilst you are supporting your baby in neonatal care. It may also mean being able to place firm boundaries around what you can and can't do in this situation right now, to enable you to cope.

SUMMARY

Being a parent or being responsible for other children whilst having a baby in neonatal care is a huge task. This chapter has looked at ways you can help your children understand what's happening, help them understand and manage their feelings, and nurture a compassionate response towards yourself in your parenting role. Remember, there are lots of people to help you as you get through this period as a family, both on and off the unit, and you are not alone in moments where it feels overwhelming and hard. Take a look at some of these selected resources to support you on your next steps.

RESOURCES

Somewhere to find more information

Nell and the Neonatal Unit is a specially designed interactive app to help siblings become familiar with the neonatal unit through stories and games. It is available from major app providers. Follow the QR code.

Something to watch

'Neonatal siblings – A perspective' is a video of children talking candidly about their experience of having a sibling in neonatal care, produced by the neonatal charity **Spoons**: www.youtube.com/watch?v=9ozodynCmPQ

Something to listen to

'Let's talk siblings!' is a vCreate 20-minute podcast about how to integrate siblings into the neonatal journey with veteran parents and an experienced neonatal nurse. It is available on Spotify, Google Podcasts and other platforms.

Something to read

My Very Little Sister and the Very Big Story by **Alina Brett** was written and illustrated by a sibling about the time her sister spent on the neonatal unit, and talks about the experience, including the emotional journey, through the eyes of a younger child.

CHAPTER 8

Important conversations about care

FINDING WAYS TO TALK ABOUT WHAT MATTERS AND MAKING SIGNIFICANT DECISIONS

Whilst every day on the unit is punctuated by conversations and interactions with the team and other parents, there are some conversations that feel different. These include conversations that approach sensitive or distressing subjects, that address issues that may affect your baby's treatment planning or that begin to touch on perhaps unspeakable fears or doubts. Conversations like these are often layered with anxiety and apprehension as well as a hope for clarity and certainty.

Talking about difficult subjects can take place between you and the neonatal team, but will also be part of discussions with your partner or close family and friends. The first part of this chapter will address how to approach and manage important conversations when things are difficult to talk about, looking at:

- The challenges of talking about topics that cause pain and distress, and how avoidance can prolong it
- How to talk to your partner or supportive others and your neonatal team when it's hard
- Managing conversations with your wider family, with a focus on where this might be difficult
- What to do if you don't feel ready to have these conversations.

Important conversations can be the precursor to a decision-making process, whether it's making a plan or a decision that's key to your baby's course of treatment. Whilst we have touched on some aspects of decision making in Chapter 4, there are some decisions that bring up a range of quite different thoughts and emotions, and there may be times when your wishes about your parental role and degree of involvement may change. In this chapter we will look at when there are more complex or challenging decisions to be made during your baby's admission, and explore ways to support your discussions and thinking. We will focus on:

- Where to start when making significant decisions about your baby
- Factors to consider in shared decision making – the practicalities and what you need to know to act in line with your parenting values.

ENGAGING IN IMPORTANT CONVERSATIONS – APPROACHING EMOTIONAL PAIN AND DIFFICULTY

For most of us there is a natural tendency to shy away from things that are painful and difficult to talk about. We may be apprehensive about what it would mean to go towards the very things we want to avoid (e.g., discussing whether the suggested treatment is working or whether we want to consent to an operation that has significant risks). This presents us with a dilemma – as circumstances around us continue to require discussion, thought and decisions, we can, on the one hand, continue to avoid them, even as the situation becomes more complex or, on the other, we can choose to move towards the things that are difficult. Coping by avoiding has limits, and the risk of putting off important conversations is that events might overtake you, leaving you less equipped when it matters.

The first task for yourself and perhaps others around you is to be honest about what the 'elephants' in the room are. As you think about your situation, what do you find yourself instinctively backing away from? It's important to do this from a place of compassionate understanding towards yourself – and others. You are asking yourself to go towards a place of pain and uncertainty, but with the motivation to alleviate some of the distress and confusion you may feel in the longer term.

Let's look at some ways that important conversations can be difficult during neonatal care for the families of baby Kian, Lottie and Hanna.

Teddy was engaged in the everyday care of his son Kian, and to some degree was feeling relaxed about being on the unit, chatting every day to the nurses, and beginning to feel more confident as a father. However, Kian had had a brain injury at birth that Teddy had not been able to think about or acknowledge. Whilst the team were flexible and trying to adapt to his pace in terms of what he could manage, as planning for home was approaching they needed to talk to Teddy about Kian's ongoing needs and plan for support. The more time went on, the more anxious the team became, and the more Teddy avoided ward rounds with the doctors. For Teddy there were other important conversations he wasn't having. At home he avoided his wife's company when they might be alone, busying himself with household tasks and watching TV late into the evening. In fact, since Kian was born they hadn't talked together about what had happened during the birth or during the admission to the unit.

Tamara and Paul's baby Lottie arrived during a difficult time in their relationship. Their discussions often resulted in arguments, and Paul found it hard to keep his temper when Tamara was anxious, finding it hard to understand and empathize with her. This had led her to withdraw from sharing how she was feeling, causing her to feel resentful and uncared for, particularly whilst she was recovering from birth. Paul wanted to find a way to talk about him seeing his friends and finding ways to cope that were different to Tamara's, but resorted to going missing for extended parts of the day instead, because he felt Tamara wasn't able to grant him permission to be absent from the unit. The tension between them was making caring for Lottie challenging, and they started to avoid time with her together.

Hanna's mum Lena felt a sense of panic every time she was asked to speak to the team in the unit's 'quiet room'. She knew there were many worries about Hanna's feeding and that the team were advising a gastrostomy tube; however, she couldn't imagine what her baby girl would look like or be like with a tube fitted. She felt the pressure to make a decision was overshadowing all her time with Hanna, and started to feel less warm towards her. Her partner Danya was keen to go ahead with the procedure, but felt that she couldn't share her opinions for fear of coming across as unsupportive.

The potential impact of avoiding or delaying difficult conversations

For all the couples, the absence of sharing and discussing what was happening for them had a number of unintended consequences, both for their personal relationships and for those with the team. In Paul and Tamara's situation their difficulties in talking together and understanding each other's perspective reduced opportunities for meaningful emotional support from each other and generated other difficult feelings such as resentment and feeling isolated, patterns that went back many years before they found themselves in hospital. These feelings they held individually also meant that they found it much harder to be compassionate to each other or motivated to help one another. Tamara was fearful that by being honest and open Paul would reject her, and Paul feared that Tamara would be unable to manage without him as a constant presence, making him unable to access what he needed. Lena's partner Danya was afraid to voice her support of a decision she felt would benefit Hanna because it may have come across as being unsupportive. Danya agonized over how to approach the subject sensitively, but often found herself frustrated with Lena and angry about the reasons for her reluctance. Meanwhile Hanna continued to struggle, and Danya felt she was failing her.

Feeling alone with emotional experiences and fears of talking about them

For Teddy and his partner, not being able to talk about the traumatic events and outcomes at Kian's birth meant that both of them had difficulty knowing what the other was really thinking and feeling about the situation. They suffered on their own with an uncertainty of how their experiences would be received or understood by each other. They both felt in their own ways that keeping things going was fundamental, and they were fearful that talking about what had happened to them and Kian would be so devastating that they wouldn't be able to cope, jeopardizing their chances of going home on schedule. At the same time, they were aware that not talking about it and what Kian would need to be looked after on discharge could also delay going home – the situation felt stuck. In reality there was no way forward that felt easy, but they recognized that capacity and opportunities for joint problem solving were significantly reduced, both with each other (in terms of how they could be helpful together in an emotionally supportive way) and with the team (who couldn't meet with Teddy to talk about his worries, as he avoided them).

Danya found that Lena's reluctance to talk to the team about moving forwards made her feel increasingly angry towards her, both as a partner and her perception that as a mother she wasn't fulfilling her role to protect her daughter. She started to talk to doctors when she was on the unit alone, and the gap in communication between her and Lena meant she was questioning how they would ever be able to parent together.

There are often many parallels between what's tricky communicating between partners and what's tricky communicating between the parents and the clinical team. Whilst there can be clear pathways around communication and formal meetings, there is often the question of when is the right time to talk about what. If the conversations are avoided, just like for the couples we've met, it can reduce the opportunity to think together with the team creatively to understand and help, and it can also lead to a situation where there is time pressure when a decision might need to be made. Being able to approach difficult conversations helps issues to be 'out in the open'. In this way, your needs and those of your baby can be met more easily and problems addressed quickly before they feel too overwhelming.

DIFFICULT CONVERSATIONS

Approaching difficult conversations with your partner or supportive others

Sometimes subjects or scenarios are so painful, traumatic or anxiety provoking that fear of talking about them is a significant fear all of its own. Remember, you would have approached them already if it had been easy. As you go towards them, remember that it will take courage, and you may want to look back at Chapter 2 ('Connecting with your compassionate mind') to remind yourself of some of the features of a compassionate response that you need for yourself.

Consider extending that compassion to others you care about – your partner or family member who is in this position with you, and your baby who is at the centre of your thinking and decision making. In this section we will talk about a partner, but there may be another family member such as a parent or auntie who holds this position in your circumstances, and much of this applies to important conversations with them too.

When having an important conversation with your partner, you might want to consider the following:

- Clarify for yourself what the difficult topics or issues are and perhaps order them in terms of how hard you find them to approach or talk about. Invite your partner to do the same.

- Let your partner know what the conversation is about so they have time to prepare: 'There are some things that weigh so heavily on my mind we haven't spoken about that I need to let you know/think about with you'.

- Find a protected and private time as much as possible.

- Let each other know what you need to make the conversation work for you: 'I'd like you to listen to my list without judging me or trying to fix it for the moment', 'I need you to respond in a way that shows me you understand how I'm thinking and feeling', 'I need you to help me feel safe right now if I start to feel very frightened'.

- Be open and honest about your fears (the very ones that may have led you to avoid the conversation to start with): 'I'm really frightened that if I share how I'm feeling you'll think I'm a bad person/parent', 'I'm worried you'll just minimize it and tell me I'm being ridiculous', 'I feel ashamed about feeling this way and can't bear the idea you'd feel the same'.

- Put some parameters around the conversation if you're fearful it will become about something else or get side-tracked: 'I know we need to think about the needs of all the children, but it's important to me we can just focus on the twins at the moment'.

- Given the conversation is likely to bring up powerful feelings, take some time to agree how you will manage these together: 'If I'm tearful, can you come and sit closer to me and hold my hand?' 'If I start getting stressed or angry, can I have a couple of minutes to calm myself and then carry on?' The key here is supportive containment and emotional connection.

- Think about what you're doing afterwards so that you feel you have the time you need to transition back into the next part of your day/evening.

- Make time to follow up on the conversation again – and stick to it. This shows a commitment to continue working on the hard things together. You may wish to make time to talk as part of your regular hospital routine.

Approaching difficult conversations with your neonatal team

The need to approach some important or difficult topics with the neonatal team may not always correlate with urgency or a big decision. Sometimes the need will be yours and sometimes the need will be theirs, and ideally discussions will be part of an ongoing relationship. Neonatal care involves a great deal of uncertainty and unpredictability, so some of the things you may wish to know may not have a straightforward answer, or there may only be an answer to the 'next step' – 'If they can manage on this new ventilator setting for the next 24 hours then this is what we will know...and then this is what we'll think about next...' What is central is the openness, honesty and compassion of everyone who cares for each other within this uncertainty and unpredictability.

It's also important to feel safe and comfortable to ask questions and voice concerns or fears. If you don't feel you are able to do this with anyone on the unit, you can ask who else within the hospital is able to help (e.g., your Patient Advice and Liaison Service, known as PALS). If you feel that there are things you are not talking about with the team that you would like to approach, the following can be helpful:

- Ask a general question in a ward round or routine discussion about how the team can support you: 'If there are things we want to discuss that are hard to ask or feel difficult to talk about, how can we do that with you?' 'Who is the best person to have this kind of conversation with on the unit?'

- A more direct approach may be needed so that the team is alerted to the need: 'I have some things weighing on my mind that we haven't talked about that are causing a lot of distress. I would find it helpful to know who can sit down with me and discuss them, and when they might be able to do that.'

- Consider making a list of the questions or topic areas so that the healthcare professional has time to think and prepare. If they are better equipped, then ultimately, so are you.

- Let the team member know how they can help you feel comfortable to talk about what matters to you by including some pointers on what they can do to support: 'I'd really value being able to express all my concerns about this even though I know the future is hard to predict at the moment', 'If I'm crying or distressed I'll let you know if I need to stop, but knowing you understand where I'm at and feel for me and our family is so important'.

- Think about who else might need to be part of the discussion, such as a spiritual or community leader or an advocate.

'What if I'm not ready to have these conversations?'

If your team would like to discuss issues with you that you don't feel ready for, it's important to be able to let them know your fears and reservations so you can work together. As we saw in the example with Teddy, being absent or continually steering conversations away from difficult areas can make it difficult for the team to know how to support the process most effectively, and they may inadvertently increase your distress by misunderstanding or misreading your situation (e.g., assuming that your absence means you are too busy rather than fearful). Remember, it is an understandable response to feel yourself pulling away from difficulty, but it is a *shared dilemma* with the neonatal team when they need to work with you.

If they raise having an important conversation that causes distress, the following can be helpful:

- Let the team know why it has been difficult for you to have the conversation to date: 'I've felt so angry we're in this situation due to a mistake that it's been hard to sit down again and feel like we can trust what you suggest next', 'Every time you suggest a review I think you're going to tell me there's nothing more you can do; it makes me terrified'.

- Establish the timelines for having the conversation so you can prepare:

'Does this need to happen right now or do I have some time?' And what it refers to specifically – further treatment options, changing direction of treatment or having surgery, for example.

- Ask if you are able to have the conversation with a consultant or other healthcare professional who you know and trust.
- Establish what the conversation is for – will it require an immediate decision or is it giving options/information?
- Ensure that there is support available for after the conversation takes place by actively making a plan together.

Important conversations with wider family and friends

The neonatal unit can feel like a 'bubble' from the outside world at times, where the intensity and detail of the discussions can be hard to convey to those who love and support you. Discussions can often be helpful and supportive with family and friends, giving you space to 'think out loud' with others as well as having a safe space to voice fears and concerns. However, there can be particular challenges when you're faced with a situation that might elicit strong views and opinions from your wider community, exerting additional pressure and distress in an already difficult situation.

Here are two mothers in very different situations with their family and wider community:

Cherry was undergoing a series of discussions about whether to consent to surgery for her little girl to have a tracheostomy (often referred to as a 'trachy'). The neonatal team felt that her daughter Destiny would be much more comfortable and be able to take part in many more activities to aid her development if she had the operation. However, Cherry's father was against the procedure and felt that the team should exhaust all further options before Cherry consented. Cherry reached out to her friends for help and advice as well as the surgical nurses on her unit who arranged with her to meet another family whose daughter had been through a similar procedure. At the same time she was receiving phone calls and messages from her parents' friends and family urging her to change hospitals and seek another opinion. Cherry struggled to express her views or needs to her parents' friends and she felt judged. She came to the neonatal team in distress, unsure how to reconcile the differences of opinion from a family who she relied on, not only emotionally but also financially.

Celia had consulted the views of her community at the church from the beginning of her stay in hospital, when she was on extended bed rest. She felt she needed their counsel and advice to cope with the decisions she was being asked to make, and found the regular chats with her pastoral team essential. When her little boy developed a severe infection requiring surgery, she asked for help in giving her strength and courage for what was ahead, but made the decisions about his care with her sister and the neonatal team.

For Cherry, her role as a mother with responsibility for her daughter was one that her family were struggling to adjust to and respect, and Cherry felt her younger age also played a part. Her family did not come into the hospital often to see her and Destiny and, despite Cherry's best efforts, they found it hard to understand the challenges she had overcome and that she faced ahead. Not only was the next step difficult due to decisions about surgery, but there was a real fear she would lose the support of her family, which added to her sense of threat and uncertainty about the future. All at once she felt she had a lot to lose whilst she battled to do what was best. For Celia, she had a community who supported her, but they did this with boundaries around what she asked and needed from them.

It's important to remember that there's no obligation to involve anyone you don't wish to be involved in important conversations or decisions. Some parents can come under considerable pressure to do so at a significant cost to their own wellbeing.

- Remember, they're *your* baby, and you are in the best position to know what's best for them. You also have a great deal more information, context and lived experience than those outside the neonatal unit who may not have encountered a preterm or unwell baby before.

- Decide where you need to put the boundaries with others – when you would like their views and when you wouldn't, limits around contact and types of contact (e.g., no phone calls or only replying to text messages at a certain time), or limits around the time, place or length of a conversation, for example. These boundaries might be part of a general picture in terms of how you would like to shape the relationships with your family now you are a parent.

- Tell those around you what you need from them explicitly: 'I need you to listen to what I am saying without judgement and to support me as a parent in this very difficult situation'.

- Give yourself permission to put the needs of your baby and yourself (or you and your partner) first. This may be new for you, and the change can feel difficult to start with. It's not selfish or uncaring to put the needs of you and your baby first; it's part of the transition in parenthood to a new set of priorities.

- Seek support from your neonatal team to help you if you're finding the dynamics with your wider family or community distressing. They can help in practical ways such as providing some information/education around clinical practice and approaches as well as working with you to limit contact, or support you with more helpful contact as needed.

- Consider giving your wider family tasks and roles that you feel comfortable with that meet their needs to be useful but in a way that feels appropriate and manageable – researching options for buggies or car seats for a baby with medical needs or looking at what support is available for you once you are back home in your area, for example.

We have thought together about navigating important discussions about difficult and distressing topics that you may have with your partner and the neonatal team and your wider community. These discussions often lead towards decisions at some juncture, and in the next section we will be exploring the process when those decisions are challenging or complex.

GETTING TO KNOW YOUR OWN DECISION-MAKING STYLE AND NEEDS

We make many thousands of decisions every day, some of which feel thoughtful and purposeful, and others that we might make instinctively or very quickly. As you are reading this chapter, you might start to think about the kind of decisions you've made at home as a parent, in your various other family roles, and in your job up to this point. You may have a particular way of making decisions or a certain style, or there may be very specific needs, such as having information presented visually rather than verbally. There is a great deal of variation in how people make decisions, including what they base those decisions on. Before arriving on the neonatal unit you will already have made many decisions about your baby's care in the course of your pregnancy and during their birth.

REFLECTING ON THE DECISIONS YOU'VE MADE SO FAR

Take a moment to reflect on the decisions you have made up to this point. You might want to consider some of these questions:

- What was making the decision/s like for you?
- Were there some that were harder than others?
- To what degree do you feel those decisions were shared with medical professionals and your family/friends, and to what degree do you feel you made them on your own?
- Did you feel like you had what you needed to help you make those decisions, and if not, what would that have looked like?
- What would have made the process of making those decisions easier?

Make a note of some of your responses and thoughts here:

....

....

....

....

....

....

....

....

....

....

The answers to these questions will be helpful in planning what you need now whilst your baby is in neonatal care, particularly as each family and each person within that family can have very different needs around decision making.

> David and Lydia felt they didn't have the information they needed antenatally to make a decision about intensive care or palliative care for their baby, and therefore they made the decision on the basis of what they had been *told* they needed

to know. Coming into the NICU had been a shock, and they experienced distress from a constant doubt they had 'done the right thing'.

Harleen felt that having many doctors and nurses giving inconsistent messages about what the next steps could be for her baby made it hard to make a joint decision. She was also unsure what she could decide, having little experience of being asked her views or thoughts in the past.

Thinking back to decisions already made often brings a range of emotions. Some parents describe feeling happy or even 'at peace' with the decisions they have made, whereas for others, thinking about previous decisions can bring some difficult feelings, such as regret, guilt, anxiety and shame. We touched on some of these feelings in Chapter 2, and how we can approach them compassionately from where we are now.

Part of the difficulty in evaluating decisions we have made in the past is that we think about them in the context of the present (perhaps when we have much more time or more information, or circumstances are very different to those the medical professionals or we could have predicted). In truth you will have made a decision that was the best you could have made at the time with the information you had and the people around you at that moment.

COMMON THEMES IN CONVERSATIONS ABOUT MAKING DECISIONS

As we come to think about making significant and complex decisions in the neonatal unit, there are themes that come up regularly for parents that might resonate with you:

- Wanting to make the decision that enables you to feel like a 'good parent' or that you have fulfilled your roles to the best of your ability
- Wanting to do the 'right' thing in your baby's best interests; this could be 'right' in the context of your ethical, moral, religious or cultural framework, and there can be conflicts between these
- Difficulties and distress when there may be a difference in viewpoint or even judgement from family and friends and/or those looking after your baby about the decisions you had made or are in the process of making

- Factors that influence your decision making that you might be aware of (such as your views about disability, life experiences around trusting those in positions of power) and those you might not be so aware of (such as how easy it might be for you to tolerate uncertainty or risk or to trust a medical professional)
- Fear of not having the right information, enough time or a way to think about the decisions you are facing
- Feeling the approaches, views and actions of the medical team are not consistent, which can lead to confusion
- Feeling too overwhelmed and in your 'threat' brain system to be able to think, reason or listen to what is being talked about.

When we think about having to make decisions, we often imagine that this will relate to just one thing or one area. In reality, the ways that decisions are made in neonatal care can be much more complex, particularly if your baby has a longer stay, which brings with it more complexity.

Let's look at the situation for Steve and Imani:

> Steve and Imani's baby Arib was born with a rare genetic condition that meant that his lifespan would be limited, but they did not have a clear sense of how long this might be or what this meant for him. They felt like the medical team were presenting information in a way that made them feel they were doing something wrong in actively pursuing treatment for him, and feared they were being talked about behind closed doors. Much of the focus of discussion was on end-of-life care and planning, but Steve and Imani also wanted to know what other choices and decisions they could make for their son. They realized that there were several parallel plans and decisions (including planning for if Arib survived his time in the neonatal unit) that would involve a lot of different professionals. They asked to have a meeting early on in his time on the unit to give them time to think through all the information and options as well as to involve key members and elders in their family and community in the process, allowing their religious and cultural values to be supported.

There's a lot of variation in how much parents want or feel able to be involved in decisions, and what kind of decisions these might be. You might have already noticed that there are some decisions you feel happier for the medical team to make, perhaps because you feel they have the knowledge and expertise in this area and therefore you feel they are best placed to make a judgement and take responsibility. There may be other areas where you feel your advocacy role as a parent is paramount and that you want to have more responsibility for the decision.

For most, when finding their way through a complex and emotionally charged decision-making process, having a consistent person or small group of people in the neonatal team who really know you and your baby and are emotionally sensitive and compassionate to help you make decisions is important. It might be helpful as you read this chapter to think about who that person or people might be in your unit.

HELP WHEN MAKING SIGNIFICANT DECISIONS ABOUT YOUR BABY

In this section we will explore the areas that are helpful to think about and/or discuss with others when faced with a significant decision about your baby. Whilst not exhaustive, these are some of the key areas that can be helpful if you aren't sure how to structure your thinking or make sense of the process.

We will explore the following:

- How able you feel to make the decision at this point in time, and the challenge of thinking at a time of high emotion
- Clarifying what the decision is you're making
- If this is a decision that can be shared with the team looking after your baby
- Thinking about what you need to know to make the decision
- Establishing your key values, beliefs, hopes and fears that inform this decision
- Working out who you need to support you in making this decision.

How able do you feel to be able to make the decision at this moment in time, and with the challenge of thinking at a time of high emotion?

Making significant decisions about your baby, whether they are ones that need to be made quickly or where you have more time, can leave many feeling in shock, overwhelmed emotionally and in a moral and/or spiritual crisis. A decision that could have lifelong or life-limiting consequences quite understandably puts you into a system of high threat, where you'll find your mind thinks in a certain way (see Chapter 2, 'The threat and self-protection system') as your whole system organizes around protection of yourself and loved ones. Whilst this can help you to escape immediate danger, it takes your 'thinking brain' offline, making it much harder to process information, pay attention and weigh up options (or any other complex mental activity involved in a multifaceted process). This is a tricky situation where you need to bring your thinking brain back online whilst still feeling a high sense of threat. At times you may have to make a decision or be part of a process when there is little time to feel calm or centred.

If you are experiencing disabling anxiety, it's important to ask your neonatal team if the decision to be made needs to be made straightaway. Remember, most decisions that involve absolute urgency are life-preserving decisions that are taken by the medical team. If the decision does need to be made or discussed imminently, you will need the team and those around you to help you be in the best state you can be to have that discussion.

FIRST STEPS TO HELP

- Recognize if you are currently unable to think (you may notice everything feeling 'fuzzy', unreal or jumbled), and let those around you know.
- Take some moments to help yourself regulate your threat response by using techniques that calm your physiological activation (such as the 'Soothing breathing rhythm' in Chapter 1 or other techniques in Chapter 2, 'Finding ways to a more soothed, safe and connected state', and the '5-4-3-2-1 grounding technique' exercise). Remind yourself compassionately that you are in a moment of extreme suffering and difficulty, and that you are doing the best you can.
- Be direct with your medical team about what they can do to help you feel more regulated (e.g., coming and sitting next to you, slowing down the pace, talking to you calmly, pausing when needed), and what is unhelpful for you right now.
- Bring others who might be in an easier position to listen to the information with you, and who know your preferences and values so they can help you articulate your wishes and summarize what is being said for you. Many parents report it being easier to take in information from those who are their closest and loved friends and family, who might also be able to summarize key messages and themes.
- Ask your team to write down or record any information that's critical so that you can look at it/listen to it when you feel more able to.
- Remember, your reactions are understandable and a reflection of how much your baby matters to you. Working with your responses as much as possible rather than judging them or 'willing them away' will help you to do the best that you can in the circumstances.

What is the decision you're making?

In the midst of complexity and many conversations, it can be easy to lose track of what you are being asked to make a decision about. Clarity around (1) what the decision/s to be made are right now and (2) what might be a further decision for another time or the next step is important so that you know where to focus your thinking, information gathering and time with healthcare professionals. You can ask the team to summarize the decisions to be made and your options and write them down where time allows. It is also helpful to understand as much as possible about the *context* of the decision being discussed – for example, when discussing options for treatment, is it one of many possibilities, is it fairly routine, or is there something more to consider about this decision, such as a significant change to a long-term outcome?

It can, of course, be extremely difficult when you are faced with several options, none of which you feel you wish to choose, and this section is designed to help 'unpack' what the options are, even in these sorts of circumstances. Typically, for decisions in specific situations that need informed consent (e.g., for a surgical procedure), there is more clarity and written information to help you. For more complex decisions or those that might be referred to as being in a 'grey area' – where there may be less of an established 'map', for example both you and the neonatal team will be holding varying degrees of uncertainty and making many decisions at multiple levels.

Is this a decision that can be shared with the team looking after your baby?

Shared decision making (SDM) is a collaborative approach where you work with your neonatal team to reach decisions about treatment in a way that recognizes your expertise as a parent (and your values and beliefs and the context of your life) and their medical knowledge and experience. In general, SDM has been found to lead to better quality decisions and provide an opportunity for decisions to best align with values, and as a result there is a move towards this as a model of good practice in the neonatal setting.

SDM is a *process*, and for some significant decisions it can be a lengthy one. Sharing a decision-making process works best in relationships with a healthcare professional where you feel you have trust and confidence in their expertise and a sense that they can be honest and open with you, as well as emotionally supportive. You are likely to have spent time establishing who those professionals are for you already in your 'core team', even if this is not a formal arrangement.

Whilst SDM can be a very helpful and important process, there may be times when you would rather the decision was made either by the neonatal team or by yourself. What you can decide on wholly by yourself will be guided by certain legal parameters in certain situations, and your team can explain these to you so you can know in an open and transparent way where your choices and decisions lie. If you have a differing view on a significant decision between you and your partner, you may need help to work your way through this, such as with a psychological professional, to think through the situation together and find a way forward. In some situations where it is difficult for you to come to an agreement, either with your neonatal team or between yourself and your partner, you may also benefit from the assistance of a medical mediator – professionals who are trained specifically to help in situations where it feels things may have reached an impasse.

There may also be circumstances where you may wish the neonatal team to make the decision for you, for example, when to move away from active treatment. Many parents feel that they don't want to have the responsibility for some decisions and need them to be taken by someone else they trust. It is always helpful to be open with your team about where you feel you're at emotionally so they can take their direction from you. Part of being open is also acknowledging that you may change your mind about your involvement, and establishing how best to manage this between you.

What do you need to know to help you make the decision?

Having thought a bit about what has been helpful in the past (see 'Getting to know your own decision-making style and needs'), consider what you feel you need to know to make decisions now. Whilst the neonatal team will have information that they will standardly share with you, it's helpful to work out what you need to know and how it's shared with you. Some like the 'big picture', others all the details, and you might also think about whether you would like the conclusion or significant decision to make at the beginning of the conversation or after all the information that puts it in context. Let your healthcare professional know so they can tailor their time with you appropriately.

If this is your first conversation, some things you may want to know could include:

- Details about the nature of the problem in simple language, and available options for treatment. It can be helpful to break this down into chunks, with regular opportunities to check everyone is at the same place in their understanding.

- The team's experience of having done something before or having been in a similar situation and/or knowledge of what happens, step by step. This can help with anxiety as there is a 'trodden path' to give you a bit of a framework.

- Statistics on risk and benefits and what the significance of these are in the short and longer term. Whilst doctors cannot give you precise statistics for your baby, they will use statistics from research with babies who share characteristics with your baby to help give a picture of outcomes.

- Where appropriate, what these outcomes might look like in everyday life terms, including what matters most to you for your family. Again, whilst doctors can't give absolutes, they can use the information they have to give you a broad picture, also acknowledging that there can be significant variability between babies.

- The experience for your baby in going through a procedure, course of treatment or redirection of care. This is important as a parent, both in terms of preparing yourself for what's to come and also thinking ahead about how you can support your baby.

- What it entails practically – in terms of length of time in hospital, level of care (which may require a move in or between units), returning home with frequent clinic visits/medical equipment or a change from active treatment to palliative care, for example.

- Next steps – what you can expect to happen next and within what period of time.

A lot of information about statistics and outcomes can be complex, and not everyone has the skills or knowledge to 'translate' these facts into something that makes sense or gives a picture of what it might look like in reality. If you find yourself wondering about these things, ask your doctor or nurse to make the translation for you in a way that is helpful. Talk to your team about *how* they give you this information in terms of format and context – for example, if you would prefer it visually such as using a pie chart, or put in a certain way such as outcomes in terms of number of children in a class/school affected.

Information gathering is not a one-way process, so don't be afraid to ask the question/s that are really bothering or frightening you – for example, 'Will my baby have a risk of dying or having a disability?' Many parents sit with these questions by themselves for a very long time, and can find they are worrying about something that is, in fact, unlikely, or that they are trying to solve or think through the implications of an outcome without having the facts to help them to do that.

There may be times when something is being explained to you where you feel you don't understand, and again, it's important to remember that no question is 'silly', even if it makes you embarrassed that you don't know the answer or feel like you've been unable to take in what's been said to you. What's important is that you feel you've found a way with those helping you to understand, even if it's many conversations down the line.

What are your key values, beliefs, hopes and fears that inform this decision?

Values, beliefs, hopes and fears underpin all our decision making, but particularly when decisions are significant and potentially life-changing. Acting in accordance with your values and beliefs is important in the short and longer term as values tend to be consistent across time, even when circumstances change. In earlier chapters we have thought together about what your values and beliefs are about parenting. Here you might be thinking about your values in relation to something specific, such as quality of life, experiences of pain and suffering, or in broad terms, about what's important for family life. You may hold beliefs around the will of a god, your purpose/role as a parent, what it means to be a 'good parent', or what happens after death. Ideally your clinical team will have learnt about your values and beliefs as part of forming a strong collaborative relationship with you; however, there may be specific aspects of your beliefs that need highlighting and clarifying – to others and perhaps also for yourself.

Once you know what decisions you are being asked to make, take some time to think about your values and beliefs, and let the team know so they can link these to what's being discussed in a meaningful way.

Let's look at Leo's story:

> Leo believed very strongly that being a good parent meant protecting his baby Storm from unnecessary suffering. What felt most meaningful to him in the discussions with the team was really understanding the options available to ensure her comfort as well as what procedures and checks were in place to spot pain or discomfort straightaway. The consultant spent time going through different ways they could help with pain, and showed him ways he could also support his baby girl.

Holding on to hope is very hard but often important to help manage. Healthcare professionals will hold hope with you, at the same time as wanting to let you know what might happen if things change – these two positions can seem like they conflict, but in fact work alongside each other. It's also possible to make a decision based on the most probable outcome, but also hold on to hope that there might be a different outcome (e.g., planning for supporting a child with likely significant motor difficulties whilst also hoping that they will make excellent progress, and doing all you can to facilitate this).

Often our hopes intersect with our values as circumstances and meanings change – for example, a 'good' parent might also be one who makes sure their baby has the best care, that they are well looked after and loved, even if they can't change the outcome.

Who do you need to support you in making this decision?

In Chapter 4 we talked about considering those on the unit you feel most comfortable and safe with, and some questions to help you identify them. Take a moment to look back at this list and think about who these people would be now that you are facing a significant decision. Talk to these people on the unit about when they will be available, and whether there is flexibility and time to have discussions when they're next on shift. You can request the presence of a religious leader or representative if this is important to you, as well as members of your support network outside the hospital. Your baby's nurse will accompany you to discussions about their care, and they are often key people who can go back through the detailed discussions bit by bit to help you process and think about them, if time allows. Many parents find talking about decisions with a peer support worker helpful, particularly one who's been through something similar and can perhaps offer a different perspective. You may also benefit from the help of a psychological professional at some or all stages of a complex decision-making process, and this is very much part of their role on a neonatal unit. They can accompany you to meetings and help the team to help you.

SUMMARY

In this chapter we have thought about how you can approach areas that may feel extremely difficult to talk about and make decisions with those around you. Whilst you will have hopefully found something helpful to start these discussions, it's important to remember that they are a process, and one that happens in the context of the relationships you have with others. It's easy to look back and think you may have chosen a different path or done something different, but remember to practise self-compassion. You've done your upmost to decide what is best for your baby and your family, often in the most difficult of circumstances.

RESOURCES

Somewhere to find more information

'Difficult conversations: 4 simple steps you can take to arrive' by **Dr Ray Owen** gives top tips on principles for difficult conversations using ideas from Acceptance and Commitment Therapy (ACT) that can be used with neonatal teams and family members: https://contextualconsulting.co.uk/resources/difficult-conversations-4-simple-steps-you-can-take-to-arrive-dr-ray-owen?utm_source=chatgpt.com

Something to watch

'Shared decision making' from **Kate Nelson** on the **Courageous Parents Network** is a useful summary from research with parents about decision making, what parents learn about being a decision maker, using peer support judiciously, and changes in the process over time: https://courageousparentsnetwork.org/video-library/video-topics/shared-decision-making

Something to listen to

'Choice and voice: Family perspectives on decision-making for children with medical complexity' is an in-depth episode for parents and professionals from **OPENPediatrics** addressing many of the issues in this chapter based on research with families: https://soundcloud.com/openpediatrics/choice-and-voice-family-perspectives-on-decision-making-for-children-with-medical-complexity

Something to read

A Parent's Guide: Making Critical Care Choices for Your Child from **Together for Short Lives**. Even if you are not facing these kinds of decisions, this is a useful guide to conversations, plans and care choices: www.togetherforshortlives.org.uk/app/uploads/2018/01/FamRes-Parents-Guide-to-Critical-Care-Choices.pdf

CHAPTER 9

Coping with difficult events on the neonatal unit

With a baby in hospital, fear of danger and change is never far away. It can be helpful to know about common difficult events to help you feel prepared ahead of time, or to manage when they happen. In this chapter we will look at coping with some of the things that happen to your baby (such as them having to have an operation) and events that you may witness (such as the death of another baby on the ward). We will think together about how you might help yourself to cope with these events, and action you can take to look after yourself emotionally.

This chapter focuses on some specific events and circumstances that can be particularly distressing and challenging:

- Moving between different areas of the unit (also applicable to other transitions such as moving between units)
- When a baby on the unit dies
- When there is an emergency on the unit
- When your baby needs surgery
- When your baby is in pain or distress.

MOVING BETWEEN DIFFERENT AREAS OF THE UNIT

Although moving from one room or area of the unit to another can seem like a simple event, it is often experienced as a mixed emotional situation at best and, at worst, anxiety provoking, even when the move is a 'good' move to a lower level of care. The unit will make every effort to let you know when your baby has been moved; however, this can happen at short notice or when you aren't present. Whilst you may be feeling relief that your baby has improved and a sense that home is closer now you are out of intensive care, you are still adapting to a significant change, even if it's only the other side of a corridor.

Here are some common challenges neonatal parents describe, and the steps they can take to help overcome these:

Challenges	Next steps to help
The space you have created for your baby as their temporary home (and yours) is disrupted and will need to be recreated.	Recreate the space as soon as is practically possible, selecting key items that need to be there first as a priority. Ensure anything that can travel with you (such as drawer units) are treated with care and privacy as they are likely to contain personal items.
Staff may change and this can cause a disruption to close and supportive relationships. You may also see a change to the staffing ratios (how many nurses look after how many babies), staffing experience and seniority, which can be anxiety provoking.	Check with your team which nurses might work across more than one area of the unit so you know whether to expect them to look after your baby again. You'll often find that those you've built close relationships with will come by to see how you are and may be able to support you via other aspects of their role (such as a breastfeeding champion). If you are worried about the experience of the nurses in the room, it can be helpful to raise this directly with them so they can let you know more about what care they are trained to provide, how this fits with what your baby needs at this moment in time, and how they can escalate concerns. Remember, help is always at hand, and anyone can raise a concern about a baby.
Parents around you who provide peer support may also change, meaning you lose those moments of connection and understanding you have had more regularly as part of being physically closer.	Support of other parents is pivotal, so be careful not to leave this to chance if you move on a unit. Schedule regular breaks and tasks together (e.g., expressing milk, memory making over a cup of tea in the parents' room) and use technology to keep the thread of connection throughout the day.
You may be mixing with parents who have had very different experiences to you (such as a shorter stay), particularly if you are stepping down from a long period in intensive care. This can bring up feelings such as loneliness, resentment and jealousy as well as that others around you aren't able to relate to your journey.	Validate the range of emotions you feel as you see those who have had a different journey to you. It's okay to feel these emotions, and they are often an expression and acknowledgement of pain and loss. Many parents find their longstanding friendships are those that matter most and that they don't form new relationships with parents in other nurseries. Others find helpful but different elements in both.

The fabric of your surroundings will change, leading to a loss of familiar anchors such as lighting, sounds or even the spacing of the room.	Take time to adjust to the impact of a new environment. You may find that the sensory changes cause a heightened level of stress or can be triggering. Share your baby's preferences and needs for their environment with your nurse, and monitor how they are coping with the adjustment so you can also plan for their needs in your new space.
The routine of the room, rhythm and pace can change, which can be a challenge when you have worked hard on being within these and may need to modify them (or they are being changed by others).	These foundational areas are when change can feel very unsettling and may produce significant anxiety. Share your routines with the team as soon as possible, and explore how they can be facilitated in your new space. If you have a summary of everything you've learnt about your baby and details about your family for new staff members, share this as soon as possible – this may be a laminated sheet for the cot/incubator or something that sits in your baby's notes.
You may be anxious that your baby will deteriorate and find it difficult to adjust to a lower level of monitoring. This can result in similar feelings to those you might have had nearer the beginning of your stay, which might feel at odds with the level of risk perceived or experienced by others.	Remember that an increase in uncertainty, fear of the unknown and loss of familiar signals of safety (such as monitors) can increase anxiety. Each adjustment takes time and can be approached in a graded way. Your neonatal team can help you to become more confident in reading your baby's cues, and to follow their enhanced ability to communicate with you and enjoy time interacting in their new state of medical need. Be gentle with your expectations of yourself and your baby as you make this adjustment and discovery together.

If you are moving back up to intensive care from a period in lower intensity, this can also be very distressing, particularly if your baby has become more unwell. Here are some common challenges that emerge with this transition, and some steps that can help to overcome them:

Challenges	Next steps to help
Fear of something catastrophic happening.	A lot of thoughts or images about scary outcomes is one product of your brain's threat system doing its best to help in a situation where things feel frightening and out of control. You can manage these thoughts in several ways, such as making a distinction between thoughts and facts, finding ways to diffuse their impact, or concentrating on activating your soothing system to help you feel safer and more contained, which will, in turn, influence how you think (look back at Chapter 2 for ideas). Remind yourself of the small gains and victories of the place you are in now with your baby, and let your team know what you need to help you through this very difficult moment. If your baby's outcome looks like it might change, this needs a different approach (you can read about this in Chapter 10).
Your baby looking very different or having much less capacity than they did to interact with you (e.g., post-surgery).	Acknowledge and validate how hard it is to lose some of the things that have given you joy and connection. Remind yourself that your baby is still the same person with the personality and character you've begun to see, even if they are unable to show you that right now. You might want to sit next to them and tell them what's happening and of all the things you're looking forward to doing again, once they're ready. Remind yourself that the equipment such as breathing support is likely to be temporary in many situations.
Feeling like all progress has been lost – for you and for your baby.	A move back to intensive care can feel like it's 'back to square one'. Remember that you and the team will know so much more about your baby now than when they were in NICU before, and that they are receiving the care they need in the right place with the right expertise. Feeling overwhelmed and experiencing some of the painful and frightening emotions you felt when they were in NICU before is very distressing. Remind yourself that it's okay to need extra support, and that if things feel worse for a while, it won't mean they stay that way forever. Think about what made the difference in helping you feel better before without putting pressure on yourself to perhaps do any more than get through each day, hour by hour, when it's tough.

You can also apply some of these principles if your baby is due to move to paediatric intensive care (PICU), a paediatric ward, or moving from one hospital to another. Think about what is important to you and your family, and share this with your current and new teams so they can help you plan the transition thoughtfully.

WHEN A BABY ON THE UNIT DIES

When a baby from another family dies on the unit, the impact can be far-ranging. You may feel extreme sadness for them and their family, anxiety that this might happen to your baby, or perhaps relief that your baby is not in the same situation. Often the feelings can make parents feel guilty – particularly when they have feelings and thoughts that centre around the theme of 'Thank goodness that wasn't my baby'. You will also be witnessing the emotional reactions of staff, and this may impact how you experience the care you receive, or at the very least, the 'emotional temperature' of the unit.

If the baby has died in the same nursery, you may have witnessed attempts to save the baby's life and the raw grief and distress of the parents. Even though these events have not happened to you, they can still leave you feeling very shaken, upset or even traumatized. You may experience intrusive thoughts about what you've seen, elevated fear and anxiety and accompanying physical reactions. For some parents the death of a baby in their nursery can mean it's very difficult to come back to the room again, and to interact and feel comfortable with another baby and family who occupy their place. Other ripple effects, such as feeling perhaps less confident in the clinical team, or feeling like the hospital is less of a safe place, are common. It is a lot to deal with in addition to your own situation, and it's important not to minimize or invalidate your experience.

What can help?

Self-criticism and feeling guilty or in some way wrong for your response can cause more distress in already difficult circumstances. Remind yourself that your range of emotions, including those that can feel 'selfish', are normal and a reflection of your desire and need to protect your own children and the safety of your family. If you are feeling very fearful about what could happen to your baby, take time to remind yourself that much as you feel for the baby who has died, the situation with your baby is most likely different. It can be helpful to make a list of all the things you know of that are dissimilar about your situation and your baby, and to remember that even if your baby's medical situation *appears* similar, there may also be many things you aren't aware of that aren't. It can be hard when the neonatal team are not able to give you the information about the baby who has died you feel might put your mind at rest, but remember that they are looking after confidential information in the same way they safeguard it for your family.

Allow yourself recovery time after the event, and be gentle with the parts of you that need to rest, regroup or perhaps need some extra care and reassurance. You might feel it's helpful to find a way to mark the death of the baby yourself, as well as express your condolences to the family, and for some this shared experience of loss and sorrow can be helpful. Equally, give yourself permission to refocus on your baby or to move back physically and emotionally from the situation if it's feeling too difficult at this point in time. It doesn't mean you don't feel or care for the baby who has died, but that you are focusing your limited energy and capacity on your own child, and limiting your exposure to further distress.

WHEN THERE IS AN EMERGENCY ON THE UNIT

When the alarm sounds, the whole unit is on alert and ready to respond. If you aren't in the nursery, there can be several disorientating and frightening minutes between hearing the alert and discovering your own baby is safe and well. At other times, you may find that it is your baby who needs urgent assistance and you may have been there watching as events unfold and the alarm is raised. Emergencies tend to happen more often in higher levels of care and are part of being in an uncertain and changing situation (you may hear the phrase 'two steps forwards and one step back' a lot). However, they take their toll as a significant event can be life-threatening. Whilst these events are well practised by the clinical team, the terror felt by parents who may be seeing something like it for the first time is undeniable.

What can help?

If the alarm sounds and it is not for your baby, compassionately acknowledge your stress response and help yourself to come back to a place of equilibrium, both emotionally and physically. You might want to hold your baby or be close to them and block out the activity around you by using a screen, or strategically placing your body or chair so you can focus on your baby. Let yourself know kindly that you were ready for action but now it's okay to stand down and that the emergency is not related to your baby. If you have found some of the calm/safe place exercises helpful (see Chapter 2, 'Safe place imagery'), this might be a good opportunity to imagine you and your baby in that safe place, away from the unit. You may wish or be asked to step out of the room whilst the team are attending to the emergency. Take this time to reconnect with anchors of safety for you and for your situation.

If it is your baby who needs an emergency intervention, remember that you are able to stay in the room if you wish (although you might be asked to give the medical team some space), or you can step outside if you choose. Many parents find these emergency events extremely distressing and can feel a range of stress responses (e.g., fight, flight, freeze, fawn or faint). It can also be particularly hard if your baby is being held by you at the time, or if you're involved in feeding or any of their 'cares'. It may feel like you're watching what's happening from far away, or things might feel 'dream like'.

These are all common responses to traumatic events, so try not to judge them – they are your brain's way of helping you to cope in extreme stress. As much as possible the clinical team will let you know what they are doing whilst they are helping your baby, although their priority and focus will be on their baby. You might find that if there is an additional member of the team in the room, they can narrate what is happening for you at the time.

Once your baby is stable again, the team will talk you through what happened and help you to understand it, which can involve putting events and information in order, and the rationale for the clinical decisions that were made. You will also be able to ask questions and raise any concerns you may have. If you don't feel able to take part in this conversation so close to the event, and need time to recover and be with your baby, you can reschedule this for another time. Bear in mind that due to shift changes you might have some time constraints if you'd like to speak to the same people who helped on the day together.

It can understandably take time to feel safe again after an emergency, and you are likely to find yourself hypervigilant (on alert and unable to relax) for a while, as well as potentially experiencing images, thoughts and other memories of the event that might come into your mind suddenly, sleep disturbance and wanting to avoid reminders such as being in the nursery, particular people, or holding your baby again if they were having a cuddle or contact with you at the time. Typically, these reactions ease over time, and you can refer back to 'First steps to help' in 'Traumatic events and experiences' and 'Finding ways to a more soothed, safe and connected state' in Chapter 2 for more on how to help.

It can help to talk through what has happened with others and to remind yourself of how the event ended, for example, what you know now. You can seek help from a psychological professional on your unit if you are struggling after an emergency, and they can support you to process what has happened and feel more comfortable being back with your baby again.

WHEN YOUR BABY NEEDS SURGERY

The need for surgery can be part of a care plan that you know about in advance or something that's required more urgently. You will have a sense from your neonatal team about how routine the surgery your baby needs is, and the degree of risk from conversations and decision making that's taken place. Although as a parent it can be inconceivable that your baby can have surgery safely when they are so small and fragile, there are specialist surgeons who are experienced in operating on babies, mostly in specialist centres. This might mean that you have to move hospital temporarily for the operation to take place, which can add to the distress of the situation (see 'Moving between different areas of the unit' in Chapter 9 and 'Transition to home via another neonatal unit or paediatric ward' in Chapter 12).

What can help?

- Meet your baby's surgeon before they operate. In most cases you can meet the person who will be performing the operation, and as well as the information they can share with you, it can be helpful to get a sense of them as another human being who will treat your baby with skill and care. It can also be helpful to see them talking and interacting with your baby, and taking the time to learn about them from you as well as the medical facts.

- Talk through with the neonatal team each step of the process, what your role is and how you can be involved. This could include whether you can be with your baby when they 'go under', when you will be required to separate from your baby (e.g., can you go down to theatre with them if you wish?), approximately how long they will be in theatre and when they will contact you after they've finished. For many parents it's important to be there to welcome their baby back to the unit, even if they are still sedated, and to keep their baby's experience in mind and in the mind of others throughout.

- Think about rituals, activities, prayers/blessings, etc. that you might want to go through with your baby before they go to theatre and when they return, such as prayers of protection, calling on guardian or protector spirits or ancestral figures or enhancing imagery that places them in the protective arms or presence of those who love them. If you have protective symbols, they may not be able to be with your baby directly, but you can discuss how they may be accommodated in the clinical environment. Spend some time planning what you'd like to do when they come back to the unit – reading them a chapter of your favourite book, singing them a special song or taking a photo for memory making that reminds you they are safe, for example. Think about what words you would like to say to them before you have to part. Often something simple like 'I love you' and 'See you soon' can make this tricky moment a little more manageable.

Finding ways to imagine your baby surrounded with love and protection when they are having an operation

- Planning ahead for the time your baby will be in theatre is key, particularly if the operation is likely to be long. Making a written plan that takes account of the time hour by hour (including what you will do beforehand and after, if you wish) can be containing when it feels like an overwhelming experience. You may not wish to leave the hospital or the nearby area, but many parents find the wait in hospital canteens or corridors creates additional stress and anxiety. If you stay in the hospital and quiet, solace and spiritual space is important, you can see if the chapel or prayer room is available to you (it is available for those who have a religion and also for those who do not). Some chapels allow you to light a candle for your baby or add their name to a book for prayer or to be held in people's thoughts. Other parents find doing something physical like taking a walk is helpful as well as soothing connection, such as the company of family and friends. You may wish to add in some time for refreshment and rest as it's often harder to leave again once your baby has returned to the ward. If anxiety impacts your appetite, try to help your body keep going through drinks such as smoothies or milkshakes, and eat small amounts rather than trying a whole meal at once.

WHEN YOUR BABY IS IN PAIN OR DISTRESS

Seeing your baby in pain or distress is one of the most difficult things for any parent to witness. You might wish you could take their place and prevent them from having to go through such a difficult course, or feel like you are failing as a parent in some way. You might also feel a fierce protectiveness that can result in anger at those who are caring for them and carrying out procedures that can be painful. You may even feel like you want to physically push others away! Looking to the animal kingdom and watching a lioness protecting her young, we can see how the instinct to protect is primal.

This often has another layer of complexity if you are someone who has experienced maltreatment or violence in your life, as seeing your baby in pain can link up with those feelings you may have had yourself at a time when perhaps no one was there to help or rescue you. Seeing your baby in pain can also bring feelings of powerlessness and helplessness, which may echo how you have felt during previous experiences in maternity, in your neonatal stay, or previous times in your life. Perhaps spend a moment to 'tune in' to what comes up for you and make a note of it here.

'TUNING IN' TO WHAT YOU NOTICE IN YOURSELF WHEN YOUR BABY IS IN PAIN

Spend some time tuning in to what comes up for you when you see your baby in pain:

....

....

....

....

....

....

As the more sick babies in the NICU can go through on average around 10 painful procedures a day (such as tape removals, heel pricks and suctioning), it's important to consider how you can manage the emotional impact for yourself and how to help your baby with the assistance of your clinical team.

What can help?

Reducing painful and stressful procedures is a growing priority for neonatal units as well as parents, so you share a common goal. There is a growing understanding that the impact of pain on babies is significant, both in the short and long term, and it is important to be aware of how babies communicate pain and distress. You are likely to have a good understanding of this for your baby from your investment in becoming an acute observer of their cues and communication (noticing things such as a change in movement, facial expression, breathing or crying), so remember, you have a lot of information that can already help your baby. How your baby shows you they are in pain will change depending on their age and how unwell they are.

Also ask your neonatal team how they assess and manage pain, so you can have a shared understanding of what the signals and strategies they use are. Sometimes your baby will need medicine to help with pain. However, there are a lot of techniques that can help your baby that do not use drugs (called 'non-pharmacological'), and there is evidence for these techniques for different types of procedures (e.g., inserting a feeding tube, eye examination). It's important to be able to feel like everyone involved will cherish, soothe and care for your baby, and hold their internal experience in mind at all times.

Techniques you may see being used commonly include:

- Using the power of parental contact. Holding your baby skin to skin or speaking to them and touching them in a soothing way so they know you're there whilst a procedure is carried out. Being close to your body and hearing your voice will help calm them and help them feel safe.
- Keeping your baby in a stable and comfortable position and providing soothing containment, such as swaddling them.
- Your baby may be encouraged to breastfeed if they are able (which gives your baby comforting touch, smell, sounds and taste) or suck on a dummy or finger, often paired with sucrose or breastmilk. The act of sucking can help them to feel soothed, manage pain and provide them with a sense of security.

Neonatal occupational and physiotherapists have a lot of expertise in this area and are involved in consulting on routine pain management, positioning and direct intervention when the situation requires additional expertise. Ask if they are available for you to talk to on your unit if you are concerned about your baby's experience of pain, and they can work with you and the team to address this.

When you see your baby in pain or discomfort, this is an important time to tap into your compassionate mind and how you can speak to those parts of yourself that are feeling distress as you are with their distress. Your empathy, attunement and sensitivity is important as your baby looks to you to help them regulate and feel contained by you at this moment of greater stress. There is a tricky balance of feeling distress about what's happening for your baby while also being able to stay in a state where you can give them what they need. This can be an incredible challenge, and not one to underestimate.

Remind yourself that what is happening right now to your baby is ultimately to help them to get better, and that this is part of your parenting role in ensuring they are cared for and have what they need. If you are finding that seeing your baby in distress is bringing up other feelings linked to abusive or harmful experiences in your past, you might find it helpful to actively bring to mind what is different about then and now – for example, that the pain they are experiencing is because someone wants to help them rather than hurt them, that they are surrounded by the care of helping professionals.

If you find that the experience is bringing up feelings of helplessness and powerlessness, remind yourself:

- You are able to advocate for your baby at all times and be their voice throughout.
- You can always be informed about what a health professional is doing and why, and they will work with you to help you feel empowered at each stage of the procedure/process.
- The neonatal team will use your knowledge and experience – you hold key information that can help your baby.
- You can stay with your baby and help them so they feel your safe and loving presence.
- You are doing what you can to assist with procedures that will help them get better, be more comfortable and healthier in the longer term.

SUMMARY

There are many difficult events and circumstances on the neonatal journey, and we have touched on just a few in this chapter. Your baby's stay in hospital is likely to be full of joyous and challenging moments, as are the events for those around you. Remember that if you come across a different difficult situation, you can take the same approach to some of the ideas you have read about here, holding in mind, above all, that your distress is valid and understandable whatever the situation, working with it compassionately rather than against yourself.

RESOURCES

Somewhere to find more information

Parents' stories from **'Providing emotional support for NICU families'**, from **Noah's Ark**, a Children's Hospital Charity, talk about some of the experiences in this chapter, including witnessing the death of other babies on the unit: https://noahsarkcharity.org/2019/04/15/13754

Something to watch

'Coping when a baby needs neonatal surgery' from **healthtalk.org** includes videos of parents talking openly about their experiences and how they coped when their baby needed surgery on the neonatal unit. The site also includes a lot of useful information: https://healthtalk.org/experiences/parents-experiences-neonatal-surgery/coping-when-baby-needs-neonatal-surgery

Something to listen to

'Unexpected beginnings: The neonatal unit' is a podcast from the **Leeds Teaching Hospitals**. Listen to parents talk about their experience of surgery when their baby became suddenly unwell: www.leedsth.nhs.uk/about/press-media/podcast-series/unexpected-beginnings-the-neonatal-unit

Something to read

'The role of parents in comfort and pain relief', produced by **Bliss** and researchers at the **University of Oxford**, will help you learn more about comforting your baby during painful procedures on the neonatal unit: www.bliss.org.uk/parents/in-hospital/being-involved-in-your-babys-care-and-procedures/role-of-parents-in-comfort-and-pain-relief

CHAPTER 10

Coping with and adjusting to your baby's long-term medical condition or disability

Anton felt jealous of, even angry towards, all those parents who were told their babies just had to grow. He knew his daughter couldn't grow out of this situation, and he felt powerless to change it, however long he waited.

Helen spent all her time sitting by her baby thinking 'This isn't the deal, this isn't fair. I've done everything right in pregnancy, everything I could on the unit, and still the life we wanted we won't have.'

Taylor felt that after a time she could feel like her daughter was still her child, that there was a baby, a person, as well as a syndrome: 'I felt like I could finally connect with her, understand and really love her – and wanted others to feel that too.'

Finding out at any point in your pregnancy or after your baby has been born that they will have longer-term challenges affects everyone differently. If you were unsure whether your baby would survive the pregnancy or their early time in neonatal care, this is likely to have been (or perhaps still is) your first focus and consideration. You may have spent many months whilst pregnant with fears about the outcome for your unborn child. The complexity and weight of holding hope whilst also holding the reality of potential loss takes its toll. You may be in a position where this uncertainty continues now your baby is born, leaving you with another set of extremely difficult tasks and feelings.

If you know that the differences for your child are not immediately life-threatening, you might find you begin to experience all sorts of other thoughts and emotions. You may be overwhelmed with loss, grief, anger or a sense of injustice, or be thinking 'Why me/our family?', 'What did I do to deserve this?', 'I didn't sign up for this', 'I won't be able to cope'. You may also have a range of feelings concerned with protection, love or acceptance, and a wish to 'rise to the challenge' or fulfil a new role. Commonly there is a mixture of many feelings, some of which feel hopeful and manageable and others that feel overpowering and hard to be with. Some may feel shareable and easy to talk about, and others you may feel you need to hide and sit with alone.

Whilst navigating your own responses, you may also start to think about the reactions of those around you to the news about your baby, even those who are strangers. The future may seem impossible to imagine or contemplate and the pressure to adjust and 'move on' immense. Pausing for the moment, be assured that there is no expectation of you as you read these pages. It is hoped, however, that there is space for you to explore how you feel and to give yourself as much time as you need. You are on no one's timeline or agenda but your own.

Some parts of this chapter are likely to resonate with you, and others may not. The aim is to cover a broad spectrum of feelings and experience with the acknowledgement that you, your baby and your situation are unique.

WHEN THINGS ARE NOT AS YOU EXPECTED OR PLANNED

Let's meet three families, each with their own experiences and challenges, but with one thing in common – the outcome for their baby was not what they had expected or planned for.

Silvia waited a long time to become pregnant, and at the 12-week scan she was delighted to see her baby on the screen. She felt that life was finally getting better after years of heartbreak and miscarriages. At the 20-week scan that she had to attend alone, she was told that her baby was not developing as they expected, and could have a genetic condition. At the time she was in shock and didn't know what this meant or how it would affect her baby. The connection she felt to her unborn child suddenly felt different. Each day was full of worry, not only for what she knew, but all that she didn't know. She felt much of the joy and happy expectation had gone and she was left with managing uncertainty and anxiety. When her son was born, on the one hand, she was desperate to finally meet him, but on the other, she was afraid to see him in case he looked very different to the baby she had imagined.

When Bob was told that his daughter had damage to her brain after birth, he couldn't accept it. He felt like the future he had imagined for himself and his family was over, and that whilst he would love her, it wouldn't be the life he really wanted. Bob felt ashamed of his feelings and hid them from his partner, who received support and felt more 'positive' about the situation. The gap between what he felt he 'should' feel and what he actually felt became larger over time, leading him to feel low and isolated. He didn't want to spend long periods of time on the unit, and felt more at peace being with his other children, where things felt more normal.

Tim and Mike had spent six months in hospital looking after their son Milo, who had been born at 24 weeks. They had seen him be resuscitated, undergo many painful procedures and surgeries, and were fearful for his survival for almost all that time. When he became stable and they realized his life was no longer in danger, they were devastated to learn that he was likely to be partially sighted and may not be able to hear. Having been elated that Milo had survived, they were now facing a different challenge as they thought about their future.

When news comes of a difference in pregnancy, the distress and range of emotional responses about what this means for your baby, for you and for your family often sits alongside immediate concerns about what it will be like when the day comes to meet your baby. What will they look like? What will they need? Will they survive? Will they be in discomfort or pain? Will they be happy and content? Will they know they are different? Will you feel the same as you did with your other children?

You will have many questions to add to this list of your own if you have been through any pregnancy where there are concerns about the health of your baby. Many parents describe these concerns and fears running through their minds constantly, at the same time as feeling helpless to do anything to change the outcome. This helplessness to be able to control or fix is particularly difficult as a parent in relation to your child. The search for reassurance can be complicated by a lack of absolute certainty, and the reassurance of friends and family that 'everything will be okay' can sometimes feel invalidating and alienating rather than helpful.

There can understandably be a lot of conflicting feelings about the relationship you now have or hope to have with your baby. Thinking back to Chapter 6, there are lots of reasons why it can be difficult to invest or feel connected to a baby who is unwell or has known difficulties. At the same time, you may feel a huge sense of responsibility for their welfare and future as you connect to their increased vulnerability and needs. Many parents struggle with feeling responsible in some way for their baby's diagnosis or predicament, or that their body or genetics have failed them in some way. Almost universally there are worries about what life will be like for their baby, or how they might look after them once they are born.

You might find that you've been able to adjust and take on some of the changed situation leading up to your baby's birth, but it's important to recognize that whatever it means to you to 'adjust', it may not apply blanketly across multiple areas. For many there are areas of ongoing distress and conflicted feelings. The few months of pregnancy, often shortened by early arrival, is not a long time to process what is happening to you and your baby and to be ready for their birth and what follows. It's important to bring your compassionate mind to this process, and whatever expectations you or others around you hold about it.

If you have found out after your baby is born that they have developed differently, or perhaps your baby has experienced an injury or event during birth that is likely to impact them long term, this is a situation that has its own challenges. You may feel at sea in where your feelings are, in shock, or unable to take on the information or facts shared with you. You might find yourself, at least in the short term, being unable to accept this has happened and carry on as if it hadn't. You may feel intense anger or rage at those who were involved in your baby's care, and this can make it extremely challenging if you have to come to the same hospital to see your baby in the neonatal unit. Each one of the emotions and reactions is in many ways its own process, with its own timeline and intensity.

We will look together at some of the areas that arise for parents who have faced similar situations, and explore what they might mean for you and ways to help.

LOSS OF THE CHILD YOU HAD IMAGINED AND PLANNED FOR

For every parent, at some point there is a disconnect between their imagined and actual child. The wish for a healthy child, however, is a starting point for every parent, and the change to this picture whenever it comes involves multiple interconnected layers of loss, whatever your beliefs around difference and disability may be. Losses can be related to immediate events such as the need for hospitalization, the need to involve people outside the family in your baby's care, and the loss of a perhaps long-awaited and uneventful newborn period.

Feelings of loss can also extend into the imagined future for your baby, and you might find yourself thinking about the things that could be different, such as key milestones and events, time spent coming into hospital and the interruption to their life, and first days at nursery or school. You may even wonder if they might meet a partner and have children of their own, and about the multiple types of potential they could hold. The emotional investment as a parent concerns an imagined lifetime well before you know the future ahead.

For many parents the space to be able to voice these complex losses is absent in the moment, or brings the realization it was never available in their family or circles. Silence around these unspoken losses can be driven and maintained by shame, anger or fear in families. Let's look at Kiera and Jing's stories:

Kiera's older brother Fred had a learning disability and was still cared for by her parents. There were periods when she was growing up where she struggled immensely with her own emotional needs not being met, as the focus was on Fred. When she found out her own baby may have a learning disability, Kiera felt she couldn't talk about her fears and disappointment with her family as they only wanted to focus on 'all the positives'.

Jing came from a family where illness and disability were not openly discussed, and she felt huge shame for having a child with a genetic disorder. Jing kept her parents away from the hospital, and struggled as much with the fears of her parents' reaction as fears about her own.

You may move into a different phase of acceptance of the child you do have and find ways to build a life that is different to the one you imagined together, but this is a *process* that takes time and is very often not linear. At the time of reading this book, you are at the very beginning of this journey. When you talk to parents further along in their journey, you might find them at various stages along their journey emotionally, but most will recall how raw, afraid and alone they felt at the start.

The sense of loss of the child you hoped for, planned for and started to form a relationship with will affect you in a number of ways and at different time points. Some find that the sense of loss becomes greater as their baby gets older, and there may be more noticeable differences between their development, physical appearance or abilities over time. In the neonatal unit, differences can be less marked as all babies need medical care in a hospital environment. This sense of shared experience with other neonatal parents can be helpful in the beginning, but there may also be a sense of injustice, jealousy, unfairness and anger that enters the picture as time goes on, as we saw in Bob's story earlier. These types of feelings can be difficult to express and even harder to share.

You might feel that your reaction is 'not like you' and that you are becoming a different person. You may be in a situation where you feel you are holding powerful emotions by yourself and that no one else feels the same way. *It's important to know that these feelings are common, and whilst this doesn't necessarily make them any less painful, it can be helpful to know that you're not alone.* Try not to compare or judge yourself against parents you may be linked with via the hospital or support groups several years into their family lives, although they can offer a huge amount of wisdom, compassion and solidarity.

WHAT WERE YOUR HOPES AND EXPECTATIONS FOR YOUR BABY?

Honestly and without censor think about what your expectations and hopes were for your baby. Then take a moment to go down your list and acknowledge how you feel about these expectations and hopes at the moment and what comes up for you. Here are a couple of examples from Danya, and some space afterwards to add thoughts of your own:

Expectations and hopes	How I feel at the moment
Having a child who would look like me and people in my family.	*I can't see anything of myself in her – I keep searching, but with no success. She doesn't feel like mine.*
I hoped that she would be able to run around with other children at nursery and make friends.	*I'm worried she won't be able to enjoy life. I can't imagine how it might be in school – will she make friends and be able to join in? It feels devastating.*

You may wish to do this exercise with your partner or other significant family members. Give space and time to each other to be able to express how you're feeling without judgement.

WHAT DOES A LONG-TERM CONDITION OR DISABILITY MEAN TO YOU?

Having a child with a long-term medical condition or disability can mean very different things to different people. Some of the beliefs and ideas you hold might be helpful in terms of coping and finding a way to move forward, but others might make this more difficult. Beliefs and ideas vary enormously and include beliefs about why it might have happened (e.g., seeing it as a punishment due to things you feel you should have known or been able to control or seeing it as a blessing/being chosen to look after a more vulnerable child). You might also hold ideas about what it means about you as a parent and a person in your own right ('I am uniquely capable to manage it', 'I've somehow deserved this', 'I am not patient or self-sacrificing enough to care for my baby') and the kind of life you might lead (e.g., feeling like your life is over, that things will never be the same again, or that you are energized to find a new route or lifestyle). Very commonly the sense of having no ending to being in hospital or dealing with difficulties can feel overwhelming, and the craving for life to return to some kind of normality is strong. You may also feel fearful and overwhelmed about everything it could mean for your future ('Will I be able to keep my job?' 'Will I ever go on holiday again?').

Many parents feel an overwhelming drive and desire to fix what has happened in some way, activating their drive/motivational system (see Chapter 2), which can be very helpful to cope and give hope, particularly in the early days. However, it can also be difficult when you may not be able to make things wholly better or find yourself at the limits of medical knowledge and treatment. There may be a point when it feels easier to find a balance between what you may be able to change or not change, but at an early stage this balance can be hard to find, particularly when you're taking on so much new information, opinions and implications.

When trying to make sense of all the 'whys' and 'hows', there can also be a tension between what you might know rationally (such as knowing that what has caused your child's difference is not your fault, is out of your control, and so on) and how you feel about it, which may be complex and bring up a range of conflicting emotions.

MAPPING MEANING, THOUGHTS AND FEELINGS

This exercise invites you to consider a series of questions about what it means to you to have a child with a long-term medical condition or disability. As in the previous exercise, try not to censor these thoughts as they arise – the point of the exercise is not to evaluate them or judge, but to give yourself permission to express them honestly and openly. You may want to imagine doing this in the presence of your compassionate companion or other resourcing figures from Chapter 2, or make your way through these with a partner or other loved one.

- What thoughts or beliefs do I hold about why this happened to me and my baby? What does it mean to me that it has happened?

....

....

....

- What does this mean about me and my life?

....

....

....

- What are my biggest fears and worries right now?

....

....

....

- What worries and thoughts do I feel I can share, and which ones am I keeping to myself?

....

....

....

- What fears, worries or disappointments do I have that relate to things that might happen (or not happen) in the future?

....

....

....

- What emotional impact is this having on me now? Are there any fears I have about the emotional impact in the future?

  ....

  ....

  ....

- What impact will this have on my relationships with my children, partner, friends and family? Are there any specific worries about these?

  ....

  ....

  ....

Note if there are any particular things that arise that cause distress or conflict within you, and then bring your compassionate mind to these areas of challenge and difficulty. Imagine what a perfectly compassionate response would be to each of your replies, and how it could offer you comfort and wisdom at this moment in time. Think about who can offer you compassion in your life in this new situation, bringing you the empathy, wisdom and understanding you need.

SUPPORTING YOUR OTHER CHILDREN

Having a new baby in the family with additional needs can bring up many challenges and opportunities and you're likely to be thinking about the impact on your other children. It is another time of adaptation for children who will have had their own hopes and expectations about what a new sibling will mean for their lives and the family. When your baby is in the neonatal unit, it's very hard to know what's ahead in a concrete way to explain to your other children. You may not know what the future holds, and this can make it difficult to answer questions or plan with your other children for times ahead. There are specific charities that support siblings (see the 'Resources' section at the end of this chapter) and can provide much more detail about what they may need and how you can help.

Here are some first steps to supporting your other children whilst you are still on the unit:

- Continue to encourage your children to build a relationship with your baby at their own pace (see some ideas for this in Chapter 7).

- Ask your children about their hopes and wishes for the new baby. This can be a helpful starting point for working out what might be different and what matters to them. You may have already had a good idea of this when you were pregnant and can build on those conversations and preparation.

- Explain any diagnoses and what they mean in simple language they can understand, calmly and clearly. Use pictures, cartoons or toys to help if your other children are very young. It can be helpful to check what they might already know and to build on this as well as having an opportunity to correct any misunderstandings. If you have access to a play specialist or family support team on the unit, they can help you.

- Your children will understand at their own pace and level. There is no 'wrong' or 'right' way for them to respond to the information – they may have no response at all, or wish to express a range of emotions. Let them know that all feelings are okay, and normalize feelings that can be hard to share (such as jealousy or anger). What's key is being sensitive to what they need emotionally over time, helping them contain big feelings, and letting them know you're there for them.

- Invite them to ask any questions and what they may be thinking. If you're not sure, ask 'What's going through your mind?' Children are naturally curious, so follow their lead in what's important to them, allowing them to speak freely.

- If your baby has medical equipment or devices, it can be helpful to normalize these and help your other children to become more familiar with them. For example, you can purchase a range of dolls that have tubes, stomas, etc., or you can give your child spare equipment to play with at home. Talking through what everything is for and what it does helps to 'demystify' things that can look and sound scary. If your baby will need medical equipment once home, introduce the idea and what this will be like, gradually leading up to discharge.

- Work with your child's teacher and other key adults in the community to inform them of the situation and plan ahead for supporting them even if there are no current signs of difficulty or distress.

- Make time for them away from your baby and do your best to honour any commitments you make.

- Let them know they are as loved and important as their baby, and find ways to keep connected when you're apart.

- You can help shape the story about your new baby with them. Think about what you'd like them to learn about who they are and their journey. You can be creative and start to make a story book or help them to make sense of the story if they are older whilst you are in hospital.

- Remember, this is a lifelong journey for them too. If your child is not interested or too young to know what's different right now, that's okay. You can make the decisions as a family about when the right time is to talk about your lives together.

It's also important to recognize for yourself the enormity of the task ahead of you, and to come to this from a place of compassion for yourself as a parent. (You might find it helpful to revisit the exercise in Chapter 7, 'Bringing compassion to yourself as a parent when it's hard'.)

THE MEANING OF A LONG-TERM DIAGNOSIS OR DISABILITY TO OTHERS AROUND YOU

It's a complex task to navigate the views and expectations of those around you whilst also attending to your own needs. In many cultures and religions, as well as within beliefs that are held in families, there are multiple views on difference and disability. You may be in a position where you share these views, share some of them, or actively disagree, but for most parents they have a significant impact.

If you feel your friends and/or family are supportive and motivated to help, it can be useful to let them know what your needs are. You might want to look back at Chapter 1 ('Building a support network') and use the same framework to think about them again in this new context. Even with good intentions and care there may be important things to establish in your network for you and your child, such as:

- **Use of language** – your preferred language concerning your child's long-term medical needs or disability and your sensitivities around some phrases or comments that may be intended to be of help but you don't find helpful

('Everything happens for a reason' or 'It is what it is' are two common examples).

- Flow of giving and receiving support. Learning that a grandchild, for example, has additional needs can be distressing, and it's important to acknowledge that it does impact the wider family. However, responsibility for causing or alleviating that distress is not yours to carry – encourage friends and family to seek their own support to help them, to enable them to focus on supporting and helping you.

- Respect for your perspective, knowledge and parenting approach. You will develop a great deal of knowledge about your baby and their needs over time. This knowledge and the parenting your baby needs will differ from what's familiar to those who haven't been in your position. It is your choice how much you wish to explain and educate those who support you, how much you can delegate the task of learning more to them, and how much you wish to share.

If views and beliefs of family or friends do not align with yours and your values, not only can this feel devastating, but it can also feel isolating when the support and solidarity you need is unavailable. For some, where differences in beliefs lead to upsetting words and behaviour, there can be additional grief, anger, hurt and a sense of abandonment.

FIRST STEPS TO HELP

- Establish clear boundaries about what you're willing to hear and discuss: 'I am happy to talk about what we have been advised to do to help Lisa's development, but I'm not prepared to discuss your opinions on a cure.'
- Enlist the help of the neonatal team to update information that may influence beliefs in your family based on current knowledge, as well as show family members what they can do to help most usefully.
- If you feel that what is said or acted on is harmful to you or your baby, you might consider reducing, suspending or stopping contact. You can discuss any worries about safety with your neonatal team, who can find the right help and support for you.

YOUR BABY IS NOT THEIR DIAGNOSIS – EVEN WHEN IT CAN FEEL LIKE IT

At the time a significant medical diagnosis is given, it can feel like it takes up all your child's identity and your sense of them as a unique individual with a heritage, personality and hopes and dreams of their own. You may struggle to see them as your baby or feel they are connected or related to you. Remember, you've also had very little time to get to know them. You may feel ambivalent about spending time with them or even feel angry towards them. This can be particularly challenging on the neonatal unit when your role in your baby's care is given such importance. It might lead you to spend less time with your baby or overcompensate in some way for feelings you're experiencing. Your baby's identity may also be obscured or changed by information that you may have been given or looked up online. Whilst this information can be helpful for some, it might also raise anxiety about what the future holds and who your child will become.

The way some neonatal healthcare professionals may talk or write about your baby to you and others can add to the feeling that they are in some way their diagnosis. You may feel over time you would like to take more control over how these discussions take place (see Chapter 8) and the language used about your baby. Not only is this language important to consider in terms of how you see them, but it also plays a significant role in how they will grow up to see themselves. Whilst you might find that in some places and in some groups there are strong views about the use of certain language and terms, what's most important is that it feels right and comfortable for you and for your child. You can start to model this language for the medical team and for your family and friends.

One way to think about the process of seeing your child and their diagnosis is to think very simply of two circles. In the very beginning you might be in a place where your baby and their diagnosis feel the same, or their diagnosis wholly obscures who they are or how they feel to you as a person. As time goes on and you get to know them there are a number of processes and events moving at different speeds and timepoints that can start to pull the two circles apart. At this point you may be able to see elements of your child that feel unique, linked to you, and help them to feel like their own person. In time there is an interaction between where you are in terms of the relationship between your child and their diagnosis and your child's own relationship with who they are as they get older. These ways of relating, identities and perspectives all interact and change over time.

If you are struggling to connect with your baby in light of a diagnosis, remember that this is understandable given the circumstances (see 'Experiences and barriers that can impact the feeling of emotional connection/bonding to your baby in neonatal care' in Chapter 6).

You may wish to consider some of the following questions:

- How do I feel right now, when I am with my baby?
- How do I feel when I am apart from them?
- Are there 'micro moments' when I feel something different when I'm with them – connected, a feeling of calm or love, for example? What contributes to these times when it feels different?
- What glimmers of their personality or sense of uniqueness do I notice?
- Is there a critical or judgemental voice towards myself in the picture? How can I respond to this compassionately?
- What do I need to hear right now that will help me in this situation?
- Who around me understands and can provide what I need emotionally?

Whilst this is a simplification of a complex process, it's important to remember that ultimately children will be themselves as they grow and develop. Parents have an essential role in nurturing them, co-creating the story they develop about themselves and their sense of self. No other family's story or information about a long-term condition or disability can capture everything there is to know or understand about a child and their life or who they will be.

As we thought about in Chapter 6, the relationship between you and your baby and how you think about them is a fluid process that changes over time. If you have recently been given a diagnosis for your baby, there is likely to be a significant adjustment process to a new reality and what can feel like a new relationship with a new child. For many it can feel like the baby they got to know and imagined in pregnancy is not the same baby as the one they have now, and that the whole process from the beginning starts again on its own trajectory. It can be helpful to remind those around you of the magnitude of these challenges, adjustments and tasks, and to let them know what they can actively do to support you.

LOSSES OF YOUR IMAGINED SELF, IDENTITY AND IMAGINED LIFE

As well as thinking about your baby's identity and life, you will also be thinking about how your life might change (e.g., your sense of identity in terms of how you view yourself and are viewed by others, flexibility and autonomy, fulfilment of hopes, goals and ambitions). When the focus is on your child, intensively so in the first few months in hospital, it might feel like your emotional needs are side-lined. There's often a worry that it is selfish to even think about the impact on yourself or what might change for you. In fact, it's very important to have space and time to acknowledge and understand this impact, and to remember that having a child with additional needs does not make your needs any less significant.

For most parents their identity and that of the children they have and imagine having are both separate and linked. Whilst for some parents their sense of their own identity remains unaffected or fairly stable, it is not uncommon to feel like a diagnosis of a long-term condition or disability for your child changes your sense of self and who you are as a parent. This can be for many reasons, such as:

- A change or disruption to seeing your child as an extension of your own hopes, aspirations and dreams
- Questioning your capability for things that you may see as core parts of you, such as your capability to love, to feel happy, to accept, to look after/care for your baby long term; this might exist alongside newly discovered capabilities or capacities
- Feeling your child's differences are a reflection of personal shortcomings or features of yourself or your experiences
- Seeing yourself as wholly a 'medical mum' or parent rather than being the parent you had planned and imagined yourself to be
- Worrying about how others may view you (e.g., you may dread a sense of pity from others)
- Worrying about how being a parent to your baby may change you emotionally (e.g., concern you may become a resentful or angry person or become someone very different from the person you were or wish to be).

EXPLORING THE IMPACT OF YOUR BABY'S LONG-TERM HEALTH CONDITION/DISABILITY ON YOUR PERSONAL AND PARENTAL IDENTITY

Take a moment to list the ways that you feel your baby's diagnosis has impacted your personal and parental identity. You may wish to come back to this at various points in time to see what may have changed and what has contributed to those changes:

....

....

....

We will think together in the following sections about the early stages in finding a way forwards. If you don't feel ready to read on just yet, allow yourself to pause and be where you're at in the process. It's important not to feel a pressure to 'move on' or ignore the complexity of your feelings. When you do read on, you might find space to allow the challenge and difficulty alongside some other thoughts, feelings and plans.

REIMAGINING, REBUILDING AND HOPE

At this stage in your family life, it may be hard to imagine how you will adjust or cope having a baby with a long-term medical condition or disability. This makes sense, as thinking into the future takes place from where you are *now* – the knowledge and experience you have now, the emotional space you are in now, and the imagined picture of who your child will be based on who they are now. Thinking about the future is also based on our own experience as a template, and it might be that you don't yet have personal experience in this area. The actual future is different and based on accumulated knowledge and experience, an emotional place that is unknown but likely to be different, and with a child who has grown, developed and you've got to know. Whilst it's normal and natural to think or worry about the future, problem solving future predicted problems isn't always useful. So what is?

Two psychologists, David Feldman and Lee Daniel Kravetz, talk about the idea of 'grounded hope', which has two parts. The 'grounded' part refers to a realistic understanding and assessment of the challenges and difficulties in a situation – in this context, knowing what these are for your baby and your family at a time and *at a pace that works for you*. The 'hope' part refers to building confidence in your capabilities to shape what happens next in the situation. This might be in taking on a role of advocacy, problem solving, finding new joy and encouragement in steps towards progress as well as finding ways to ensure your own support to sustain you in a life that may look very different to the one you had planned for.

As part of building hope there can be a process of making new goals or wishes for your baby, for yourself and your future, that align with your values and preferences. These may be different to those you and the team might have had in mind in the beginning, and this can be a difficult adjustment. For example, moving focus from a cure or living without a medical condition to living with it is not a straightforward process. There is a large area between the positions of 'doing everything' and 'doing nothing', and the intricacies of this often become more visible over time. It may feel like you're giving up or somehow not fighting for your child if you change your goals. It may feel like you're being asked to stop hoping if the conversations change with your neonatal team, or that you are being asked to accept a new type of 'normal'. It can be helpful to take a position of holding both, ensuring you honour the role of hope and also thinking about what's needed in the here and now to help your baby.

What can be helpful is revisiting the parenting roles you feel are most important to you (see Chapter 4, 'Will my baby think of me as a nurse and not a parent?', which looks in detail at parenting roles, and Chapter 5, 'Identifying what your values are as a parent and putting them into action') as well as potentially new goals around medical care, and to think about how they can be fulfilled and honoured in this new situation. You might also want to do this with your partner, particularly if you find yourselves taking different approaches or having very different emotional reactions.

There is also a process in relation to wishes and hopes that's part of moving into a different version of 'normal life'. Whilst these seem simple, even pragmatic in nature, they can be fraught with grief as well as hope. Entering into the complexity and ever-changing emotions with your compassionate mind 'online' will equip you little by little to be alongside the changes and complexities, and from this place of wisdom allow hope in its own way to grow.

Another part of hope can be focused on how you think about and share your child's identity. Many parents whose babies have gone through adversity talk about them as brave, courageous and being 'a fighter'.

✓ THINKING ABOUT HOW YOU VIEW YOUR BABY'S IDENTITY

Take a moment to think about the journey of your baby, and jot down some of the words that come to mind:

....

....

....

....

....

Your baby will reveal a lot about themselves over time. You will grow to know and understand them in a way that no one else can. Whilst it may feel like a more one-sided process now, your future and how you build this is something you can do together.

LEARNING MORE AND PLANNING AHEAD

As you read this chapter you are likely to be finding yourself in a situation that's outside what you have planned for, imagined or understood about your life and the life of your baby. After the upheaval and trauma of neonatal care, your reality has changed again. It can be very hard to make long-term plans or predictions as you are in a different world that is largely unknown. It may be helpful to remind yourself that you have already adapted and changed perhaps more than you realize since the very early days of your baby's birth. At the same time, the tasks ahead of you are significant.

Many find planning and finding out information empowering and helpful, *but there is a limit to how much you will be able to take in and act on at any one time.* When a diagnosis is new, it may be something you have never heard of before. Your expertise and knowledge will grow over time, but it can be hard having to make decisions or act on little knowledge in the beginning. There is also a balance between planning ahead and planning so far ahead it's in a time that's impossible to know with much certainty what you're planning for, as it's likely that many other things will have changed by then. Plan for small and more manageable periods of time, focusing on what you can do now when it feels overwhelming. Remember that the degree to which we ever know what is in store for any of our children or people we love is limited.

There may be an element of feeling responsible for the outcome for your baby, and this can feel particularly daunting as you are faced with new things to learn about their care and ways to help their development. Whether you experience these as demands or expectations, it can be helpful to remember:

- All new skills can be learnt gradually over time. Be clear about what you feel ready to know and when. Be explicit about your worries and fears with the neonatal team.

- The exact outcomes for your baby are not written in stone. There will be a lot you can do to help them, and medical knowledge is changing all the time.
- Connecting with other parents who have a child with a similar condition or issues can help as they share their wisdom and expertise with the perspective of being ahead of you in their journey.

Finding support from other parents and families

Support from other parents can be invaluable and offer a sense of solidarity and hope. At the same time, it doesn't always follow that those parents will be those you may naturally befriend or who hold your beliefs or values. Take time to find parents you genuinely connect with and who can offer you the hand of friendship. Equally, support online and reading forums can be helpful when you feel parents understand your situation and can offer counsel and practical advice. Sometimes, however, it can be overwhelming to read about older children and the future, and it's often the case that parents seek online support only when they're struggling. Take time to find the right community and people for you.

MAKING THE JOURNEY TOGETHER

Whatever the journey ahead for you and your baby, remember you're making it together. You will be a key person in creating and shaping the narrative they have about themselves as they grow and in how they navigate their world. Even though their life may be different or briefer than the one you imagined, they are growing into their own story as themselves from the very beginning.

✓ THINKING ABOUT SUPPORTING YOUR BABY AND THE STORY THEY DEVELOP ABOUT THEMSELVES

Here are some questions to ask yourself about your baby. You may want to return to these at different time points as they grow. You may also wish to share these questions with your partner, family member and other people who have a key role in shaping their world:

- What is important for them to know about themselves?

....

....

....

....

- What's the story you would like them to hear about their journey so far?

....

....

....

....

- How would you like them to feel about their medical condition or difference?

....

....

....

....

- How can you show them what they mean to you?

....

....

....

....

- How can you support them best, even when you may be struggling yourself?

....

....

....

....

- How can others around them support you to support them?

....

....

....

....

SUMMARY

Finding out that your baby has a long-term medical condition or disability can be a time of intense and mixed emotions. In this chapter we have thought about some of the challenges and processes you may be going through at this point where all is new, and some of the ways to find a way forwards for the future. You may wish to come back to some of the exercises and sections in this chapter as things change over time, and look again at where you're at with your baby, your family and yourself. Remember, you are not alone in your situation, and finding the right people to be your 'village' now and in the future will help you cope and feel more supported. Also remember that you have a significant role in shaping the story of your child for others and for themselves.

RESOURCES

Somewhere to find more information

'Supporting parents of disabled children and adults', from **Affinity Hub**, offers emotional support for parents of children with additional needs: www.affinityhub.uk/1/Welcome.html

Together for Short Lives offers support for families where their child's life is expected to be short, including a helpline: www.togetherforshortlives.org.uk

The charity **Sibs** is an excellent resource for siblings of adults and children with disabilities. They have numerous free guides including how to talk to your children about their feelings, and helping your siblings to have a positive relationship. They also have links to further support on their website: www.sibs.org.uk

Something to watch

'How do I cope with my child's new diagnosis?' from **Exceptional Lives**. Watch a couple talk about their experience of receiving a diagnosis for their child a little later on and how they coped: https://exceptionallives.org/blog/my-child-has-a-new-disability-diagnosis-now-what

Something to listen to

The Skies We're Under is a candid, honest, supportive podcast and community created by and for parents of people with disabilities. It is hosted and created by **Rachel Wright** (an author and a qualified nurse) with the aim of 'bridging the gap between the life we expected and the one we're actually living': www.bornattherighttime.com/the-skies-we-are-under-podcast

Something to read

Day by Day: Emotional Wellbeing in Parents of Disabled Children by **Joanna Griffin** is a book that focuses on looking after your emotional wellbeing as a parent of a child with additional needs across the transitions and different stages of their lives. Joanna is a psychologist and parent herself of a disabled child, offering a wealth of personal and professional knowledge and wisdom.

CHAPTER 11

When your baby is not expected to live long or dies (including the death of a twin or triplet)

There is little more devastating for a parent than the news that your baby has little time to live or is dying. Whether this is your own experience or that of other parents you have met in neonatal care, this chapter will talk about how incredibly difficult and overwhelming this experience can be. I have written this chapter, like the rest of the chapters in this book, addressing you, the reader and the parent, as you. Even if this is not your own experience with your baby, I hope that you will find insight here and ways you can support others who may be going through this.

The death of a baby for many is like losing a part of themselves, and it brings complex and overpowering emotions. It can feel incomprehensible and cruel that death can even be a possibility at a time that is usually so full of the energy of new life. At many points on your journey, if this is what is happening, you will have hoped that there may be a different outcome, and this hope often lasts to the very end.

This chapter aims to be a companion alongside some events, moments and situations that might feel inconceivable to imagine. It's here if you don't know what to do next, to gently suggest ways to navigate what's ahead. In this situation there is no right or wrong to how you may feel or want things to be; you're doing the very best you can in the most difficult of circumstances. By being with your baby, letting them know you are there for whatever comes, you are helping them to feel safe, cherished and loved in every moment you have together, even when that time is painfully short. You might want to share some of the contents of this chapter with others to help them understand and support you the best they can.

THINKING ABOUT THE UNTHINKABLE

When the conversation changes to talking about limits on treatment for your baby and their survival comes into question more urgently, it can often feel unbelievable or unreal. Many parents describe feeling far away, or as if everything is happening in a fog. It can be hard to focus or listen to the words that are spoken. You may feel intense anger coupled with despair, giving an overwhelming energy to fight for your baby or wanting to seek another opinion. You may find yourself thinking it's all a mistake or a bad dream. Many parents focus on the hope that there will be a miracle, and this helps them to keep going through each moment. For others the feeling of devastation is paralysing, and makes actions and decisions feel impossible.

You are in a situation where there will be many people and systems around you to help, but wherever you are in the process you will be facing the agony of thinking about the unthinkable. No one ever anticipates they will outlive their children or have to contemplate what their last few months or moments will be like, particularly at a time so close to birth. The idea of physical separation can be overwhelming, particularly when you have been pregnant and felt your baby grow as part of your body. *Remember that you do not have to go through this alone.* This is a time to draw those who love you and understand your suffering around you, and also to lean on the neonatal staff who will do their upmost to support and guide you.

In some circumstances towards the end of life you will have time to think and plan a little about what might happen. This may be with the help of specialist teams (such as a palliative care service) or through the process of advanced care planning.[1] These teams and conversations may have been part of the picture for a while, where the outcome for your baby has been uncertain, to help plan for different outcomes, hopes and wishes. In other circumstances, you may have very little time and events may be changing course extremely quickly.

If time is short, read on to the next section first. If you have longer, there is more to consider from 'When you have more time' which follows, including if you have more than one baby to think about.

1 An advanced care plan is made collaboratively between you and the neonatal team to think about your hopes and preferences for your baby and all their possible outcomes. It is an ongoing process rather than a 'one-off conversation', and will likely change according to the circumstances. It can be helpful as a reference point and as a way of bringing together what's meaningful at a time when things can feel overwhelming.

WHEN TIME IS SHORT

When things change rapidly, you're likely to be in a state where it's hard to think or function. You may be flooded with feelings or feeling emotionally detached and cut-off. All these experiences are your brain and body's way of trying to manage an overwhelming level of distress. This will also show up in your body, so it's particularly important to ensure your basic physical needs are met, if you can, even if this is basic hydration and a safe chair to support your body when it's fragile.

At this time your clinical team will be focusing on caring for your baby so that they are as comfortable and as close to you as possible. They will make every attempt to move you into a private space or room. When there is a sudden change, your baby is most likely to stay in the neonatal unit and be cared for by those who have already been looking after them and know you. If there is a specific team member you'd like to be with you, ask if this is possible. Often a familiar person who is compassionate, containing and knowledgeable can make a significant difference when everything feels overwhelming. Whilst circumstances vary, they will be trying their upmost to make sure they give your baby what they need whilst also giving you the time to be with them in the way that you want.

When you have very little time, your neonatal unit will be there to guide you through, and whilst local procedures may vary, these are some general principles:

- Hold yourself gently and compassionately in this situation. There is no 'right' way to go through what's ahead. You're doing your very best by being with your baby in the midst of such pain in any way you can. If you would like more direction on what to do or what needs to happen when, ask. The team will take your lead.

- Think about who you would like to be with you – this can include family, friends and faith/community leaders. A member of the neonatal team can usually contact people on your behalf to allow you more time with your baby.

- Consider what ways you would like to be together as a family and how you would like to make those memories (for more details, see 'Legacy building, memory making and memorializing'). This may include creating tangible mementos such as hand and footprints, collecting items from your baby's care (often collated in a memory box) as well as experiences you would like to have together. The unit will have many ways to facilitate these. You may not feel you are in a place to make choices, but you may also find that there are unexpected things that feel meaningful and special to you that you'd like to ensure happen.

- If there are specific rites of passage, rituals or religious ceremonies that need to take place and time is short, you can ask your hospital chaplaincy/spiritual care team to assist. Whilst some of the team will be focused on your baby's medical needs, they'll also consider what you need to ensure events take place as much as possible in alignment with your belief system before, during and after death. You don't need to have a religion to access spiritual care, however; they will also support you if you have no faith or are unsure of what you believe.

- It can be helpful to know what changes you might see in your baby in the process of dying. Whilst this can feel impossible to contemplate, it can help make what you experience with them a little less frightening, and so you know how to be with them and soothe them at each stage.

- Experiencing a powerful mix of emotions and reactions is normal. You may feel you want to be very close to your baby and then need to step away, or feel very afraid about what's to come. You are doing what you can to get through. Focus on small time periods and let those around you know what you need, if you can. Just as there is no right or wrong way to be, there is no right or wrong way to feel.

- The team will work around you to do what is medically necessary as unobtrusively as possible to allow your focus to be on your baby. They can help you make choices about when and how to remove equipment and fulfil your wishes, such as holding your baby skin to skin without any wires or tubes.

- You may want time with your baby alone to be close to them without feeling observed and being able to express your emotions as you wish.

- You don't need to rush in any way after your baby has died. There are many ways to keep you together in the hospital or to spend some time together at home, and you may wish to have some time holding them in a way that feels less clinical, such as cuddling in a bed together. This can be especially important when you may not have had time to do everything you wanted to with your baby when they were alive. There are still opportunities in most cases to do a range of important things after their death.

WHEN YOU HAVE MORE TIME

However much time you have ahead of the end of your baby's life, when you know that death is the end point of your journey, it's impossible to feel fully prepared emotionally or that there is ever enough time. Everyone will manage this time in their own way and cope differently. It's important to acknowledge the distress of uncertainty in this situation, with many parents describing being in a state of unbearable 'limbo'. You may not know what you can plan for or look forward to, struggle with what or how to feel, be unsure about whether your baby may be suffering and what this means, be uncertain what to invest in or even what you 'should' do or how to be. Feelings can seem contradictory but are, in fact, part of the complexity of the situation. For example, you may be feeling a lot of grief in anticipation of what is to come, and feel 'cut-off' or detached, which can make it hard to connect back to your baby at a time when you might also feel anxious about time passing.

Take a moment to take stock of what you are holding emotionally in this moment whilst also trying to fulfil all your roles and tasks. Pause and bring compassion to your situation as you do so, remembering that this is a moment of immense suffering and difficulty.

In this emotional space there will be a lot of conversations that will take place between you and your care team as you think through options and preferences and who is important to be part of those. Some of these are outlined in the 'Palliative Care Information for Parents' booklet (see 'Resources' at the end of this chapter). Like any difficult conversation, it's helpful to find ways to bring yourself into a window where you feel you can think and take in what's been said (see Chapter 8, 'Approaching difficult conversations with your neonatal team') whilst acknowledging that these times may be fleeting.

If you have some space to think and explore further about what matters and is meaningful, consider some of the following for yourself and in discussion with your partner, friends and family.

✓ QUESTIONS TO ASK YOURSELF AND DISCUSS WITH OTHERS: WHAT MATTERS AND WHAT'S MEANINGFUL?

- What matters to me as a parent right now, and what might matter in the future? (Think back to the parenting roles and values you have identified previously (in Chapter 4, 'Will my baby think of me as a nurse and not a parent?', and Chapter 5, 'Identifying what your values are as a parent and putting them into action') to help you.)

....

....

....

- When you think about the future, what would you want your baby to have experienced and known about your thoughts and actions (e.g., 'That I explored every option for you', 'I was with you when you needed me')?

....

....

....

- How do you want to be there for your baby now? What helps you to be able to do this? Who do you need around you to help, and how? What journey do they need to go on, and how can you help them to make it?

....

....

....

- How do you want to weave your baby into the landscape of your life and others in this period of time? (This can be through the experiences they have with others or particular places or activities. You may wish to ask grandparents and siblings what this would look like for them in terms of meaning and significance. For some it's grounding and comforting to consider intergenerational traditions, stories and rituals they would like to incorporate. How will your baby always be part of those? For others, it's about creating new and meaningful traditions, stories and rituals.)

....

....

....

....

....

....

RESOURCING YOURSELF EMOTIONALLY FOR WHAT'S TO COME

No one feels emotionally prepared for going through the process of their baby dying. It can, however, be helpful to think about what inner strength or capacity could help you get through what's ahead, and how to create a sense of that to be with and alongside you.

Kian felt overcome by total devastation and was very afraid he wouldn't be able to stay with his baby as they died or even be in the room, even though a part of him was desperate to. He identified courage as a resource he wanted to strengthen to enable him to do what he needed to do. Other resources often include needing a sense of protection, compassion, strength and hope.

IDENTIFYING FEARED FEELINGS OR REACTIONS AND WHAT STRENGTH OR CAPACITY YOU NEED

- Ask yourself, 'What's the most difficult or distressing part of what's to come for me?' This may be something you are worried about feeling or something you need to do, such as 'I'm most worried about holding my baby while they take out the breathing tube'.

- Think about a strength or capacity you need that would help you with this. If this feels too abstract or difficult you can think about what feeling or belief you would like to have to be able to help you. It might also be helpful to think about a person or a being that embodies this for you: 'I would like to believe I can do very hard things to help my baby', 'I need a sense of protection from the pain for that moment'.

- Once you have this resource in your mind, imagine what it would feel like to have it flowing through your body, using as many of your senses as you can to make it vivid. Notice how it feels emotionally and how you are thinking when it's present.

- Imagine going into the situation you identified at the beginning, with this resource flowing through every part of you. You may want to find an object that symbolizes this resource that you can keep with you when you go into the situation you find hard to connect back to, such as a special stone or picture.

You can use resourcing at any point of difficulty as your needs and situations change. You may find you mix several together or have very specific resources for particular things.

LEGACY BUILDING, MEMORY MAKING AND MEMORIALIZING

Memory making happens throughout your baby's stay in neonatal care, but takes on a special significance at the end of life. The task can feel enormous, with a sense of needing to make a lifetime of memories in a very short space of time. You may feel ambivalent about what's suggested to you or be unsure about what you want to capture. If you haven't had a lot of time with your baby to get to know them, you may not feel like you are in a position to guide how you shape how they might be remembered and their legacy. For many parents this process takes place in a 'fog', as part of the whole experience feeling unreal. There can also be anxiety about 'getting it right'. In truth, there is no perfect way to make these memories. You can only be guided by what you feel you need in the moment.

Some things to consider include:

- You might choose to be very involved in memory making, but it may also feel too painful and difficult. If you need to give this task to the team or others for now, that's understandable. The unit will have plenty of ways to do this, and you can choose how much you wish or are able to be part of it.

- There are many tangible ways to make a record of your baby. You might also want to consider how they are remembered in the context of your family and those who love them – making handprints of everyone with theirs, or having family photos together, for example. This can also be helpful later if you're struggling to hold on to a memory of them as part of you and your world. Many parents worry how they should look in photos, or again, what's 'right'. Ultimately photos focus on capturing the relationship and love between you and your baby, love that is inevitably infused with grief.

- If your baby has spent a lot of time in an incubator or your access to a sense of their body feels limited, consider taking time to make a sensory map of their body and their being when there are less barriers. Take your time to hold them and make your way through each part of their body. Focus on how they feel, and also any other senses such as their smell, or the details of how each part of them looks. This may be particularly important to do without any wires or equipment. Talk to your team about how they could help with this.

- Think about how you can incorporate elements that are most meaningful to you and your baby. These may be particular stories or characters that hold significance, music or writing that you'd like to be part of this time, or the presence of specific people. This may also include making memories of routines or rituals around their care, such as giving them a bath or going through a bedtime routine.

- You may want to hold on to items that have been related to their care in the unit such as their name band and also their clothing, bonding square or blankets that have been close to them. If your baby hasn't had the opportunity to wear clothes, consider if you'd like to dress them, which may include any special items you had planned.

Katie had a christening dress that was passed down through generations in her family, which felt symbolic and powerful for her baby to wear when she was christened by the hospital chaplain.

- Items that link you and your baby can also be important as they act as a physical focus and point of connection – having two of the same blanket you can wrap them in, so that one can stay with them and one with you, for example. Teddy bears, two-part jewellery and any other meaningful and creative ways you can find to maintain this connection can be helpful. Spend time linking those objects with your baby in your mind and through your senses, as well as thinking about what rituals or activities can help strengthen their connective properties.

Indigo said a blessing over the teddies that talked about their symbolism of never being alone in the journeys that were to come, which helped her with her grief later on, particularly when she felt the separation acutely.

- If your baby is in a hospice or at home at the end of their life, there is more scope to make memories that involve much more of your lives outside of hospital. The teams that will be working with you, if this has been offered as an option, can talk you through what's possible.

- You may wish to donate breast milk to help other babies, as a gift from you and your baby. It is possible to have your milk made into a memento such as a pendant for a necklace, and this can be a meaningful reminder of your baby and what you gave in their memory held against your skin. In some regions there are also communities and collective ways to remember and honour this gift, which can be an ongoing source of meaning and support.

- In some cases you may also be asked about organ and body tissue donation. Whilst for some families this feels unthinkable, for others it's another legacy of their baby's life to be able to save someone else's.

- Remember, it's never too late to find ways to remember your baby, even when there may be a fear of forgetting. What happens at the time of their death is a start in what can be a lifelong process of finding new ways to mark their time in the world and their continued memory and presence in your life. This can be publicly by having tangible memorials that others can see and be part of (such as planting a shrub, creating and tending a garden, having a plaque on a bench) and those that are more individual (such as a special piece of jewellery or a tattoo).

- Every year, on the 15th of October, there is a global 'Wave of Light'[2] where everyone across the world joins together to light a candle and remember babies who have died. This collective way of remembering can be powerful – to know you are not alone in your loss and your suffering at the same time as remembering your baby with others.

HONOURING AND INCORPORATING YOUR BELIEFS

Whether they come through your religion, set of cultural practices, broader spirituality or your own belief system, you will have ideas and beliefs about the process of death and what happens afterwards, even if you perhaps aren't aware of them explicitly. You may also have very clear guidance around what needs to happen when and what's most important. Take some time to ask yourself about your own beliefs in the following exercise. You may also wish to consider these questions with your partner, close family member or friend, particularly if it's helpful to clarify your own thoughts.

2 See https://babyloss-awareness.org/wave-of-light

✓ YOUR BELIEFS ABOUT DEATH AND DYING

- What do I believe happens in the process of dying and afterwards? Knowing this, what's important for me, my baby and others?

....

....

....

- What absolutely *must* happen in this process? And have I let the team caring for us know?

....

....

....

- What are my wishes for what happens before, during and after death?

....

....

....

- What do the team need to understand to help me best in line with my beliefs?

....

....

....

- Who else needs to be here to be able to help this take place?

....

....

....

The team will make every effort to work within your beliefs and preferences and to work out with you what's possible. This can also be a time, however, when some of the beliefs and ideas you might have held undergo adjustment or change.

WHEN BELIEFS AND WORLD VIEWS ARE CHALLENGED

Whilst beliefs can offer comfort and help to make sense of what's happening for some, it's not uncommon to find that facing the death of your child upturns much of what you thought was true, right or bearable. It can often feel a frightening and alienating place to be in an already painful situation, and rather than find comfort, you find confusion or fear.

It can be important to talk through this experience, if there is time, with a psychological professional or faith leader. They can help you to find a way through the immediate situation and challenges you face, such as the implications for decision making or coping hour to hour. Longer term, they may also play a role in helping you make sense of what's happened in the context of shifting beliefs about the world, yourself and others.

RITUALS AND RITES OF PASSAGE

Around the world particular points in life and death are marked by rituals and rites of passage. It's profoundly painful when your baby's birth is so close to the time of their death. However, rituals and rites of passage can:

- Provide a structure and some control within a bewildering experience
- Help with maintaining a connection or bond to your baby – both in terms of how they are connected to you, and also their wider family and community
- Help you find ways to support key transitions for your baby (such as to an afterlife) and yourself (into a different state of being)
- Give you ways to honour and memorialize your child.

If you are part of a particular religion, you will find that there are perhaps quite specific ways in which some of these elements are woven into practices, such as mourning rituals, prayers of passage to the afterlife and a blessing for your baby and activities that take place in a specific way. Many parents find they are central to what happens, both in the process of death and afterwards.

Rituals don't always need to be part of a particular belief system or need to make sense to others. What matters is that they hold meaning for you and your baby. Here's an example from Talia who found meaning in rituals she created for herself after her baby died:

Talia was not religious but she believed in an afterlife. In the first few weeks and months after her baby girl Lara died, she wanted to find ways to feel connected to Lara, and to help her know that she was there for her wherever she was in the universe. Waking up in the morning was a particularly devastating time of day, when the reality of Lara's loss was acutely painful, so she also needed rituals to help her begin her day. Talia started the day with looking through her photos and reading aloud poems and cards that had been given to her. She went through each of her items from her memory box and spoke to Lara as she did so, connecting with her sense of her through the physical objects. She told Lara what she was going to do that day, step by step, asking her to be alongside her, and wore a bracelet of her finger prints at all times as a symbol of their bond.

BEING WITH YOUR BABY WHEN THEY ARE DYING

Many parents describe the array of complex feelings and thoughts that arise when being with their baby as they die, for example, simultaneously wanting it to happen quickly so that they don't suffer, but also to slow down so they have more time. You may be hoping for a miracle up to the end, or finding that if your baby survives longer than anticipated you are depleted of resources to cope for longer. There is often a complex mix of relief and devastation in cycles, along with almost unbearable emotional and physical exhaustion as well as fear about what the process will be like for you and for them.

It can be an important act to be able to fulfil what you wish in your role as a parent at this time. Think about what you would like your baby to feel in this situation, and what their needs are. For many this involves being able to comfort and be with their baby so they feel loved and close in the process of dying. You may want them to feel that you are there to ease their transition into the afterlife, or that you're there to peacefully and lovingly hand them into the arms of their ancestors and those who have gone before them. Your neonatal team can help you to know what to expect at each stage as your baby dies. Remember, there is no 'perfect' way to be in such unimaginable circumstances. You are doing your very best to be with your baby in any way that you can until the very end, and for whatever comes next.

THINKING ABOUT WHAT MATTERS IMMEDIATELY AFTER DEATH

For many parents it's incredibly important to be able to spend some time with their baby after they have died and to be close to them. There is no rush to separate, and it's important you feel you can have the time you need with your baby, if you wish. You may want to spend time with them skin to skin, or holding them close and talking to them. You may also be thinking about things you would like to do with them outside the hospital, which might involve some meaningful time at home or in a hospice. These might be important to you in lots of ways – things you dreamed of doing in pregnancy or longed for when your baby was being cared for on the unit as well as helping with the sense that they existed.

Some of the things you might want to do include:

- Time sleeping with your baby in a double/family bed and other intimate times as a family without the presence of a healthcare professional
- Bathing and putting your baby to bed in the hospital or in their own cot at home
- Taking your baby for a walk in a pram or driving with them in their car seat
- Having time with your baby doing 'everyday' things at home so they're part of your household more concretely in your memory; this may also involve other children, pets or relatives
- Having time for important rituals and rites of passage in a more intimate and private space
- Taking your baby to a place of religious or spiritual significance.

What's possible to facilitate may differ by area and the context of your baby's death, so finding out your options can help you know what's available. Again, there is no 'right or wrong' way to spend time with your baby after they have died, even if your wishes don't align with those around you. What's most important is your time and what you want. Think about what the *need* is behind the requests you are making, so that if the specific location or activity isn't possible, you can brainstorm with healthcare professionals about meaningful alternative options – for example, if you need time together physically close as a family, could that happen in a hospice setting if it's not possible at home?

At the same time as thinking about this time with your baby, it's important to recognize that their body will start to undergo changes after they have died, and this can be difficult to experience. It can be helpful to know a little of what to expect and how to position or hold them as well as what might happen over what timescale. If you want to spend a longer time with them, there are cold cots/mattresses that help to keep the baby's body at a cool temperature, and in some cases hospices have a room for this purpose.

If their death has happened very unexpectedly, there may be many things undone or unsaid that you would like time for. Whilst extra time with your baby can be helpful for some, it equally doesn't take away from the reality of feeling like you will never have the time you need. It may feel inconceivable to imagine being apart from them, even after death. At these moments ways to maintain a bond are not a replacement for the loss, but a thread of connection that you can start to weave into your life in time.

One of the most difficult moments can be if your baby needs to spend some time in the mortuary at the hospital. This often conjures up cold, frightening images from dramas on TV, or may bring distressing memories of your own. Common worries and questions include: 'Will my baby be by themselves?' 'Who will look after them and how?' 'Where do I see them?' Your baby will be gently and lovingly cared for by staff whilst they are in the mortuary as much as they were before their death. This includes really thinking about where they are placed, and who is with them. Often babies are alongside other babies or younger children, or with a teddy bear or other items you feel connect you both. You may have the opportunity to take your baby to the mortuary yourself and meet the people who will look after them and let them know what's important to you, for example, that they are spoken to and touched tenderly and lovingly. When you want to see your baby when they've spent time in the mortuary, this happens in a family room, often a bedroom, where you will have time and privacy together.

GETTING THROUGH THE FIRST HOURS AND DAYS WHEN YOU LEAVE THE HOSPITAL

When your baby has died, the immediate time that follows can feel agonizing. It can be inconceivable that the world could go on at the same time as such a tragedy has happened. Many parents describe a sadness and a fury that people in the hospital can continue about their day, that the buses still run, that the coffee machine still works...

Jan's experience after the death of her little girl captures some of these feelings:

> 'I left the unit without her, and I saw a couple coming out of the maternity unit with their newborn, happy and smiling. I felt a sudden flood of anger and distress – couldn't they see? How was it even possible that life and death were happening either side of a corridor? I hated the man in the lift tapping his foot to his music; nothing seemed right. I felt an intense loneliness, that no one was ever going to understand how I felt again, that I'd never be back in this world that felt so entirely lost to me.'

This period can also feel surreal, and it may be difficult to remember what's happening from moment to moment. This can be hard as there will be decisions to make, paperwork and processes to go through before you leave. You may feel like it's hard to know where you belong or where you should go, as if nowhere is anywhere without your baby. If you have experienced the death of a twin or triplet there can be a paralysing pull between feelings of grief and not wanting to return to the unit or home and feeling the need to return to the hospital to see your other baby/babies. Remember, this is so painful because in truth no one is equipped to have to manage these feelings in such a situation.

If you are not bringing your baby home, you may want to consider the following:

- Do you want to return to your family home at this juncture, or do you feel time with extended family/friends would be easier? For some, home takes on a very different significance, which is hard to cope with straightaway.
- Is it important to you to have cards and baby items around at home? Or would you rather someone put them aside for now?
- Where and with whom would you like to sleep, and what rooms feel possible for you to use? Some parents find sleeping with their other children comforting, and this also helps allay anxiety about their wellbeing.
- Do you want to have something symbolic of your baby's presence at home (e.g., a lit candle) as a focal point?

PHYSICAL SENSATIONS AFTER YOUR BABY'S DEATH

Loss is experienced in the body in many ways, and many parents describe how their body doesn't know what to do or how to function. The physical yearning and pain of separation from your baby, the exhaustion and heartache of what you've experienced, the pain of emotional pain often shows up in the body. You may experience still feeling your baby inside you, or hear and feel other sensations related to their body and their presence. You might find this disturbing and hard to make sense of, or it can feel like your baby is with you in some way – whether in spirit or in another realm connecting with you – and this can be comforting.

You might find it helpful to have a physical object such as a teddy[3] to hold at this stage or reconnect with how your baby felt, both in your body when pregnant and when you were with them. In many ways it can be hard to feel like there's a state that's at all familiar, settling or soothing when the loss is so great. In the early days you may find you experience transient moments where the enormity of what's happened shifts a little in your body, but for many the physical impact continues to take a toll. Be gentle and kind with your body as it holds so much for you and your baby.

In addition to the physical impacts of loss, you may be experiencing the effects

3 See, for example, www.achingarms.co.uk

of having recently given birth, such as cramping, or you may still be producing milk. Your bereavement team in the unit will help you with some of the practical aspects of this stage and talk you through choices. There are a lot of differences between mothers in terms of what feels right or possible. Remember, it's your body and your unique situation – so be guided by what you feel you need.

IMMEDIATE GRIEF REACTIONS AFTER THE DEATH

Responses to the death of a baby are psychological, emotional and physical. Many parents wonder if they can survive what has happened, like their whole being and world has shattered. You may feel numb, as if things are not real, with a disconnectedness in your body as well as your mind, or like it's all happening to someone else. For some this continues long after they come home from hospital, and can often be misinterpreted as 'coping well', but it is, in fact, a way of coping with overwhelming pain. You may have needed to 'cut off' to function around the time of your baby's death, to allow you to be with them.

Often underneath this is a well of strong feelings – grief, sadness, despair, loneliness/isolation, rage/injustice, fear, uncertainty, panic, guilt, hopelessness. These are a lot to bear, and you may find you and your partner and family deal with them very differently. There can be an additional layer of managing the expectations of others or helping them to manage their grief, which can complicate or invalidate your own experience.

FIRST STEPS TO HELP

- At this stage it may be about making it through one minute or one hour at a time, setting expectations of yourself to the bare minimum.
- Attend to your basic needs when you can – sleep, rest, food, drink. You may find these are very disrupted for a time – you are only able to eat very small amounts or sleep for small periods of time, for example.
- Make a list or even rota people who can be with you who are supportive and who are able to be with you in your grief, who you know can reliably be present.
- Delegate tasks to others that don't feel like they have meaning or that are essential for you as much as possible.
- Make a structure for your day. This may include simple tasks like eating or going for a walk, even if you don't feel like it. This can help anchor you in emotional turmoil with the sometimes-overwhelming expanse of time ahead.

- If you feel it's hard to talk about what you're experiencing, explore ways to express it through writing, music, drawing or physical movement/activity.
- Connect with what gives you meaning and prioritize this. This may be religious or spiritual ideas and practices, rituals or continuing to produce milk to donate to others, for example.

What the ongoing impact of your grief may be is hard to know in these early days. Listen to yourself in terms of what you feel and how you're able to manage. There are many places and people you can go to for help, and they often have experience of baby loss themselves (see 'Finding further help').

FEELING IN CRISIS

The death of a baby can feel so overwhelming for some parents that they feel they have lost all hope of being able to live with the loss. You may be feeling like you cannot imagine tolerating even being awake with the pain of what has happened, like there is no future that will not be full of anguish and longing, or you may even wish that you were able to join your baby. You are in new territory, and it is understandable that you may feel you have no reserves or capacity to manage or know where to turn to next.

Ensure that you are surrounded by people who know how you are feeling and who have a good idea of what you need to continue to keep you safe and feel loved, even if you're not sure yourself. It can feel lonely that not everyone may understand the depths of how you feel, but they may be able to help you find ways to cope, even if it's just minute to minute. Reduce any expectation of yourself to be in any particular way. You may simply be focusing on the absolute basics for survival, and that's okay. If you don't feel you can keep yourself safe, let someone know and refer to Chapter 2, 'What if I don't feel I can keep myself safe?', for how to access additional help to support you.

PLANNING FOR FUNERALS AND HOW TO COPE AT THE TIME

No one expects to be attending the funeral of their own baby. Whilst it's something most parents want to plan and be there for, it can feel overwhelming knowing what to do or how to be. Common worries include:

- Being overwhelmed and unable to participate in or remember any of the funeral

- Getting it 'right' – a feeling that it has to be perfect, as the one opportunity to show everything you feel about your baby .
- Being concerned you haven't known your baby long enough to make the funeral feel personal
- Being able to physically manage being there – worries about fainting, being unable to speak, talk or move, for example
- Being worried about the reactions of others, meeting expectations or showing emotions in public
- If you have another baby who is still on the neonatal unit, worrying about something happening to them on the day of the funeral and being unavailable, feeling guilty or disloyal to not be focused on them, or concerned about losing the significance of being one of multiple babies in the funeral proceedings.

✓ YOUR FEARS AND CONCERNS ABOUT THE FUNERAL

Take a moment to think about what your own fears or concerns are about your baby's funeral. These may be general or very specific based on your own life and circumstances:

....

....

....

....

....

....

....

....

....

....

....

....

When you look at your list, ask yourself:

- Who do I need to understand my fears and provide practical assistance? (For example, keeping the number of people I talk to at a manageable level, making sure there is seating nearby at all times if I feel faint, having a backup person who can take over any aspect of the proceedings if needed, having someone to look after my other children if they attend.)
- What matters most to me? What do I need to do for me and my baby? (These can be helpful to know so that if you are overwhelmed you can focus on these elements as a priority.)
- What resources do I need to help me get through? (This might be a mixture of emotional resources, specific people, rituals, prayers and blessings or practical planning for each step. It is helpful to consider these ahead of the day and discuss them with your close family and friends.)
- What information do I need? (The time between your baby's death and their funeral will depend on your beliefs, as will the amount you might be able to personalize what happens. Funeral directors have a lot of expertise and gentleness when it comes to helping families plan around the death of a baby, and specialist charities such as Sands (see 'Resources' at the end of this chapter) can also help, advise and demystify the process.)

Remember that what happens doesn't need to be expensive, grand or perfect to capture your baby's imprint on you and the world. You will have as much time as you need to nurture and grow their memory and find ways to keep your connection.

THE DEATH OF A BABY FROM A MULTIPLE PREGNANCY

The death of a baby from a multiple pregnancy presents a particularly challenging situation to any parent – grieving for your baby who has died whilst also caring for your baby/babies who go on living. It's often described as an impossible task emotionally, and you may feel like you're inhabiting a strange emotional place where there is little capacity for either. This landscape is complex, and the list of challenges is long. Whilst not in any way comprehensive, some common things you may feel if one or more of your babies has died from a multiple pregnancy include:

- A loss of the special status that comes from being a parent of multiples.

You may feel that this important part of your identity is obscured or lost when one of your babies dies. This loss of identity, purpose and role can be an aspect of grief in and of itself.

- Feeling like you have to put your grief 'on hold' for your baby who has died – consciously or unconsciously – while you look after your other baby/babies. You might worry that your sadness or thoughts about your baby who has died will in some way harm your baby/babies who are alive. You may also be concerned that any positive emotions are in some way not allowed or mean that you do not feel the grief for your baby who has died.

Judy was concerned that smiling in any photos would be viewed as having 'got over' her baby's death. She was unsure how to encourage her surviving baby and celebrate their milestones, and became anxious about what appeared acceptable to others, often feeling she couldn't get it right.

- Feeling like the death of your baby is minimized by others (e.g., 'At least you have one baby') because you have another baby/other babies who are alive. This may also extend to feeling obligated to feel grateful or lucky, which can put extreme pressure on you when you're grieving.

- Feeling angry or resentful towards the baby/babies who have survived. This can be difficult to acknowledge and often goes unspoken as there is a fear that it is 'unacceptable', which can lead to feelings of shame and a sense of having to hide what you're truly feeling.

- Feeling very anxious about the wellbeing of your baby/babies who have survived. You may feel like they are in increased danger, feel alert to small changes that may signal a catastrophic outcome or like their death is in some way inevitable.

- Experiencing difficulties bonding with your surviving baby/babies. This can be for a multitude of reasons and is understandable from many perspectives, such as fearing getting too close will make it more painful if they were to die, therefore holding back on investing emotions to protect yourself. You may find it very difficult to focus your attention on your surviving baby/babies or even be on the unit with them.

- The impact of similarity and difference between your baby/babies who have died and those who have survived. It may be alarming or comforting – perhaps both, at different times – to see the similarities between them. It may also be difficult if there are differences that feel significant in some way that may signal further danger.

Adie's baby boy who died was always talked about as the strongest and biggest twin. After his death Adie was certain that his twin was at increased risk as they were smaller and still ventilated.

- Feeling triggered by coming back to the neonatal unit when you have experienced the death of a baby there. The unit itself may trigger difficult or traumatic memories, you may feel that it's an unsafe place, or certain people or places may hold very difficult associations. It can be particularly hard to see other multiples on the unit, or to come back to the same nursery where your babies were together. Remember, this is a huge ask of any parent, and if you're finding it difficult it's understandable, wherever that difficulty arises from.

- Being worried about being far away from your other baby/babies when attending the funeral of your baby who's died.

FIRST STEPS TO HELP

- Nurture compassion towards yourself in what you are holding at a time of immense suffering, struggle and complex feelings. There is little that's straightforward or simple about what's ahead of you.
- Identify causes of additional distress that may be avoidable or preventable, such as having other twins in the same room or being in the same nursery where your babies were together. Talk with your team about things that may seem less obvious that have a significant impact, so they can work with you to alleviate suffering where possible.
- Your unit may attach a purple butterfly[4] to the cot of your surviving baby/babies to share with others that they are part of a multiple pregnancy. This can help others honour and acknowledge all your children, and ensure that they are thought about in all care and interactions.
- Think about what each part of you needs at this moment in time – the grieving

4 See www.neonatalbutterflyproject.org

part, the fearful part, the angry part, the part of you that is trying to care for and connect with your surviving baby/babies. Rather than see these needs as incompatible, recognize that they are all valid and need tending to.

✓ IDENTIFYING PARTS OF YOURSELF AND THEIR NEEDS

After Martha's example, there is space for you to add your own words.

Part of myself and emotion	What that part of me needs
Grieving part: full of sadness, unable to focus, chest feels hollow, don't know what to do next.	*Comfort, reassurance, no judgement about how I am, physical closeness.*
Angry part: raging at the injustice of the situation, angry at people whose babies are okay, angry at still having to come to the hospital.	*Understanding: listen to me, hear me out; help me to know it's okay to feel.*
Fearful part: scared about being able to leave my other baby, scared they will die too, scared to know how to be in the world with all this grief.	*Patience. Don't minimize my fear, don't tell me it's all okay when it's not. Help me learn when it's safe, show me what I need to see to feel differently.*

SUPPORTING YOUR OTHER CHILDREN

Talking to your other children about the death of their baby can be one of the hardest conversations to have as a parent. It can feel uncomfortable, anxiety provoking and difficult when you are already in a state of emotional turmoil. Families come to this conversation through many routes, and you may have little time to explain what's happening to them. There will be many people on the neonatal unit or in another setting such as a hospice who have expertise in helping children around the death of their brother or sister, and there are many resources available to you.

As a parent your priorities can be pulled in different directions when you want to be with your baby and you may not feel there is much left to give to your other children. However, it's important to think about their experience, and helping them make sense of it so that they can process what's happening and what it means, in both the short and long term. In practice this is likely to be many conversations over time, so don't feel the pressure to have to say everything or have a firm answer for their questions in the beginning – just be open to what they bring.

Whilst every child is unique and at different stages of development and understanding, you might want to consider the following as a starting point:

- Share information to help them prepare if death is a likely outcome so that they can start to anticipate what is going to happen.

- Let them know in simple terms why death might happen: 'Their heart is different to your heart and mine. The doctors tried to fix it, but they couldn't make it work properly again.'

- Use simple, straightforward language, avoiding euphemisms such as 'They have gone to sleep' or 'They are in a better place' as these can generate further worries about what might happen to them or to you.

- Discuss what your family beliefs/stories are about death and what happens. Children can be worried about their baby being safe, loved and cared for after they have died. It can be reassuring to go through many times what will happen – and this can also be helpful for you, as a parent.

- Talk to your child about emotions and what they might see in you and in others. Raw distress can be frightening for children, so it can be helpful to let them know what it means and that you are not in danger. Equally, they are likely to pick up on changes in you even if you try to hide your feelings – openness and honesty is helpful, appropriate to their age and level of development. Often young children are responding to the distress and changes they see in others more than the death itself.

- Every child is unique and there are no hard and fast rules when it comes to being involved in funerals or memorials. Talk to them about what they can expect and how they may wish to be involved – for many children, contributing something that is meaningful can be helpful, such as choosing music, balloons to be released or photos that they like. Children may also want to be close to you more than usual and might find being apart when they are grieving difficult, even for short periods. Try to incorporate choice within each option, with the ability to allow them to change their mind at short notice.

- Be compassionate with yourself as you navigate the death of your baby with your other children. You may not feel like you have huge capacity to be the parent you want to be at a time of such emotional devastation. By being present and alongside them even when you are struggling, you are sharing an important message that no one needs to be alone in grief or overwhelming feelings, even when it's messy and hard.

CHANGES TO IDENTITY

The death of a baby often leads to seismic shifts in identity, both in terms of how you might think about yourself and how you see your identity as a parent. There can often be a sense or expectation of having to return to 'normal', at least eventually, but for many their sense of self is irreversibly changed. At this point in time you may not know what the impact will be longer term, but it can be helpful to reduce pressure to return to a point before your baby was in your life. It's often a long and unknown process of working out your sense of self in relation to all that has happened.

Your identity as a parent also undergoes major shifts after your baby's death. There is no official word in English for a parent whose baby has died, which perhaps reflects how difficult society finds it to even think about. This can be particularly painful when you have no other children, as your status and identity appears to change from the outside, but remember, you are and always will be a parent.

How you process and negotiate the changes in your identity as a parent, in terms of what alters and what remains, and doing this in a way that is right for you, is a long, perhaps lifelong, process. It may be important to maintain your parenting role through rituals (such as celebrating birthdays and tending your baby's grave) as a way of still caring for your child. At the same time, you will be facing the painful differences to caring for a living child. You may be considering where and how you invest with those still living, including your other children. Whilst others may have an opinion on how you find the balance between these, focus on what's right for you at this time. The balance will change as it needs to, but at your own pace.

FINDING FURTHER HELP

The death of a baby can devastate your world, and many parents find they need additional help in many forms to get through such a life-shattering event. There are many charitable organizations that provide help and support for you and your family, and a link to a list of these can be found in 'Resources' at the end of this chapter. If you feel like you need professional help you can ask a psychological professional or member of the bereavement team on your neonatal unit to speak with you about services in your area.

Support from parents who have been through a similar experience can often be transformative as they 'get it' in a way that can feel you're not alone or 'losing your mind'. Being part of a group of bereaved parents can also help with the feeling of being an 'outsider' to other people and in places that may suddenly not feel familiar or safe. Peer support is available in many ways through charities and religious and community organizations tailored to your needs at the time. Think about who you need around you and build a net of support that's there to hold you.

SUMMARY

We have thought together in this chapter about some of the things to think about when you are facing the death of your baby and what you might do after they've died. No one can be truly prepared for this tragedy and the new territory it puts you in, whenever and however it happens. In being able to consider some of what matters now, you've made a start in investing in the future for yourself and your ongoing relationship with your baby after death. Take time to keep considering what you need as time goes on, and surround yourself with those who truly understand.

RESOURCES

Somewhere to find more information

Sands exists to reduce the number of babies dying and to support anyone affected by the death of a baby, before, during or shortly after birth, whenever this happened and for as long as they need support: www.sands.org.uk

Baby Loss Awareness Alliance, for support that's right for you: https://babyloss-awareness.org/support

Something to watch

'Remembering your baby' is a special video made by the charity **Tommy's** where parents whose baby has died talk about how they remember their baby, how they talk to their children about what's happened and how their baby continues to be a part of their life: www.tommys.org/baby-loss-support/neonatal-death-information-and-support/spending-time-with-your-baby or www.youtube.com/watch?v=iRKaqfF5Eqk

'How to give support', part of the **Baby Loss Series**, is another video produced by **Tommy's** about how others may be able to best support you: www.tommys.org/baby-loss-support/neonatal-death-information-and-support/how-to-support-family-friends-and-colleagues-after-their-baby-dies

Something to listen to

The Lullaby Trust lists a range of podcasts about aspects of baby loss from different voices and perspectives: www.lullabytrust.org.uk/bereavement-support/how-we-can-support-you/bereavement-resources/bereavement-podcasts

Something to read

'Neonatal death stories' on **Tommy's** website are real stories of families who have experienced a neonatal death. They include a mix of parents' letters to themselves at the time of loss, the ways families have chosen to remember their babies and accounts of the mix of emotions of being a parent of a surviving twin: www.tommys.org/baby-loss-support/stories/neonatal-death

Palliative Care Information for Parents, from **Bliss** and **Together for Short Lives**, has more information on palliative care where your baby's future may be uncertain or they are not expected to live long. It can help support a conversation you have with your care team, your options and your choices: https://s3.eu-west-2.amazonaws.com/sr-bliss/images/Palliative-Care-Information-for-Parents-PDF.pdf

Empty Cradle, Broken Heart: Surviving the Death of Your Baby by **Deborah L. Davis** offers reassurance to parents who struggle with anger, guilt and despair, during and after such a tragedy.

CHAPTER 12

The road to home and making sense of your journey

The *'H' word*, the idea of going home with your baby, is something you might find impossible to think about in the early days of admission and cautious to ask about as your stay progresses. Many parents find the tension between hope for home and fear of letting themselves think about it, should it not happen, constant throughout their hospital stay, even at the very end. It's not unusual to feel like something may happen to change the outcome even as you prepare to make the final exit through the doors, whether you're going home from the unit directly or via another ward in the hospital.

Whilst going home brings with it much joy and relief, it can also bring other more mixed emotions. It is a *significant adjustment* for you, your family and your baby. This chapter aims to help you consider how to navigate this next stage of your journey.

In this chapter we'll look together at:

- How you may be feeling as going home conversations start to happen for your baby
- How to start to plan and make the most of your remaining time in hospital to make the transition to home as smooth as possible, including going home via another neonatal unit or paediatric ward
- Identifying your needs and what can help in this new period of significant adjustment
- Making sense of what's happened, telling your story and opportunities for personal growth.

HOW YOU MAY BE FEELING – 'EXCITED' *AND* 'TERRIFIED'

Tina surveyed the room as the nurses organized the final bits of training for her and her partner to complete before they took their baby home. She was excited – she had waited for weeks in the hospital watching John struggle to breathe, surrounded by equipment, living with constant uncertainty. Now was the moment to leave and finally be alone as a family. She could introduce their baby to her parents and friends, one of the many losses she had felt as they weren't allowed into the hospital to visit. At the same time as this excitement, Tina also felt a growing unease and anxiety. She knew that learning how to resuscitate her baby was part of what she had to do to make sure she was prepared at home, but she was terrified about the idea. Rather than feeling empowered, all that ran through her mind was the image of her baby not breathing, creating panic. She felt like these last few days on the unit were a bit like a 'test', and she'd never been good with those before.

Sahil's baby girl was doing well, but she was going home on oxygen. This had always been a possibility, but Sahil had hoped that the unit were giving him the worst-case scenario and that it wouldn't happen. He was worried about how he'd cope with the equipment, but mainly about how people would view his baby when he went out with her. He saw himself as a private person and had never liked questions about him or his family. Now he felt that everyone would want to know what had happened and ask him about an experience he felt should only be shared between his close family and friends.

Daira's baby had a lifelong condition, which meant frequent stays in hospital were something she knew she'd have to get used to – although how she would be able to juggle all her baby's medical needs and support herself financially was still unclear. Daira had been well supported in the neonatal unit, and felt like many of the nurses were friends – certainly some of the only people she had been able to see during the pandemic. Leaving the support and familiar faces began to feel daunting, and Daira feared being lonely. She also felt that whilst her baby's condition was accepted in hospital, other people outside may not respond the same way. She felt more 'normal' in the 'abnormal' situation of being in hospital – it was all she had known as a mother – and now she was out on her own.

One of the themes we have talked about is the way in which feelings often exist alongside each other – even emotions that are seen as opposites. The key word here is *and* – allowing space for them all to exist and be held as valid. It can be helpful to acknowledge this to yourself and to let those around you know as well. News of home can come with great joy, which is often shared by family and friends. However, the pressure to feel *only* joy or relief can bring its own set of difficulties as you may feel you need to hide other parts of your experience. Some parents report that they are made to feel as if 'negative' emotions are in some way unacceptable

– for example, negative emotions are perceived as an indicator that they aren't 'grateful enough' or are not excited.

IDENTIFYING HOW YOU FEEL ABOUT GOING HOME

Take a moment to listen in to what is happening for you emotionally as you think about going home. Give yourself permission to let any feelings come up, without judging them if you can. If you do notice a critical voice or a judgement about how you are feeling arise, just acknowledge that that is there, too, as part of the here and now. Write down some thoughts here.

STARTING TO WORK OUT WHAT THOSE FEELINGS ARE 'MADE UP OF'

It can be helpful to gently explore with yourself what is contributing to the emotions you are experiencing now, and how much of an impact they have on you. For example, if you are feeling anxiety, does that feeling mean you are unable to sleep and constantly have anxious thoughts or images running through your mind? Or does it feel like it comes and goes and is manageable with the support of your family and friends?

Most people have a sense of whether what they are experiencing is overwhelming or unusual for them, so it's important to listen to yourself. When you think about the feeling, it's also useful to explore what themes come up as you think about it. For example, is the anxiety about something very specific, such as managing a feeding tube? Or is it something more general, such as being at home on your own?

> Once you know what might be behind your feelings, you will be in a position to start taking action with those around you whilst your baby is still in hospital and the expertise and time of the neonatal team is at your fingertips. Remember, you can start this process when it feels right for you – you don't have to wait for anyone else's timescales.

TRANSITION TO HOME VIA ANOTHER NEONATAL UNIT OR PAEDIATRIC WARD

Going home via your local neonatal unit

Often your baby's route to home will be full of turns and changes rather than a straight line. It can be an isolating and painful experience to see others around you have a more straightforward journey home if yours is long and difficult. A common route is moving from a regional neonatal unit to one closer to home – your local neonatal unit (or LNU) – which you will hear referred to as 'repatriation'. The reasons for this include your local hospital getting to know your baby, making it easier to spend time with them as you near discharge, and making sure your baby is cared for 'in the right place, at the right time'. Ideally this is something that will have been discussed with you towards the beginning of your stay, although it can often come as a shock, especially when it happens quickly.

Moving units can be a time of huge emotional upheaval and adjustment. Some of the things you might be feeling and experiencing may include:

- Anxiety about the change in the neonatal team's knowledge and expertise, which can lead to a lack of confidence in your baby's care
- Getting used to new ways of doing things and a new environment; even small changes can feel overwhelming, and this is a big change
- Loss of your community – your peer group on the unit and familiar members of staff
- Worry about what might happen if your baby becomes unwell again
- Concerns about returning to a hospital where you may have had a previously traumatic or difficult experience.

FIRST STEPS TO HELP

- Help the team to understand and plan around your needs, and let them know about causes of distress or concerns that may not be obvious (e.g., returning to the place of a traumatic birth). They can think together with you about what can be done to help once they understand the issues.
- Virtual/in-person visits (often with the help of a repatriation link nurse on the unit) can help the new unit become more familiar, which can reduce anxiety. Planning important details, such as who will travel with your baby in the ambulance when they're taken to the new unit, can also feel containing.
- Take steps to start creating a personalized space for your baby on your new unit straightaway, to reduce differences for them and for you (see Chapter 1, 'Personalizing your baby's space and finding pockets of "normal" in hospital').
- Whilst the environment is important, it's the people who often make the most difference to a unit move. If possible, invest in key relationships ahead of time, to provide a sense of continuity and safety for you and for your baby.
- Decide what you need to get out of the time on the new unit. Often reframing the local unit as a different chapter with different goals and purpose can help with the loss and sense of difference from your regional unit.
- If you've been receiving psychological support on your journey so far, it's important for this to be ongoing in the short term to support you over the transition period. If your LNU has psychological professionals, they might arrange a joint session or a comprehensive handover to support you going forwards.

Going home via a stay on a paediatric ward

Paediatric wards can be difficult to adjust to for many reasons, and this is another significant transition that needs planning. You will find that there's often a mix of ages and reasons that children and young people are there, and it's a significant change to be out of a 'baby only' environment that's tailored to their needs. The move from a baby focus may not only be practical but also mirrored in the expertise and understanding of needs. You may feel like there's a lack of recognition of expertise in looking after your baby, or like you have to 'prove' your skills and competency again, which can feel disempowering and frustrating. You may also be struggling with the loss of your peers as you move to being alongside new parents who've not had a similar experience. This can be extremely isolating and difficult.

Similar principles in all transitions can be applied to the move to paediatrics, and when the wards are typically in the same hospital, use the opportunities to visit in person and to link up members of staff. You might find that those you have been close to on the neonatal unit can come and see you, and that can be helpful, both in terms of information sharing and a sense of familiarity.

A TIME OF SIGNIFICANT ADJUSTMENT

'Being in survival mode until now', 'Just holding my breath', 'Not daring to even think about it' are some of the ways parents describe this period. Behind this are many parallel changes and shifts to navigate in the process of going home at the same time as taking on a lot of new information.

> The adjustment is not only momentous for you as you integrate your world in hospital with the world outside in a new way, but also a significant one for your baby as, up until this point, being in hospital is all they have ever known. Whilst you may be connecting with aspects of your pre-neonatal life gradually, your baby will need help to make the transition to an entirely new environment.

Your baby will have a lot of tasks to coordinate and master (regulating their body systems, learning how to sleep and feed, managing the new sensory environment). It's often hard as your baby may seem different to the one you have cared for in hospital, and this can cause alarm and anxiety, or even feel like rejection if they are struggling to regulate themselves around you, feed or don't seem to settle. It can also be exhausting, both mentally and physically, to look after your baby.

FIRST STEPS TO HELP

- Give the adjustment to going home the time and importance it deserves. You are not inconveniencing anyone by your need to plan, gain knowledge and meet the needs of you and your baby.
- Gain a sense of the timescales of each step, and what is negotiable within those and what might not be. This can help with more effective planning and managing expectations.
- Talk with those overseeing your discharge about these challenges for your baby and how you may be able to support them. This helps them understand what you're seeing in the same way you did when they were on the neonatal unit – noticing when your baby is becoming unsettled due to overwhelming

noise or doing more than one thing at a time, for example. This can often reduce some of the difficult feelings that arise in yourself, and help you feel more regulated to help your baby and be emotionally available.

- Link up with healthcare professionals who will be looking after you in the community before you leave, and think about what you need them to know so they can care for you best. You may have an opportunity for a discharge planning meeting where you can make these connections in person or meet some of the people who will be looking after your baby in your home if they require extra care.
- Help manage the expectations and wishes of your family and friends. Whilst they may hope that the hospital stay is now behind you, they can help most empathically and effectively if they understand that going home is simply the next chapter on your journey, and not the end.

Remember, you and your baby are making this adjustment together. Neither of you will always find it easy, but there will be new moments of joy and connection too as you find new ways of being.

Making a detailed plan for going home that covers what's important to you and addresses your needs is an essential step. This can be made alongside the programmes or processes from your unit.

MAKING A GOING HOME PLAN

Here is an example of some of the areas and questions to think about. You may want to work on this plan with your partner or close friends to look at what needs you have in common and those that could differ as well as adding to it as you go along.

- What are my needs practically in the next few weeks?

  ....

  ....

  ....

- What do I want to happen most when we are home? Are there any barriers to this that need addressing (e.g., managing the expectations of family visits, childcare)?

  ....

....

....

- What am I most worried about? Is there a way to address some of these worries?

....

....

....

- What am I looking forward to, and how do I make time and space for this?

....

....

....

- How would I know if I wasn't coping? What would I notice first? What would others around me notice and need to look out for?

....

....

....

- Who do I need around me to support me and how? (Gather contact details and put them in an accessible place.)

....

....

....

- What's most important for healthcare professionals to know about me and my baby?

....

....

....

- If there are carers coming into my home, what do they need to know about how we live, the way we parent our baby, how we wish them to be cared for and how we can work together?

....

....

....

- What matters most to me in this next period of time?

....

....

....

TAKING A GRADED APPROACH TO THINGS THAT FEEL DAUNTING

Even when you've been used to caring for your baby whilst they've been in hospital, parents often feel daunted and anxious at the idea of being in sole charge of their baby outside of a medical environment. This huge increase in responsibility is often one of the hardest psychological shifts. You go from a position of having this shared by a large and experienced team to being in sole charge without the immediate back-up of a neonatal team. Acknowledging the magnitude of this adjustment, most units have a process such as a 'road to home' or a similar map that illustrates what your baby needs to be able to do before they are able to be discharged. This can help to frame the final period in hospital and to anticipate where the focus of the neonatal team will be in their time with you. You may have a community outreach team who are there specifically to look after you and your baby during the transition to home and for a short period after you are home.

Alongside the journey for your baby is a series of steps for you, as a parent. For example, if there are stages related to establishing feeding, it's helpful to know what the unit needs you to do, such as to be present on the unit for most of the day. You may also have some basic training such as resuscitation or in becoming more confident reading your baby's cues and caring for them, particularly in this new phase where medical support is reduced. Whilst you are still on the unit, it might be helpful to think of this period as a transition stage where you can practise new tasks and take on new elements of your parenting role, with the 'safety net' of the neonatal team, should you need it. Just as you started to learn how to take care of your baby in the early days, the same approach can be applied now.

Here is an example of Rachel's graded approach to helping her feel less anxious ahead of being home with her baby without monitors:

Rachel's baby Tim was in NICU for many months and was resuscitated several times in that period. In the early days of being on the unit she found it hard to leave his side or to take her eyes away from the machines. Having the numbers and beeps was how she knew her baby was safe, and she felt this also meant the staff knew what was happening too. Tim improved rapidly after a period of little change, and the move to special care came as a shock. Adjusting to caring for Tim and being confident in his care from others was a transition that needed some extra support from the team.

Here's an example of a plan Rachel made with help from the team:

My steps to being without monitors

1. Watch Tim for a few hours with the monitors attached and notice how often they alarm now. Is this different or the same to how often they used to alarm in NICU? How does he show me he is hungry/hot/uncomfortable/needs me? Note down these cues, which might be different now from when he was very unwell.
2. Watch other babies in the special care nursery – what happens to them without alarms? How do their parents notice if something isn't right?
3. Talk to the doctors and nurses about why they feel confident to reduce monitoring for Tim. Make a note of their answers to return to if I feel anxious, to remind myself of the rationale. Also ask them about what would happen if they identified a problem with Tim so I know what to expect if he is causing concern.
4. With the support of the nurse, try half an hour of time with Tim off the monitors. Note down what I expected would happen. Note down what actually happened. What did I learn from this?
5. Work out a schedule with the nurse to gradually lengthen the time Tim spends off the monitor.
6. Identify things to do with Tim that he enjoys. Notice what happens to my anxiety/vigilance when I am engaged in these activities with him.

At the end of this graded approach Rachel felt more confident and relaxed without a monitor for Tim. She was happy for him to be without a monitor during the day, but still needed one at night for the first few weeks at home. After a few weeks, she took a similar approach with sleep/not watching Tim, and was able to regain a more restorative sleep pattern, which, in turn, helped her to feel less hypervigilant overall.

Many units have 'rooming in' opportunities where leading up to discharge you spend a few nights with your baby on your own, but with help if you need it. This can provide another opportunity to take a graded approach to fears and worries. Talk to your team about how they can support you and what time you feel you need.

THE REALITY OF HOME, MAINTAINING KEY RELATIONSHIPS AND THE 'NEW NORMAL'

The idea of home and what being there looks like may have been something you've thought about for weeks or months. Once the exit from the unit and the elation of making it through the door for the final time has passed, being back in the 'outside world' can bring up feelings that may surprise or unsettle you. At the same time as many victories and gains, the loss of a familiar team of people around you and other parents who truly understand you and your experience can be painful. Many parents feel these relationships create unique bonds that aren't possible to recreate with their regular social groups and family. It's important to think about how to maintain links where you can with those who have been through the journey with you. You may also find that connecting with parents who've been through the neonatal journey through online forums and support groups can help you feel less alone and more understood. Remember that in every class of children in school, three will have had some time in neonatal care. Your community is bigger than you might think.

Most units will also welcome you back to visit and enjoy seeing how you're doing. Whilst in time it may seem like they may not remember you, families leave an imprint on staff, particularly if your stay has been long. Keeping in touch helps them to reconnect with a sense of purpose and meaning too, and helps them continue to care for families into the future.

Don't be surprised if the reality of home brings up some difficult emotions and revisiting of losses you have incurred on your journey. There can also be a sense of loss around the child you were expecting to take home and the one you are – and the implications of this for how life might look now, even if these are temporary. Your baby may not be able to manage a lot of regular daily activities, such as when you go shopping, going to the park or having a lot of people in the house straightaway. This can feel isolating and impact how you feel in yourself as your days are restricted. It may also be difficult if you have other children as you balance their desire to get back to their regular activities and routine after a period of disruption, only to be disappointed this can't happen as quickly as they would like. It can be helpful to think of this time as a period that everyone can join in with, helping your baby adapt, and employing some creativity to what's possible at each stage. Children can benefit from having roles and jobs (e.g., noise monitor) to make the process meaningful for them.

If your baby has ongoing medical needs, it can sometimes be hard to find the 'new normal' when it may feel like your time is very focused around tasks to care for your baby's physical needs. You may not know what 'normal' is for anyone for a long time. Adjusting to finding the balance between your responsibilities and ways to enjoy time that's made up of the things that matter – for you and for your baby – is an ongoing task. You might find that you're just about juggling their care to start with, so give yourself some grace to find your way with the rest.

MANAGING THE INCREASE IN RESPONSIBILITY AND FEARS OF THE UNKNOWN

The change in level of responsibility for the wellbeing of your baby can feel substantial once they leave the hospital. Whilst being in sole charge can bring a sense of new-found freedom, it can also increase anxiety. For some parents this is manageable with some graded approaches, but there are many reasons why it can be particularly hard:

- Being in a situation where you're caring for your baby alone
- Being the parent of a baby with ongoing medical needs that may be significant and/or life-threatening
- Having an uncertain future or outcome for your baby
- Living in accommodation that makes it difficult to care for your baby in the way you'd wish – exposure to mould and overcrowding, for example.

Whilst some of these issues once raised can be addressed, at least partially, by practical support, there remains a difficult balance between addressing real and perceived risks. Your sense of what might happen will be heightened as you have witnessed and experienced many times when the feared outcome does, in fact, happen when your baby has been in neonatal care. A raised sense of threat is therefore very adaptive to ensure your baby's survival, but a continued sense of threat can take its toll. While each situation will vary, some principles can be helpful:

- Remind yourself that you have spent many weeks or perhaps months parenting your baby and getting to know them. Whilst they may take time to adapt to being at home, they are still the same child, and your skills and knowledge as a parent will only grow.

- Recap your 'going home plan' and all the points of contact you've listed to help you – in the everyday and in an emergency. Many parents need more help than they've first anticipated to manage at home, and that's okay. Gathering support around you benefits everyone.

- Be prepared for events, even if they are unlikely, by planning through what would happen, step by step. Although the fear of what could happen can sometimes make it easier to avoid thinking about it, this leaves you less equipped to cope if the time comes.

- Share responsibility, where possible, with a broader range of people, even if this is for a short period while you build up confidence. You may consider training up a grandparent or close friend in some tasks so that for periods of time they can hold the responsibility with you. You don't need to take on everything at once if this feels overwhelming.

- Remind yourself that there is a lot that's unknown about what the future holds – but that you have just managed a whole period of time where this has been the case, however hard. Draw on what's helped you so far, and remember your strengths.

TELLING AND RETELLING YOUR STORY

The stories we tell ourselves and others about our lives and experiences help us process and make sense of them. You may have had little time to stop and think about what you make of what's happened to you and your baby during your time in hospital. Taking stock once you're home and starting to map out your story can be a healing and helpful process.

You can map your story in several ways, either by writing it – perhaps several times – drawing it, or perhaps certain parts of it that are key, or making a timeline. Here's an example of a timeline exercise:

MAKING A TIMELINE OF YOUR EXPERIENCES TO HELP ORDER AND MAKE SENSE OF THEM

- Take a piece of ribbon as a timeline of your experience – it can start and end where you like.

- Use stones to mark difficult times on your timeline, what happened at that point, and what it meant to you: 'When Lottie went back to NICU after making progress: it felt like she would never come off the ventilator; I felt like hope was very far away.'

- Use buttons or stickers to mark times that were in some way positive for you, what happened and what it meant: 'When she first opened her eyes: she looked at the world for the first time and I was there. I felt she could finally know me.'

- Once you have your timeline, tell your story to yourself right from the beginning, and choose who else you can share it with. Ask them to tell you what stood out for them, and what they've learnt about you and your baby. Notice as you tell your story if these things change for you, too, or whether new things come to light.

Remember, your story will continue to change and grow over time, which may reveal new meaning or perspectives.

BRINGING COMPASSION TO YOUR JOURNEY THROUGH WRITING A LETTER TO YOURSELF AND TO YOUR BABY

We have talked many times about the power of compassion in the face of suffering and difficulty. Writing yourself a letter as you take stock of your journey and all you've been through can be a powerful testament to your experience, bring compassion to what you've suffered, and help you think about the future.

Here is a short guide to writing yourself a compassionate letter. This doesn't have to be a one-off process; you may find that you write many letters over time, perhaps as things change, or you want to write letters about specific challenges or to parts of yourself (e.g., the part that struggles with ongoing uncertainty or the part that's angry about what's happened to you and your family).

WRITING A COMPASSIONATE LETTER TO YOURSELF

Before you start to reconnect with the qualities of compassion that are most important to you, such as wisdom, kindness and non-judgement (look back to Chapter 2, 'Connecting with your compassionate mind', for a list), and remember you are writing from this place.

- Let yourself know that you're writing to yourself or a part of yourself because you want to help and you know what's hard.

- Start writing to the 'you' at the beginning of your time on the neonatal unit – how you felt then, what your fears and hopes were, what you carried with you. Then work your way through your experiences, again writing to yourself at each of those times. You will notice all sorts of feelings as you write – let them be and try and describe them as they were.

- Bring kindness, empathy and non-judgement for what you have been through: 'You've had to manage things that were unthinkable, that made you feel you couldn't cope, and this has been hard for so long – you didn't get a break or let-up for months. No wonder it felt overwhelming then as it does at times right now. It was a lot to have to deal with when you were afraid and exhausted; how you were feeling wasn't your fault.'

- Tune into your compassionate voice that understands and wants to help. What would it say to you at this moment reading all that you've written from your heart? Think about the most compassionate and kind people you know around you. What would they say to you as they read what you have written? Write these things down in full. Notice if you start to creep into a more critical or less warm and compassionate tone, and bring yourself back to focusing on the most important qualities.

- End your letter on what you wish for the future, if you could be alongside your difficulties compassionately. What do you hope for? What do you need to support you?

Read your letter out loud to yourself and notice how it feels. You may also choose to read it to others, and this can be an important way for them to witness a different part of your personal journey as well as understand its impact.

WRITING A LETTER TO YOUR BABY: 'WHAT I WANT YOU TO KNOW'

This can be a powerful exercise at this stage in your journey, as you reflect on what's important for your baby to know. You may want to include some of the following sections in your letter:

- What happened to you
- How I cared for you
- How people helped
- What you taught me
- What I know now
- What I want you to carry with you
- How I want our future to be.

List other things you wish to include here:

....

....

....

Once you have completed your letter, it can be powerful to share it with your baby by reading it out loud. As they get older, you may want to choose a moment when they can understand it to share it again and what they mean to you.

Here's an example of a letter that Janis wrote to her baby Helga after a long and difficult neonatal stay:

> My dearest fighter girl, you are home from the battle at last. You came into the world so poorly and so small, and the doctors and the nurses worked very hard to first save your life and then to help you become bigger and stronger. Every day I was so worried for you but was by your side, watching you keep going, and every so often give them a happy surprise when you did even better than they thought you would.
>
> Darling girl, I came every day to be with you as much as I could. I held you and sang to you and read you so many stories. You would have been proud at the times I stood up for you, like a mama bear – and that's now what everyone calls me! I wanted only the best to help you get well, and I never gave up that you'd come home.
>
> I want you to know that you were born strong and feisty, that you have a determination that made me constantly amazed. You are full of love, and you kept me calm and able to go on too, in some moments that were so hard. You're my light, always shining, showing me the way, like a lighthouse. You are and will always be incredibly special.
>
> I want you to carry with you that sense of strength and love your whole life, and

that you're never on your own – there will always be me and many people around you who will be your cheerleaders and have your back. I hope that in the future you'll be able to meet those people who saved your life.

We have so much to explore now we're out in the big wide world! Here's to a life of adventure. Love Mummy (Mama Bear)

MAKING SENSE, FINDING MEANING AND OPPORTUNITIES FOR PERSONAL GROWTH

Letters, timelines, talking through and other creative methods are all different elements of sense making. For some, positive changes and perspectives emerge within these processes (alongside distress and difficulty). These can relate to how you feel about life, your relationships with others, personal strength and aspects of spiritual change. They don't happen for everyone, and may be many months or years away for you on your journey – but you may want to scan the following questions and notice your responses:

- Are there ways that you might choose to live differently after your neonatal experience?
- What beliefs have changed during this time? Or become stronger?
- What has this experience shown you about yourself, your partner/family and your baby? What really stands out?
- What things have become more meaningful or changed in meaning?
- What has changed in your relationships with others?

For some parents, finding meaning and opportunities for personal growth gives a sense of purpose and direction once they are home from neonatal care. You might find yourself re-evaluating parts of your life or what you've learnt about yourself. It may be simply that you've realized something different that you can take forwards into your life post neonatal care – for example, 'There are people in my life who care about me' or 'I don't always have to be strong all the time'. You may wish to come back to these questions years after you've been home and ask them again, noticing what changes and what stays the same over time.

SUMMARY

To have survived a neonatal stay and been through what most people can't even imagine is life-changing. As you return home, we have thought together about how you can start to make sense of what you, your baby and your family have been through, and to make steps to build for the future. It's important to acknowledge that there will always be a legacy of your time in neonatal care, and that this point in time is not the end. Take time to work out what you need, allow those needs to change as your life changes, and bring compassion to all that you experience.

RESOURCES

Somewhere to find more information

'Going home from the neonatal unit' is **Bliss**'s dedicated section on their website, including how you may feel and what support is available: www.bliss.org.uk/parents/going-home-from-the-neonatal-unit

Something to watch

'A stay in neonatal care – Preparing to take your baby home' from the **NICU Foundation**. This animation takes you through the stages of discharge from the unit, step by step, how you may feel, the healthcare professionals involved as well as some practical tips: www.youtube.com/watch?v=kThECxW1zbw

Something to listen to

Dear NICU Mama has an excellent range of podcasts that cover the whole experience, offering a supportive community and many opportunities to reflect and talk about the neonatal experience: www.dearnicumama.com

Something to read

'Relief, fear, survivor's guilt: What it's like to bring your baby home from NICU' by **Charlie Bond** for **HuffPost**. This article outlines some of the complex emotions and experiences parents face when coming home from the neonatal unit: www.huffingtonpost.co.uk/entry/bringing-your-baby-back-from-nicu_uk_627e3286e4b010453ae433c5

Final thoughts and next steps

At the start of this book a journey began with the arrival of your baby into the world, beginning their life in neonatal care. As the author Joan Didion once famously wrote in *The Year of Magical Thinking*, 'Life changes fast. Life changes in the instant', and no more so than when you are faced with inhabiting a landscape of life and death every day. Each chapter in this book has aimed to shine a spotlight on the challenges, joys and tasks you've faced as you've needed a type of intensive care of your own.

In many of the chapters we've thought together about how to make sense of your emotional experience as someone's parent, someone's partner and someone's child. You've faced many tasks in each of these roles – being a parent in the most unimaginable situations, learning a whole new world of medical terminology and knowledge, working out how to be a partner under extreme stress, and have conversations and make decisions you never expected, and building a relationship with your baby and perhaps meeting them and saying goodbye in a painfully short period of time. You've come to this experience bringing everything from your life before, and it will play a part in shaping who you are in your life to come.

Each part of the book has aimed to take you through a new experience or set of circumstances, step by step, breaking down the tasks ahead of you, to help you in finding your way in new territory. The exercises and techniques have been drawn from a range of therapeutic approaches, and you might want to think about what has been most helpful for you going forwards. Many times you have been encouraged to explore and lean into difficult emotions as they arise, compassionately listening to yourself and your needs, helping you to find ways to lessen your distress and walk alongside it. At many times in your neonatal journey you may have found it hard to be compassionate to yourself, perhaps much harder than you've found it to be compassionate towards others. At this point, as you look towards the future, think about what you would like for your baby as they grow, or perhaps what you would have wanted for your baby if they died during your time in neonatal care. Most times when we think about how we'd like our children to treat themselves and how we would like them to relate to their emotional worlds, we can learn to extend, bit by bit, that same tenderness to ourselves.

Another major theme of the book has been about relationships with others – building communities, building a network of people around you who can meet your needs at different times. Although these needs will change as your neonatal stay becomes further away in time, the need for others will remain. It's an important task to keep monitoring your sense of connectedness to others and how supported you feel and to listen to your needs. You may wish to come back to some of the exercises in this book again at different points, to keep investing in key relationships as time goes on. Just as your relationships with others change and grow, your relationship with your baby will do the same.

As you navigate your roles and the different journeys ahead in each of them, it's important to acknowledge that the neonatal experience leaves its mark on everyone in the family. Perhaps you may only now be in a position to start to process what you and your baby have been through.

SEEKING PROFESSIONAL HELP AND PEER SUPPORT IF YOU ARE STRUGGLING

For many parents, psychological challenges remain or begin once their baby is discharged from neonatal care, even when they've been well supported. Whilst there can be pressure from others to feel better, especially if your baby is now well, this isn't always how it feels. There are times when things can get harder. You might find that you are experiencing a delayed reaction now that you are in a position of relative safety, with the reality of what you've been through only just sinking in. This is not uncommon, particularly if you've been in a supportive role to your partner or felt like you've had to keep going to hold your family together. You've survived and done what you could and needed to do at the time. But it's also okay to think about your own needs, especially now. Struggling with the effects of trauma, low mood, anxiety, difficulties feeling bonded to your baby and difficulties with adjustment and loss are things many neonatal parents describe once home. You may need the help of a mental health professional to work things through and to start to feel better.

Whilst it may be impossible to think where and how you'd find the time now that you're home with all the demands and logistics this involves, investing in your wellbeing matters for you, and is also an investment for your baby. Your neonatal outreach team, health visitor and GP are some of the first people who may ask you about how you are feeling, and they can refer you to your local mental health team. If you have a psychological professional on your unit, you can often get in touch with them to help guide you to find help once you're home. Not every professional has experience of what life on a neonatal unit is like, but they will be willing to understand and make sense of it with you and work towards alleviating the distress you're carrying.

Also remember that connecting with peer support can be extremely powerful, whether this is through your unit parent groups, your local maternity and neonatal voices partnership (MNVP) group, charities or others. Being with people who understand where you're at and what you've been through first hand means there's much you won't need to explain. They have wisdom and experience as individuals and as a group, and you may find this community becomes your village into the future.

Whatever route you take and however long it is, you are not alone.

MY FINAL WISHES FOR YOU

I hope you have found this book helpful as you've gone on your neonatal journey. You are now on your way to the next chapter in your life, full of the messiness, joy and uncertainty we all face as human beings together, helping each other find our path. I wish you well.

I hope that you find true compassion for yourself.
I hope you find a sense of safety.
I hope you find a sense of hope.
I hope you find peace.

Index